Founding
Fathers

Founding Fathers

The Essential Guide to the Men Who Made America

Encyclopædia Britannica

BICENTENNIAL
1807
WILEY
2007
BICENTENNIAL

John Wiley & Sons, Inc.

Library of Congress Cataloging-in-Publication Data

Founding fathers : the essential guide to the men who made America.
    p. cm.
    "Encyclopædia Britannica."
    Includes bibliographical references.
    ISBN 978-0-470-11792-7 (pbk.)
    1. Statesmen—United States—Biography—Dictionaries. 2. Politicians—United States—Biography—Dictionaries. 3. United States—History—Revolution, 1775–1783—Biography—Dictionaries. 4. United States—History—1783–1815—Biography—Dictionaries. 5. United States—Politics and government—1775–1783—Dictionaries. 6. United States—Politics and government—1783–1809—Dictionaries. I. Encyclopædia Britannica.

    E302.5.F68 2007
    973.3092'2—dc22
    [B]   2007006001

Contents

Note to the Reader

"The history of our Revolution will be one continued lie from one end to the other," wrote John Adams in 1790. "The essence of the whole will be that Dr. Franklin's electrical rod smote the Earth and out sprung General Washington. That Franklin electrified him with his rod, and thence forward these two conducted all the policy, negotiations, legislatures, and war." Adams may have failed to foresee the way historians of the future would concentrate on his own role in American history, but he sagely predicted posterity's obsession with the Founding Fathers. Biographer H. W. Brands makes this very point in his classic essay in *The Atlantic Monthly* (September 2003) called "Founders Chic," while acknowledging, to his credit, his own contribution to the Founders' cachet with his acclaimed biography *The First American: The Life and Times of Benjamin Franklin* (2000).

So, with a cornucopia of books on the Founding Fathers to choose from, where do readers begin, especially readers wanting an introduction to the Founders, a good overview of the men, and a survey of the key issues of their day? In fact, which statesmen actually constitute this hallowed group? What did they accomplish? What did they patently *fail* to do? And did not some women, in particular First Ladies, contribute mightily to the country in its early days and to the establishment of a national ethos? The volume that follows, the latest in the "Essential Guide" series published by Britannica in conjunction with John Wiley & Sons, provides a wonderful starting point for readers wanting answers to these very questions.

Encyclopædia Britannica is in a prime position to bring you this information. Its legendary print set, first published in 1768, is the oldest continuously published and revised work in the English language, and it was the basis for the first encyclopedia on the Internet (*Britannica Online*) in 1994. Today Britannica publishes a wide array of digital products and provides online services to children, students, and readers of all ages, in multiple languages worldwide. More than 100 Nobel Prize winners have written for Britannica.

The entries in this volume derive from Britannica's exhaustive coverage of American history, edited and managed by Britannica's editors Jeffery Wallenfeldt and Michael Levy, and they range in type from biographies and special essays to summaries of treaties and primary documents. They were written by leading scholars, including Forrest McDonald ("The Presidency of the United States of America"), Henry Graff (coauthor: "George Washington"), Betty Boyd Caroli ("Abigail Adams" and "Dolley Madison"), and Pulitzer Prize–winning authors Gordon Wood ("Benjamin Franklin"), Allan Nevins (coauthor: "George Washington"), Samuel Flagg Bemis ("James Monroe"), and Joseph J. Ellis ("John Adams," "Thomas Jefferson," and "The Jefferson-Hemings Paternity Debate"); Professor Ellis also wrote the fine introduction that follows.

The entries are arranged alphabetically for easy access to specific subjects. Many readers, however, will doubtless read this book straight through, from beginning to end, and we have developed the entries with this in mind. So whether you choose to skip around or to read the book cover to cover, we trust you will find the information you are looking for.

With this wide array of articles and easy-to-use format, this volume should offer a quick, concise, and informative overview of the lives and legacy of the Founding Fathers. And if still more information on the Founders is desired, there is an extensive bibliography of additional sources at the end of this book. We also invite you to visit www.britannica.com, where authoritative answers—and even a multimedia "spotlight" on the American presidency—are just a click away.

Theodore Pappas
Executive Director
Encyclopædia Britannica, Inc.

Introduction

Joseph J. Ellis

"Founding Fathers" refers to the most prominent statesmen of America's revolutionary generation, responsible for the successful war for colonial independence from Great Britain, the liberal ideas celebrated in the Declaration of Independence, and the republican form of government defined in the United States Constitution. While there are no agreed-upon criteria for inclusion, membership in this select group customarily requires conspicuous contributions at one or both of the American foundings: during the rebellion against Great Britain, when independence was won, or during the Constitutional Convention, when nationhood was achieved.

Although the list of members can expand and contract in response to political pressures and ideological prejudices of the moment, the following 10, presented alphabetically, represent the "gallery of greats" that has stood the test of time: John Adams, Samuel Adams, Benjamin Franklin, Alexander Hamilton, Patrick Henry, Thomas Jefferson, James Madison, John Marshall, George Mason, and George Washington. There is a nearly unanimous consensus that George Washington was the Foundingest Father of them all.

The Debate

Within the broader world of popular opinion in the United States, the Founding Fathers are often accorded near mythical status as demigods who occupy privileged locations on the slopes of some American version of Mount Olympus. Within the narrower world of the academy, however, opinion is more divided. In general, scholarship over the last three decades has focused more on ordinary and "inarticulate" Americans in the late 18th century, the periphery of the social scene rather than the center. And much of the scholarly work focusing on the Founders has emphasized their failures more than their successes, primarily their failure to end slavery or reach a sensible accommodation with the Native Americans.

The very term "Founding Fathers" has also struck some scholars as inherently sexist, verbally excluding women from a prominent role in the founding. Such influential women as Abigail Adams, Dolley Madison, and Mercy Otis Warren made significant contributions that merit attention, despite the fact that the Founding Fathers label obscures their role.

As a result, the Founding Fathers label that originated in the 19th century as a quasi-religious and nearly reverential designation has become a more controversial term in the 21st. Any assessment of America's founding generation has become a conversation about the core values embodied in the political institutions of the United States, which are alternatively celebrated as the wellspring of democracy and a triumphant liberal legacy, or demonized as the source of American arrogance, racism, and imperialism.

For at least two reasons, the debate over its Founders occupies a special place in American history unlike the history of any European nation-state. First, the United States was not founded on a common ethnicity, language, or religion that could be taken for granted as the primal source of national identity. Instead, it was founded on a set of beliefs and convictions, what Thomas Jefferson described as self-evident truths, that were proclaimed in 1776 and then embedded in the Bill of Rights of the Constitution. To become an American citizen is not a matter of bloodlines or genealogy, but rather a matter of endorsing and embracing the values established at the founding, which accords the men who invented these values a special significance. Second, the American system of jurisprudence links all landmark constitutional decisions to the language of the Constitution itself and often to the "original intent" of the framers. Once again, this legal tradition gives the American Founders an abiding relevance in current discussions of foreign and domestic policy that would be inconceivable in most European countries.

Finally, in part because so much always seems to be at stake whenever the Founding Fathers enter any historical conversation, the debate over their achievement and legacy tends to assume a hyperbolic shape. It is as if an electromagnetic field surrounds the discussion, driving the debate toward mutually exclusive appraisals. In much the same way that adolescents view their parents, the Founders are depicted as heroic icons or despicable villains, demigods or devils, the creators of all that is right and all that is wrong with American society. In recent years the Founder whose reputation has been tossed most dramatically across this swoonish arc is Thomas Jefferson, simultaneously the author of the most lyrical rendition of the American promise to the world and the most explicit assertion of the biological inferiority of African Americans.

Since the late 1990s a surge of new books on the Founding Fathers, several of which have enjoyed surprising commercial and critical success, has begun to break free of the hyperbolic pattern and generate an adult rather than adolescent conversation in which a sense of irony and paradox replaces the old moralistic categories. This recent scholarship is heavily dependent on the massive editorial projects, ongoing for the last half-century, which have produced a level of documentation on the American Founders that is more comprehensive and detailed than the account of any political elite in recorded history.

While this enormous avalanche of historical evidence bodes well for a more nuanced and sophisticated interpretation of the founding generation, the debate is likely to retain a special edge for most Americans. As long as the United States endures as a republican government established in the late 18th century, all Americans are living the legacy of that creative moment and therefore cannot escape its grand and tragic implications. And because the American Founders were real men, not fictional legends like Romulus and Remus of Rome or King Arthur of England, they will be unable to bear the impossible burdens that Americans reflexively, perhaps inevitably, need to impose upon them.

The Achievement

Given the overheated character of the debate, perhaps it is prudent to move towards less contested and more factual terrain, where we might better understand what the fuss is all about. What, in the end, did the Founding Fathers manage to do? Once we brush aside both the inflated and judgmental rhetoric, what did they achieve?

At the most general level, they created the first modern nation-state based on liberal principles. These include the democratic principle that political sovereignty in any government resides in the citizenry rather than in a divinely sanctioned monarchy; the capitalistic principle that economic productivity depends upon the release of individual energies in the marketplace rather than state-sponsored policies; the moral principle that the individual, not the society or the state, is the sovereign unit in the political equation; and the judicial principle that all citizens, regardless of class or gender, are equal before the law. Moreover, this liberal formula has become the preferred political recipe for success in the modern world, vanquishing the European monarchies in the 19th century and the totalitarian regimes of Germany, Japan, and the Soviet Union in the 20th century.

More specifically, the Founding Fathers managed to defy conventional wisdom in four unprecedented achievements: first, they won a war for colonial independence against the most powerful military and economic power in the world; second, they established the first large-scale republic in the modern world; third, they invented political parties that institutionalized the concept of a legitimate opposition; fourth, they established the principle of the legal separation of church and state, though it took several decades for that principle to be implemented in all the states. Finally, all these achievements were won without recourse to the guillotine or the firing-squad wall, which is to say without the violent purges that accompanied subsequent revolutions in France, Russia, and China. This was the overarching accomplishment that the British philosopher Alfred Lord North Whitehead had in mind when he observed that there were only two instances in the history of Western civilization when the political elite of an emerging empire behaved as well as one could reasonably expect: the first was Rome under Caesar Augustus, and the second was the United States under the Founding Fathers.

The Failure

Slavery was incompatible with the values of the American Revolution, and all the prominent members of the revolutionary generation acknowledged that fact. In three important areas they acted on this conviction: first, by ending the slave trade in 1808; second, by passing legislation in all the states north of the Potomac that put slavery on the road to ultimate extinction; third, by prohibiting the expansion of slavery into the Northwest Territory. But in all the states south of the Potomac, where some nine-tenths of the slave population resided, they failed to act. Indeed, by insisting that slavery was a matter of state rather than federal jurisdiction, they implicitly removed the slavery question from the national agenda. This decision had catastrophic consequences, for it permitted the enslaved population to grow in size eightfold (from 500,000 in 1775 to 4,000,000 in 1860), mostly by natural reproduction, and to spread throughout all the southern states east of the Mississippi River. And at least in retrospect, their failure to act decisively before the slave population swelled so dramatically rendered the slavery question insoluble by any means short of civil war.

There were at least three underlying reasons for this tragic failure. First, many of the Founders mistakenly believed that slavery would die a natural death, that decisive action was unnecessary because slavery would not be able to compete successfully with the wage labor of free individuals. They did not foresee the cotton gin and the subsequent expansion of the Cotton Kingdom. Second, all the early efforts to place slavery on the national agenda prompted a threat of secession by the states of the Deep South (South Carolina and Georgia were the two states who actually threatened to secede, though Virginia might very well have chosen to join them if the matter came to a head), a threat especially potent during the fragile phase of the early American republic. While most of the Founders regarded slavery as a malignant cancer on the body politic, they also believed that any effort to remove it surgically would in all likelihood kill the young nation in the cradle. Finally, all conversations about abolishing slavery were haunted by the specter of a free African American population, most especially in those states south of the Potomac where in some locations blacks actually outnumbered whites. None of the Founding Fathers found it possible to imagine a biracial American society, an idea that, in point of fact, did not achieve broad acceptance in the United States until the middle of the 20th century.

Given these prevalent convictions and attitudes, slavery was that most un-American item, an inherently intractable and insoluble problem. As Jefferson so famously put it, the founders held "the wolfe by the ears," and could neither subdue him nor afford to let him go. Virtually all the Founding Fathers went to their graves realizing that slavery, no matter how intractable, would become the largest and most permanent stain on their legacy. And when Abraham Lincoln eventually made the decision that, at terrible cost, ended slavery forever, he did so in the name of the Founders.

The other tragic failure of the Founders, almost as odious as the failure to end slavery, was the inability to implement a just policy toward the indigenous inhabitants of the North American continent. In 1783, the year the British surrendered control of the eastern third of North America in the Treaty of Paris, there were approximately 100,000 American Indians living between the Alleghenies and the Mississippi. The first census (1790) revealed that there were also 100,000 white settlers living west of the Alleghenies, swelling in size every year (by 1800 they would number 500,000) and moving relentlessly westward. The inevitable collision between these two peoples posed the strategic and ultimately the moral question: How could the legitimate rights of the Indian population be reconciled with the demographic tidal wave building to the east?

In the end, they could not. Although the official policy of Indian removal east of the Mississippi was not formally announced and implemented until 1830, the seeds of that policy—what one historian has called "the seeds of extinction"— were planted during the founding era, most especially during the presidency of Thomas Jefferson (1801–09).

One genuine effort to avoid that outcome was made in 1790 during the presidency of George Washington. The Treaty of New York with the Creek tribes of the early southwest proposed a new model for American policy toward the Indians, declaring that they should not be regarded as a conquered people with no legal rights, but rather as a collection of sovereign nations. Indian policy was therefore a branch of foreign policy, and all treaties were solemn commitments by the federal government not subject to challenge by any state or private corporation. Washington envisioned a series of American Indian enclaves or homelands east of the Mississippi whose borders would be guaranteed under federal law, protected by federal troops, and bypassed by the flood of white settlers. But, as it soon became clear, the federal government lacked the resources in money and manpower to make Washington's vision a reality. And the very act of claiming executive power to create an Indian protectorate prompted charges of monarchy, the most potent political epithet of the age. Washington, who was accustomed to getting his way, observed caustically that nothing short of "a Chinese Wall" could protect the Native American tribes from the relentless expansion of white settlements. Given the surging size of the white population, it is difficult to imagine how the story could have turned out differently.

The Explanations

Meanwhile, the more mythical rendition of the Founders, which continues to dominate public opinion outside the groves of academe, presumes that their achievements dwarf their failures so completely that the only question worth asking is: How did they do it? More specifically, how did this backwoods province on the western rim of the Atlantic world, far removed from the epicenters of learning and culture in London and Paris, somehow produce thinkers and ideas that transformed the landscape of modern politics?

Two historical explanations have been offered, each focusing on the special conditions present in revolutionary America favorable to the creation of leadership. The first explanation describes the founding era as a unique moment that was "postaristocratic" and "predemocratic." In the former sense, American society was more open to talent than England or Europe, where hereditary bloodlines were essential credentials for entry into public life. The Founders comprised what Jefferson called "a natural aristocracy," meaning a political elite based on merit rather than genealogy, thus permitting men of impoverished origins like Hamilton and Franklin, who would have languished in obscurity in London, to reach the top tier. In the latter (i.e., "predemocratic") sense, the Founders were a self-conscious elite unburdened by egalitarian assumptions. Their constituency was not "the people" but "the public," which they regarded as the long-term interest of the citizenry that they—the Founders—had been chosen to divine. Living between the assumptions of an aristocratic and a democratic world without belonging fully to either, the founders maximized the advantages of both.

The second explanation focuses on the crisis-driven pressures that forced latent talent to the surface. When Jefferson concluded the Declaration of Independence by proclaiming that all the signers of the document were wagering "our lives, our fortunes, and our sacred honor" on the cause, he was engaging in more than a rhetorical flourish. When Washington departed Mount Vernon for Philadelphia in May 1775, for example, he presumed that the British would burn his estate to the ground once war was declared. An analogous gamble was required in 1787–88 to endorse the unprecedented viability of a large-scale American republic. The founding era, according to this explanation, was a propitious all-or-nothing moment in which only those blessed with uncommon conviction about the direction in which history was headed could survive the test. The severe and unforgiving political gauntlet the Founders were required to run eliminated lukewarm patriots and selected for survival only those leaders with the hard residue of unalloyed resolve.

This was probably what Ralph Waldo Emerson meant when he cautioned the next generation of aspiring American leaders to avoid measuring themselves against the Founders. They had the incalculable advantage, Emerson observed, of being "present at the creation" and thus seeing God "face to face." All who came after them could only see him secondhand.

A Diverse Collective

Thus far we have viewed the identity, achievements, and failures of the Founding Fathers as if they were the expression of a composite personality with a singular orientation. But this is wildly misleading. The term "Founding Fathers" is a plural noun, which in turn means that the face of the American Revolution is a group portrait. To be sure, Washington was *primus inter pares* within the founding generation, generally regarded, then and thereafter, as "the indispensable figure." But unlike subsequent revolutions in France, Russia, and China, where a single person came to embody the meaning of the revolutionary movement— Napoleon, Lenin/Stalin, Mao—the revolutionary experience in the United States had multiple faces and multiple meanings that managed to coexist without ever devolving into a unitary embodiment of authority. If one of the distinctive contributions of the American political tradition was a pluralistic conception of governance, its primal source was the pluralistic character of the founding generation itself.

All the Founders agreed that American independence from Great Britain was nonnegotiable and that whatever government was established in lieu of British rule must be republican in character. Beyond this elemental consensus, however, there was widespread disagreement, which surfaced most dramatically in the debate over ratification of the Constitution (1787–88). Two prominent founders, Patrick Henry and George Mason, opposed ratification, claiming that the Constitution created a central government that only replicated the arbitrary power of the British monarchy and Parliament. The highly partisan politics of the 1790s further exposed the several fault lines within the founding elite. The Federalists, led by Washington, John Adams, and Hamilton, were opposed by the Republicans, led by Jefferson and Madison. They disagreed over the proper allocation of federal and state power over domestic policy, the response to the French Revolution, the constitutionality of the National Bank, and the bedrock values of American foreign policy. These disagreements often assumed a hyperbolic tone because nothing less than the "true meaning" of the American Revolution seemed at stake. In what became the capstone correspondence of the revolutionary generation, Adams and Jefferson both went to their Maker on July 4, 1826—arguing quite poignantly about their incompatible versions of the revolutionary legacy.

The ideological and even temperamental diversity within the elite leadership group gave the American founding a distinctly argumentative flavor that made all convictions, no matter how cherished, subject to abiding scrutiny that, like history itself, became an argument without end. And much like the doctrine of checks and balances in the Constitution, the enshrinement of argument created a permanent collision of juxtaposed ideas and interests that generated a dynamic and wholly modern version of political stability.

Religion and Posterity

Although the Declaration of Independence mentioned "Nature's God" and the "Creator," the Constitution made no reference to a divine being, Christian or otherwise, and the First Amendment explicitly forbade the establishment of any official church or creed. There is also a story, probably apocraphyl, that Benjamin Franklin's proposal to call in a chaplain to offer a prayer when a particularly controversial issue was being debated in the Constitutional Convention prompted Hamilton to observe that he saw no reason to call in foreign aid. If there is a clear legacy bequeathed by the founders, it is the insistence that religion is a private matter in which the state should not interfere.

In recent decades Christian advocacy groups, prompted by motives that have been questioned by some, have felt a powerful urge to enlist the Founding Fathers in their respective congregations. But recovering the spiritual convictions of the Founders, in all their messy integrity, is not an easy task. Once again, diversity is the dominant pattern. Franklin and Jefferson were deists, Washington harbored a pantheistic sense of providential destiny, John Adams began a Congregationalist and ended a Unitarian, and Hamilton was a lukewarm Anglican for most of his life but embraced a more actively Christian posture after his son died in a duel.

One quasi-religious conviction they all shared, however, was a discernible obsession with living on in the memory of posterity. One reason the modern editions of their papers are so monstrously large is that most of the Founders were compulsively fastidious about preserving every scrap of paper they wrote or received, all as part of a desire to leave a written record that would assure their secular immortality in the history books. (When John Adams and Jefferson discussed the possibility of a more conventional immortality, they tended to describe heaven as a place where they could resume their ongoing argument on earth.) Adams, irreverent to the end, declared that if it could ever be demonstrated conclusively that no future state existed, his advice to every man, woman, and child was to "take opium." The only afterlife that they considered certain was in the memory of subsequent generations, which is to say us. In that sense, this very introduction is a testimonial to their everlasting life.

Joseph J. Ellis is a professor of history at Mount Holyoke College and the author of American Sphinx: The Character of Thomas Jefferson *(1997),* Founding Brothers: The Revolutionary Generation *(2000), and* His Excellency: George Washington *(2004), among other works.*

Adams, Abigail

An American first lady (1797–1801), the wife of John Adams, second president of the United States, and mother of John Quincy Adams, sixth president of the United States, Abigail Smith (1744–1818) was a prolific letter writer whose correspondence gives an intimate and vivid portrayal of life in the young republic.

Born to William Smith, a Congregational minister, and Elizabeth Quincy Smith, Abigail was the second of four children. Educated entirely at home, she read widely in her father's large library, and the constant flow of interesting, intelligent, and well-educated guests at the Smith home turned her into a learned, witty young woman. For her introduction to great literature, she credited her brother-in-law, Richard Cranch.

Abigail's plans to marry John Adams, a Harvard-educated lawyer nine years her senior, did not gain the immediate approval of Smith, who considered a lawyer's prospects inadequate. When they married on October 25, 1764, the bride's father, who performed the ceremony, amused the guests by citing a passage from the Book of Luke: "John came neither eating bread nor drinking wine and some say he has a devil in him." During the first 10 years of their marriage Abigail gave birth to five children, including a daughter who died in infancy and John Quincy Adams.

She managed the second decade of her marriage on her own, as John participated in

Abigail Adams, engraved from a painting by Gilbert Stuart.

the colonial struggle for independence as a member of the Continental Congress and later as a representative of his country in France. Their correspondence during these years, especially when added to the spirited letters penned earlier, during their courtship, provides a rich account of their activities and thinking as well as their love and devotion to each other. It is from these letters that historians, including the Adamses' grandson Charles Francis Adams, have concluded that Abigail played a significant role in her husband's career, particularly in managing the family farm and his business affairs. Because of her, the Adamses avoided the financial ruin that befell some other early presidents, such as Thomas Jefferson, after they left office.

As the revolutionary spirit swept through the colonies, Abigail firmly supported the movement for independence. In March 1776, when her husband prepared to gather with his colleagues to write a statement of principles that would soon be adopted by the Continental Congress as the Declaration of Independence, she asked him to "remember the ladies and be more generous and favourable to them than your ancestors." Although this letter has often been cited, correctly, as evidence of her fervent desire for women's rights, she did not champion, then or later, the right of women to vote, a position virtually unheard of at the time. She did, however, strongly support a woman's right to education, and in 1778 she wrote her husband that "you need not be told how much female education is neglected, nor how fashionable it has been to ridicule female learning." She also favored the abolition of slavery.

In 1784 Abigail joined her husband in Europe, when he began serving as American minister to Britain. Her letters from Paris and London contain descriptive musings on British royalty, French customs, and the superiority of the quiet life of an American farmer. She wrote in early 1788 that she much preferred her "own little farm" to "the court of Saint James's where I seldom meet with characters so inoffensive as my Hens and chickings." Later that year the Adamses returned to the United

States; when John assumed the vice presidency in 1789, Abigail divided her time between the capital city (first New York City and then, in 1790, Philadelphia) and the family home in Massachusetts. She missed her husband's presidential inauguration in March 1797 in order to care for his sick mother, and during his presidency she often stayed in Massachusetts to look after family matters.

As first lady, she kept a rigorous daily schedule, rising at 5:00 A.M. to manage a busy household and receive callers for two hours each day. Unlike Martha Washington, who had been a gracious hostess but avoided all political discussions, Abigail involved herself in the most interesting debates of the day. As the two major political factions, the Federalists and the Anti-Federalists (later the Jeffersonian Republicans), developed into political parties in the 1790s, she pointed out her husband's friends and foes in both groups. About Alexander Hamilton, who along with Adams was a leading Federalist, she wrote that she saw in his eyes "the very devil . . . lasciviousness itself." She judged Albert Gallatin, a Republican opponent of her husband, "sly, artfull . . . insidious." Her critics objected that the wife of the president should not insinuate herself in political discussions; Gallatin wrote, "She is Mrs. President not of the United States but of a faction. . . . It is not right."

In November 1800, just as the election that denied John Adams a second term as president was being held, Abigail oversaw the Adamses' move from Philadelphia to the newly constructed presidential mansion in Washington, D.C. Her letters to family members showed her displeasure at finding the building roughly finished and unfurnished, but she warned her daughter not to reveal her thoughts, since people would think her ungrateful. On New Year's Day 1801 she opened the mansion, soon to be known as the White House, to visitors, continuing a tradition begun by the Washingtons and maintained by every subsequent first lady until 1933.

After leaving office, Abigail and John retired to their home in Massachusetts. She continued a lively correspondence with many people and even resumed writing to Thomas Jefferson, from whom she had been estranged as a result of political differences. She died in October 1818 and was buried in the First Church of Quincy; her husband, who died in 1826, was buried beside her.

Until the 20th century few first ladies shared Abigail Adams's interest in politics or in the treatment of government leaders by the press. She vigorously objected to what she considered inaccurate reporting on her husband and son. But she was not altogether surprised by the "lies [and] Falshoods," writing in 1797 to her sister that she "expected to be vilified and abused, with my whole family." Although her approach to the office of first lady was in many ways advanced, her fame rests primarily on her thousands of letters, which form an eloquent and evocative description of her life and times.

Adams, John

John Adams (1735–1826) was the eldest of the three sons of Deacon John Adams and Susanna Boylston of Braintree, Massachusetts. His father was only a farmer and shoemaker, but the Adams family could trace its lineage back to the first generation of Puritan settlers in New England. A local selectman and a leader in the community, Deacon Adams encouraged his eldest son to aspire toward a career in the ministry. In keeping with that goal, Adams graduated from Harvard College in 1755. For the next three years, he taught grammar school in Worcester, Massachusetts, while contemplating his future. He eventually chose law rather than the ministry and in 1758 moved back to Braintree, and then soon began practicing law in nearby Boston.

In 1764 Adams married Abigail Smith, a minister's daughter from neighboring Weymouth. Intelligent, well-read, vivacious, and just as fiercely independent as her new husband, Abigail Adams became a confidante and political partner who helped to stabilize and sustain the ever-irascible and highly volatile Adams throughout his long career. The letters between them afford an extended glimpse into their deepest thoughts and emotions and provide modern readers with the most revealing record of personal intimacy between husband and wife in the revolutionary era. Their first child, Abigail Amelia, was born in 1765. Their first son, John

John Adams, oil painting by Gilbert Stuart, 1826 (in the National Collection of Fine Arts, Washington, D.C.).

Quincy, arrived two years later. Two other sons, Thomas Boylston and Charles, followed shortly thereafter. (Another child, Susanna, did not survive infancy.)

By then Adams's legal career was on the rise, and he had become a visible member of the resistance movement that questioned Parliament's right to tax the American colonies. In 1765 Adams wrote "A Dissertation on the Canon and Feudal Law," which justified opposition to the recently enacted Stamp Act—an effort to raise revenue by requiring all publications and legal documents to bear a stamp—by arguing that Parliament's intrusions into colonial affairs exposed the inherently coercive and corrupt character of English politics. Intensely combative, full of private doubts about his own capacities but never about his cause, Adams became a leading figure in the opposition to the Townshend Acts (1767), which imposed duties on imported commodities (such as glass, lead, paper, paint, and tea). Despite his hostility toward the British government, in 1770 Adams agreed to defend the British soldiers who had fired on a Boston crowd in what became known as the Boston Massacre. His insistence on upholding the legal rights of the soldiers, who in fact had been provoked, made him temporarily unpopular but also marked him as one of the most principled radicals in the burgeoning movement for American independence. He had a penchant for doing the right thing, most especially when it made him unpopular.

In the summer of 1774, Adams was elected to the Massachusetts delegation that joined the representatives from 12 of 13 colonies in Philadelphia at the First Continental Congress. He and his cousin Samuel Adams quickly became the leaders of the radical faction, which rejected the prospects for reconciliation with Britain. His *Novanglus* essays, published early in 1775, moved the constitutional argument forward another notch, insisting that Parliament lacked the authority not just to tax the colonies but also to legislate for them in any way. (Less than a year earlier, Thomas Jefferson had made a similar argument against parliamentary authority in *A Summary View of the Rights of British America*.)

By the time the Second Continental Congress convened in 1775, Adams had gained the reputation as "the Atlas of independence." Over the course of the following year, he made several major contributions to the patriot cause destined to ensure his place in American history. First, he nominated George Washington to serve as commander of the fledgling Continental Army. Second, he selected Jefferson to draft the Declaration of Independence. (Both decisions were designed to ensure Virginia's support for the revolution.) Third, he dominated the debate in the Congress on July 2–4, 1776, defending Jefferson's draft of the declaration and demanding unanimous support for a decisive break with Great Britain. Moreover, he had written *Thoughts on Government*, which circulated throughout the colonies as the major guidebook for the drafting of new state constitutions.

Adams remained the central figure of the Continental Congress for the following two years. He drafted the Plan of

Treaties in July 1776, a document that provided the framework for a treaty with France and that almost inadvertently identified the strategic priorities that would shape American foreign policy over the next century. He was the unanimous choice to head the Board of War and Ordnance and was thereby made in effect a one-man war department responsible for raising and equipping the American army and creating from scratch an American navy. As the prospects for a crucial wartime alliance with France improved late in 1777, he was chosen to join Benjamin Franklin in Paris to conduct the negotiations. In February 1778 he sailed for Europe, accompanied by 10-year-old John Quincy.

By the time Adams arrived in Paris, the treaty creating an alliance with France had already been concluded. He quickly returned home in the summer of 1779, just in time to join the Massachusetts Constitutional Convention. The other delegates, acknowledging his constitutional expertise, simply handed him the job of drafting what became the Massachusetts constitution (1780), which immediately became the model for the other state constitutions and—in its insistence on a bicameral legislature and the separation of powers—a major influence on the Constitution of the United States.

The Congress then ordered Adams to rejoin Franklin in Paris to lead the American delegation responsible for negotiating an end to the war with Britain. This time he took along his youngest son, Charles, as well as John Quincy, leaving Abigail to tend the farm and the other two children in Braintree. Not until 1784, almost five years later, was the entire family reunited in Paris. By then Adams had shown himself an unnatural diplomat, exhibiting a level of candor and a confrontational style toward both English and French negotiators that alienated Franklin, who came to regard his colleague as slightly deranged. Adams, for his part, thought Franklin excessively impressed with his own stature as the Gallic version of the American genius and therefore inadequately attuned to the important differences between American and French interests in the peace negotiations. The favorable terms achieved in the Treaty of Paris (1783) can be attributed to the effective blend of Franklin's discretion and Adams's bulldog temperament. Adams's reputation for emotional explosions also dates from this period. Recent scholarly studies suggest that he might have suffered from a hyperthyroid condition subsequently known as Graves' disease.

In 1784 Jefferson arrived in Paris to replace Franklin as the American minister at the French court. Over the next few months, Jefferson became an unofficial member of the Adams family, and the bond of friendship between Adams and Jefferson was sealed, a lifelong partnership and rivalry that made the combative New Englander and the elegant Virginian the odd couple of the American Revolution. Jefferson also visited the Adams family in England in 1785, after Adams had assumed his new post as American ambassador in London. The two men also joined forces, though Adams as the senior figure assumed the lead, in negotiating a $400,000 loan from Dutch bankers that allowed the American government to consolidate its European debts.

Because he was the official embodiment of American independence from the British Empire, Adams was largely ignored and relegated to the periphery of the court during his nearly three years in London. Still brimming with energy, he spent his time studying the history of European politics for patterns and lessons that might assist the fledgling American government in its efforts to achieve what no major European nation had managed to produce—namely, a stable republican form of government.

The result was a massive and motley three-volume collection of quotations, unacknowledged citations, and personal observations entitled *A Defence of the Constitutions of Government of the United States of America* (1787). A fourth volume, Discourses on Davila (1790), was published soon after he returned to the United States. Taken together, these lengthy tomes contained Adams's distinctive insights as a political thinker. The lack of organization, combined with the sprawling style of the *Defence*, however, made its core message difficult to follow or fathom. When read in the context of his voluminous correspondence on political issues, along with the extensive marginalia he recorded in the several thousand books in his personal library, that message became clearer with time.

Adams wished to warn his fellow Americans against all revolutionary manifestos that envisioned a fundamental break with the past and a fundamental transformation in human nature or society that supposedly produced a new age. All such utopian expectations were illusions, he believed, driven by what he called "ideology," the belief that imagined ideals, so real and seductive in theory, were capable of being implemented in the world. The same kind of conflict between different classes that had bedeviled medieval Europe would, albeit in muted forms, also afflict the United States, because the seeds of such competition were planted in human nature itself. Adams blended the psychological insights of New England Puritanism, with its emphasis on the emotional forces throbbing inside all creatures, and the Enlightenment belief that government must contain and control those forces, to construct a political system capable of balancing the ambitions of individuals and competing social classes.

His insistence that elites were unavoidable realities in all societies, however, made him vulnerable to the charge of endorsing aristocratic rule in America, when in fact he was attempting to suggest that the inevitable American elite must be controlled, its ambitions channeled toward public purposes. He also was accused of endorsing monarchical principles because he argued that the chief executive in the American government, like the king in medieval European society, must possess sufficient power to check the ravenous appetites of the propertied classes. Although misunderstood by many of his contemporaries, the realistic perspective Adams proposed—and the skepticism toward utopian schemes he insisted upon—has achieved considerable support in the wake of the failed 20th-century attempts at social transformation in the communist bloc. In Adams's own day, his political analysis enjoyed the satisfaction of correctly predicting that the French Revolution would lead to the Reign of Terror and eventual despotism by a military dictator.

Soon after his return to the United States, Adams found himself on the ballot in the presidential election of 1789. He finished second to Washington (69 votes to 34 votes), which signaled three political realities: first, his standing as a leading member of the revolutionary generation was superseded only by that of Washington himself; second, his combative style and his recent political writings had hurt his reputation enough to preclude the kind of overwhelming support Washington enjoyed; third, according to the electoral rules established in the recently ratified Constitution, he was America's first vice president.

This meant that Adams was the first American statesman to experience the paradox of being a heartbeat away from maximum power while languishing in the political version of a cul-de-sac. Adams himself described the vice presidency as "the most insignificant office that ever the Invention of man contrived or his Imagination conceived." His main duty was to serve as president of the Senate, casting a vote only to break a tie. During his eight years in office, Adams cast between 31 and 38 such votes, more than any subsequent vice president in American history. He steadfastly supported all the major initiatives of the Washington administration, including the financial plan of Alexander Hamilton; the Neutrality Proclamation (1793), which effectively ended the Franco-American Alliance of 1778; the forceful suppression of an insurrection in western Pennsylvania called the Whiskey Rebellion (1794); and the Jay Treaty (1795), a highly controversial effort to avoid war with England by accepting British hegemony on the high seas. When Washington announced his decision not to seek a third term in 1796, Adams was the logical choice to succeed him.

In the first contested presidential election in American history, Adams won a narrow electoral majority (71–68) over

Jefferson, who thereby became vice president. Adams made an initial effort to bring Jefferson into the cabinet and involve him in shaping foreign policy, but Jefferson declined the offer, preferring to retain his independence. This burdened the Adams presidency with a vice president who was the acknowledged head of the rival political party, the Republicans (subsequently the Democratic-Republicans). Additional burdens included: inheritance of Washington's cabinet, whom Adams unwisely decided to retain, and whose highest loyalty was to Washington's memory as embodied in Hamilton; a raging naval conflict with the French in the Caribbean dubbed the "quasi-war"; and the impossible task of succeeding—no one could replace—the greatest hero of the revolutionary era.

Despite Washington's plea for a bipartisan foreign policy in his farewell address (1796), the "quasi-war" produced a bitter political argument between Federalists, who preferred war with France to alienating Britain, and Democratic-Republicans, who viewed France as America's only European ally and the French Revolution as a continuation of the American Revolution on European soil. Adams attempted to steer a middle course between these partisan camps, which left him vulnerable to political attacks from both sides. In 1797 he sent a peace delegation to Paris to negotiate an end to hostilities, but when the French directory demanded bribes before any negotiations could begin, Adams ordered the delegates home and began a naval buildup in preparation for outright war. The Federalist-dominated Congress called for raising a 30,000-man army, which Adams agreed to reluctantly. If Adams had requested a declaration of war in 1798, he would have enjoyed widespread popularity and virtually certain reelection two years later. Instead, he acted with characteristic independence by sending yet another, and this time successful, peace delegation to France against the advice of his cabinet and his Federalist supporters. The move ruined him politically but avoided a costly war that the infant American republic was ill prepared to fight. It was a vintage Adams performance, reminiscent of his defense of British soldiers after the Boston Massacre, which was also principled and unpopular.

If ending the "quasi-war" with France was Adams's major foreign policy triumph, his chief domestic failure was passage of the Alien and Sedition Acts (1798), which permitted the government to deport foreign-born residents and indict newspaper editors or writers who published "false, scandalous, and malicious writing or writings against the government of the United States." A total of 14 indictments were brought against the Republican press under the Sedition Act, but the crudely partisan prosecutions quickly became infamous persecutions that backfired on the Federalists. Although Adams had signed the Alien and Sedition Acts under pressure from the Federalists in Congress, he shouldered most of the blame both at the time and in the history books. He came to regard the Sedition Act as the biggest political blunder of his life.

The election of 1800 again pitted Adams against Jefferson. Adams ran ahead of the Federalist candidates for Congress, who were swept from office in a Republican landslide. However, thanks to the deft maneuvering of Aaron Burr, all 12 of New York's electoral votes went to Jefferson, giving the tandem of Jefferson and Burr the electoral victory (73–65). Jefferson was eventually elected president by the House of Representatives, which chose him over Burr on the 36th ballot. In his last weeks in office, Adams made several Federalist appointments to the judiciary, including John Marshall as chief justice of the United States. These "midnight judges" offended Jefferson, who resented the encroachment on his own presidential prerogatives. Adams, the first president to reside in the presidential mansion (later called the White House) in Washington, D.C., was also the first—and one of the very few—presidents not to attend the inauguration of his successor. On March 4, 1801, he was already on the road back to Quincy.

At age 65 Adams did not anticipate a long retirement. The

fates proved more generous than he expected, providing him with another quarter-century to brood about his career and life, add to the extensive marginalia in his books, settle old scores in his memoirs, watch with pride when John Quincy assumed the presidency, and add to his already vast and voluminous correspondence. In an extensive exchange of letters with Benjamin Rush, the Philadelphia physician and patriotic gadfly, Adams revealed his preoccupation with fame and developed his own theory of the role ambition plays in motivating man to public service. Along the way he placed on the record his own candid and often critical portraits of the other vanguard members of the revolutionary generation.

In 1812, thanks in part to prodding from Rush, he overcame his bitterness toward Jefferson and initiated a correspondence with his former friend and rival that totaled 158 letters. Generally regarded as the most intellectually impressive correspondence between American statesmen in all of American history, the dialogue between Adams and Jefferson touched on a host of timely and timeless subjects: the role of religion in history, the aging process, the emergence of an American language, the French Revolution, and the party battles of the 1790s. Adams put it most poignantly to Jefferson: "You and I ought not to die, before We have explained ourselves to each other."

More than the elegiac tone of the letters, the correspondence dramatized the contradictory impulses generated by the American Revolution and symbolized by the two aging patriarchs. Adams was the realist, the skeptic, the principled pessimist. Jefferson was the idealist, the romantic, the pragmatic optimist. As if according to a script written by providence, the "Sage of Quincy" and the "Sage of Monticello" died within hours of each other on July 4, 1826, the 50th anniversary to the day of the Declaration of Independence.

Although Adams was regarded by his contemporaries as one of the most significant statesmen of the revolutionary era, his reputation faded in the 19th century, only to ascend again during the last half of the 20th century. The modern edition of his correspondence prompted a rediscovery of his bracing honesty and pungent way with words, his importance as a political thinker, his realistic perspective on American foreign policy, and his patriarchal role as founder of one of the most prominent families in American history.

Adams, Samuel

Samuel Adams (1722–1803) was a second cousin of John Adams, second president of the United States. He graduated from Harvard College in 1740 and briefly studied law. He failed in several business ventures; as a tax collector in Boston, for example, he neglected to collect the public levies and to keep proper accounts.

Although unsuccessful in conducting personal or public business, Adams took an active and influential part in local politics. By the time the English Parliament passed the Sugar Act (1764) taxing molasses for revenue, Adams was a powerful figure in the opposition to British authority in the Colonies. He denounced the act, being one of the first of the colonials to cry out against taxation without representation. He played an important part in instigating the Stamp Act riots in Boston that were directed against the new requirement to pay taxes on all legal and commercial documents, newspapers, and college diplomas.

Samuel Adams, American revolutionary, patriot, and political agitator

His influence was soon second only to that of James Otis, the lawyer and politician who gained prominence by his resistance to the revenue acts. Elected to the lower house of the Massachusetts general court from Boston, Adams served in that body until 1774, after 1766 as its clerk. In 1769 Adams assumed the leadership of the Massachusetts radicals. There is some reason to believe that he had committed himself to American independence a year earlier. John Adams may have erred in ascribing this extreme stand to his cousin at so early a time, but certainly Samuel Adams was one of the first American leaders to deny Parliament's authority over the Colonies; and he was also one of the first—certainly by 1774—to establish independence as the proper goal.

John Adams described his cousin as a plain, modest, and virtuous man. But in addition, Samuel Adams was a propagandist who was not overscrupulous in his attacks upon British officials and policies, and a passionate politician as well. In innumerable newspaper letters and essays over various signatures, he described British measures and the behavior of royal governors, judges, and customs men in the darkest colors. He was a master of organization, arranging for the election of men who agreed with him, procuring committees that would act as he wished, and securing the passage of resolutions that he desired.

During the crisis over the Townshend Acts (1767–70), the import taxes on previously duty-free products proposed by Cabinet Minister Charles Townshend, Adams was unable to persuade the Massachusetts colonists to take extreme steps, partly because of the moderating influence of Otis. British troops sent to Boston in 1768, however, offered a fine target for this propaganda, and Adams saw to it that they were portrayed in the colonial newspapers as brutal soldiery oppressing citizens and assailing their wives and daughters. He was one of the leaders in the town meeting that demanded and secured the removal of the troops from Boston after some British soldiers fired into a mob and killed five Americans. When news came that the Townshend duties, except for that on tea, had been repealed, his following dwindled. Nevertheless, during the years 1770–73, when other colonial leaders were inactive, Adams revived old issues and found new ones; he was responsible for the foundation (1772) of the committee of correspondence of Boston that kept in contact with similar bodies in other towns, in whose establishment he also had a hand. These committees later became effective instruments in the fight against the British.

The passage by Parliament of the Tea Act of 1773, which granted the East India Company a monopoly on tea sales in the Colonies, gave Adams ample opportunity to exercise his remarkable talents. Although he did not participate in the Boston Tea Party, he was undoubtedly one of its planners. He was again a leading figure in the opposition of Massachusetts to the execution of the Intolerable (Coercive) Acts passed by the British Parliament in retaliation for the dumping of tea in Boston Harbor; and as a member of the First Continental Congress, which spoke for the 13 Colonies, he insisted that the delegates take a vigorous stand against Britain. A member of the provincial congress of Massachusetts in 1774–75, he participated in making preparations for warfare should Britain resort to arms. When the British troops marched out of Boston to Concord, Adams and the president of the Continental Congress, John Hancock, were staying in a farmhouse near the line of march; and it has been said that the arrest of the two men was one of the purposes of the expedition. But the troops made no effort to find them, and British orders called only for destruction of military supplies gathered at Concord. When Gen. Thomas Gage issued an offer of pardon to the rebels some weeks later, however, he excepted Adams and Hancock.

As a member of the Continental Congress, in which he served until 1781, Adams was less conspicuous than he was in town meetings and the Massachusetts legislature, for the congress contained a number of men as able as he. He and John

Adams were among the first to call for a final separation from Britain, both signed the Declaration of Independence, and both exerted considerable influence in the congress.

Adams was a member of the convention that framed the Massachusetts constitution of 1780 and also sat in the convention of his state that ratified the Federal Constitution. He was at first an anti-Federalist who opposed the ratification of the Constitution for fear that it would vest too much power in the federal government, but he finally abandoned his opposition when the Federalists promised to support a number of future amendments, including a bill of rights. He was defeated in the first congressional election. Returning to political power as a follower of Hancock, he was lieutenant governor of Massachusetts from 1789 to 1793 and governor from 1794 to 1797. When national parties developed, he affiliated himself with the Democratic-Republicans, the forerunner of the Democratic Party. After being defeated as a presidential elector favoring Thomas Jefferson in 1796, he retired to private life.

Alien and Sedition Acts

The Alien and Sedition Acts (1798), four internal security laws passed by the U.S. Congress, restricted aliens and curtailed the excesses of an unrestrained press in anticipation of an expected war with France. After the XYZ Affair (1797), in which French agents suggested American officials pay a bribe to the French foreign minister to secure a commercial agreement to protect U.S. shipping, war appeared inevitable. Federalists, aware that French military successes in Europe had been greatly facilitated by political dissidents in invaded countries, sought to prevent such subversion in the United States and adopted the Alien and Sedition Acts as part of a series of military preparedness measures.

The three alien laws, passed in June and July, were aimed at

French and Irish immigrants, who were mostly pro-French. These laws raised the waiting period for naturalization from 5 to 14 years, permitted the detention of subjects of an enemy nation, and authorized the chief executive to expel any alien he considered dangerous. The Sedition Act (July 14) banned the publishing of false or malicious writings against the government and the inciting of opposition to any act of Congress or the president—practices already forbidden by state statutes and the common law but not by federal law. The federal act reduced the oppressiveness of procedures in prosecuting such offenses but provided for federal enforcement.

The acts were the mildest wartime security measures ever taken in the United States, and they were widely popular. Jeffersonian Republicans vigorously opposed them, however, in the Virginia and Kentucky Resolutions, which the other state legislatures either ignored or denounced as subversive. Only one alien was deported, and only 25 prosecutions, resulting in 10 convictions, were brought under the Sedition Act. With the war threat passing and the Republicans winning control of the federal government in 1800, all the Alien and Sedition Acts expired or were repealed during the next two years.

American Revolution

The American Revolution (1775–83) was an insurrection by which 13 of Great Britain's North American colonies won political independence and went on to form the United States of America. The war followed more than a decade of growing estrangement between the British crown and a large and influential segment of its North American colonies that was caused by British attempts to assert greater control over colonial affairs. Until early in 1778 the conflict was a civil war within the British Empire; afterward it became an international war as France (in 1778), Spain (in 1779), and the Netherlands (in 1780) joined the colonies against Britain. From the beginning sea power was vital in determining the course of the war, lending to British strategy a flexibility that helped compensate for the comparatively small numbers of troops sent to America and ultimately enabling the French to help bring about the final British surrender at Yorktown.

Americans fought the war on land essentially with two types of organization, the Continental (national) Army and the state militias. The total number of the former provided by quotas from the states throughout the conflict was 231,771 men; the militias totaled 164,087. At any given time, however, the American forces seldom numbered over 20,000; in 1781 there were only about 29,000 insurgents under arms throughout the country. The war was therefore one fought by small field armies. Militias, poorly disciplined and with elected officers, were summoned for periods usually not exceeding three months. The terms of Continental Army service were only gradually increased from one to three years, and not even bounties and the offer of land kept the army up to strength. Reasons for the difficulty in maintaining an adequate Continental force included the colonists' traditional antipathy to regular armies, the objections of farmers to being away from their fields, the competition of the states with the Continental Congress to keep men in the militia, and the wretched and uncertain pay in a period of inflation.

By contrast, the British army was a reliable, steady force of professionals. Since it numbered only about 42,000, heavy recruiting programs were introduced. Many of the enlisted men were farm boys, as were most of the Americans. Others were unemployed persons from the urban slums. Still others joined the army to escape fines or imprisonment. The great majority became efficient soldiers owing to sound training and ferocious discipline. The officers were drawn largely from the gentry and the aristocracy and obtained their commissions and promotions by purchase. Though they received no formal training, they were not as dependent on a book knowledge of military tactics as were many of the Americans. British generals, however, tended toward a lack of imagination and initiative, while those who demonstrated such qualities often were rash.

Because troops were few and conscription unknown, the British government, following a traditional policy, purchased about 30,000 troops from various German princes. The Landgrave of Hesse furnished approximately three-fifths of this total. Few acts by the crown roused so much antagonism in America as this use of foreign mercenaries.

The war began in Massachusetts when General Thomas Gage sent a force from Boston to destroy rebel military stores at Concord. Fighting occurred at Lexington and Concord on April 19, 1775, and only the arrival of reinforcements saved the British original column. Rebel militia then converged on Boston from all over New England. Their entrenching on Breed's Hill led to a British frontal assault on June 17 under General William Howe, who won the hill but at the cost of more than 40 percent of the assault force.

General George Washington was appointed commander in chief of the American forces by the Continental Congress. Not only did he have to contain the British in Boston but he had also to recruit a Continental army. During the winter of 1775–76 recruitment lagged so badly that fresh drafts of militia were called up to help maintain the siege. The balance shifted in late winter, when General Henry Knox arrived with artillery from Fort Ticonderoga in New York, which had been captured from the British in May 1775. Mounted on Dorchester Heights, above Boston, the guns forced Howe, who had replaced Gage in command, to evacuate the city on March 17, 1776. Howe then repaired to Halifax to prepare for an invasion of New York, and Washington moved units southward for its defense.

Meanwhile, action flared in the north. In the fall of 1775 the Americans invaded Canada. One force under General Richard Montgomery captured Montreal on November 13. Another under Benedict Arnold made a remarkable march through the Maine wilderness to Quebec. Unable to take the city, Arnold was presently joined by Montgomery, many of whose troops had gone home because their enlistments had expired. An attack on the city on the last day of the year failed, Montgomery was killed, and many troops were captured. The Americans maintained a siege of the city but withdrew with the arrival of British reinforcements in the spring. Pursued by the British and decimated by smallpox, the Americans fell back to Ticonderoga. General Guy Carleton's hopes of moving quickly down Lake Champlain, however, were frustrated by Arnold's construction of a fighting fleet. Forced to build one of his own, Carleton destroyed most of the American fleet in October 1776 but considered the season too advanced to bring Ticonderoga under siege.

As the Americans suffered defeat in Canada, so did the British in the south. North Carolina patriots trounced a body of loyalists at Moore's Creek Bridge on February 27, 1776. Charleston, South Carolina, was successfully defended against a British assault by sea in June.

Having made up its mind to crush the rebellion, the British government sent General Howe and his brother, Richard, Admiral Lord Howe, with a large fleet and 34,000 British and German troops to New York. It also gave the Howes a commission to treat with the Americans. The Continental Congress, which had proclaimed the independence of the colonies, at first thought the Howes empowered to negotiate peace terms but discovered that they were authorized only to accept submission and assure pardons.

Their peace efforts getting nowhere, the Howes turned to force. Under his brother's guns, General Howe landed troops on Long Island and on August 27 scored a smashing victory. Washington evacuated his army from Brooklyn to Manhattan that night under cover of a fog. On September 15 Howe followed up his victory by invading Manhattan. Though checked at Harlem Heights the next day, he drew Washington off the island in October by a move to Throg's Neck and then to New Rochelle, northeast of the city. Leaving garrisons at Fort Washington on Manhattan and at Fort Lee on the opposite shore of the Hudson River, Washington hastened to block Howe. The latter, however, defeated him on October 28 at Chatterton Hill near White Plains. Howe slipped between the American army and Fort Washington and stormed the fort on November 16, seizing nearly 3,000 prisoners, guns, and supplies. British forces under Lord Cornwallis then took Fort Lee and on November 24 started to drive the American army across New Jersey. Though Washington escaped to the west bank of the Delaware River, his army nearly disappeared. Howe then put his army into winter quarters, with outposts at towns such as Bordentown and Trenton.

On Christmas night Washington struck back with a brilliant riposte. Crossing the ice-strewn Delaware with 4,000 men, he fell upon the Hessian garrison at Trenton at dawn and took nearly 1,000 prisoners. Though almost trapped by Cornwallis, who recovered Trenton on January 2, 1777, Washington made a skillful escape during the night, won a battle against British reinforcements at Princeton the next day, and went into winter quarters in the defensible area around Morristown. The Trenton-Princeton campaign roused the country and saved the struggle for independence from collapse.

Britain's strategy in 1777 aimed at driving a wedge between New England and the other colonies. An army under General John Burgoyne was to march south from Canada and join forces with Howe on the Hudson. But Howe seems to have concluded that Burgoyne was strong enough to operate on his own and left New York in the summer, taking his army by sea to the head of Chesapeake Bay. Once ashore, he defeated Washington badly but not decisively at Brandywine Creek on September 11. Then, feinting westward, he entered Philadelphia, the American capital, on September 25. The Continental Congress fled to York. Washington struck back at Germantown on October 4

French engraving showing the surrender of Burgoyne at Saratoga. Saratoga (1777) was a significant turning point in the American Revolution. Not only were British hopes for an early victory smashed and American morale boosted, but, more importantly, France was convinced that the Americans were worthy of open support.

but, compelled to withdraw, went into winter quarters at Valley Forge.

In the north the story was different. Burgoyne was to move south to Albany with a force of about 9,000 British, Germans, Indians, and American loyalists; a smaller force under Lieutenant Colonel Barry St. Leger was to converge on Albany through the Mohawk valley. Burgoyne took Ticonderoga handily on July 5 and then, instead of using Lake George, chose a southward route by land. Slowed by the rugged terrain, strewn with trees cut down by American axmen under General Philip Schuyler, and needing horses, Burgoyne sent a force of Germans to collect them at Bennington, Vermont. The Germans were nearly wiped out on August 16 by New Englanders under General John Stark and Colonel Seth Warner. Meanwhile, St. Leger besieged Fort Schuyler (present Rome, New York), ambushed a relief column of American militia at Oriskany on August 6, but retreated as his Indians gave up the siege and an American force under Arnold approached. Burgoyne himself reached the Hudson, but the Americans, now under General Horatio Gates, checked him at Freeman's Farm on September 19 and, thanks to Arnold's battlefield leadership, decisively defeated him at Bemis Heights on October 7. Ten days later, unable to get help from New York, Burgoyne surrendered at Saratoga.

The most significant result of Burgoyne's capitulation was the entrance of France into the war. The French had secretly furnished financial and material aid since 1776. Now they prepared fleets and armies, although they did not formally declare war until June 1778.

Meanwhile, the Americans at Valley Forge survived a hungry winter, which was made worse by quartermaster and commissary mismanagement, graft of contractors, and unwillingness of farmers to sell produce for paper money. Order and discipline among the troops were improved by the arrival of the Freiherr von (baron of) Steuben, a Prussian officer in the service of France. Steuben instituted a training program in which he emphasized drilling by officers, marching in columns, and using firearms more effectively.

The program paid off at Monmouth Court House, New Jersey, on June 28, 1778, when Washington attacked the British, who were withdrawing from Philadelphia to New York. Although Sir Henry Clinton, who had replaced Howe, struck back hard, the Americans stood their ground.

French aid now materialized with the appearance of a strong fleet under the comte d'Estaing. Unable to enter New York Harbor, d'Estaing tried to assist Major General John Sullivan in dislodging the British from Newport, Rhode Island. Storms and British reinforcements thwarted the joint effort.

Action in the north was largely a stalemate for the rest of the war. The British raided New Bedford, Massachusetts, and New Haven and New London, Connecticut, while loyalists and Indians attacked settlements in New York and Pennsylvania. On the other hand, the Americans under Anthony Wayne stormed Stony Point, New York, on July 16, 1779, and "Light-Horse Harry" Lee took Paulus Hook, New Jersey, on August 19. More lasting in effect was Sullivan's expedition of August 1779 against Britain's Indian allies in New York, particularly the destruction of their villages and fields of corn. Farther west, Colonel George Rogers Clark seized Vincennes and other posts north of the Ohio River in 1778.

Potentially serious blows to the American cause were Arnold's defection in 1780 and the army mutinies of 1780 and 1781. Arnold's attempt to betray West Point to the British miscarried. Mutinies were sparked by misunderstandings over terms of enlistment, poor food and clothing, gross arrears of pay, and the decline in the purchasing power of the dollar. Suppressed by force or negotiation, the mutinies shook the morale of the army.

The Americans also suffered setbacks in the south. British strategy from 1778 called for offensives that were designed to take advantage of the flexibility of sea power and the loyalist sentiment of many of the people. British forces from New York and St. Augustine, Florida, occupied Georgia by the end of January 1779 and successfully defended Savannah in the fall against d'Estaing and a Franco-American army. Clinton, having withdrawn his Newport garrison, captured Charleston, and an American army of 5,000 under General Benjamin Lincoln in May 1780. Learning that Newport was threatened by a French expeditionary force under the comte de Rochambeau, Clinton returned to New York, leaving Cornwallis at Charleston.

Cornwallis, however, took the offensive. On August 16 he shattered General Gates's army at Camden, South Carolina. The destruction of a force of loyalists at Kings Mountain on October 7 led him to move against the new American commander, General Nathanael Greene. When Greene put part of his force under General Daniel Morgan, Cornwallis sent his cavalry leader, Colonel Banastre Tarleton, after Morgan. At

Cowpens on January 17, 1781, Morgan destroyed practically all of Tarleton's column. Subsequently, on March 15, Greene and Cornwallis fought at Guilford Courthouse, North Carolina. Cornwallis won but suffered heavy casualties. After withdrawing to Wilmington, he marched into Virginia to join British forces sent there by Clinton.

Greene then moved back to South Carolina, where he was defeated by Lord Rawdon at Hobkirk's Hill on April 25 and at Ninety-Six in June and by Lieutenant Colonel Alexander Stewart at Eutaw Springs on September 8. In spite of this, the British, harassed by partisan leaders such as Francis Marion, Thomas Sumter, and Andrew Pickens, soon retired to the coast and remained locked up in Charleston and Savannah.

Meanwhile, Cornwallis entered Virginia. Sending Tarleton on raids across the state, he started to build a base at Yorktown, at the same time fending off American forces under Wayne, Steuben, and the marquis de Lafayette.

Learning that the comte de Grasse had arrived in the Chesapeake with a large fleet and 3,000 French troops, Washington and Rochambeau moved south to Virginia. By mid-September the Franco-American forces had placed Yorktown under siege, and British rescue efforts proved fruitless. Cornwallis surrendered his army of more than 7,000 men on October 19. Thus, for the second time during the war the British had lost an entire army.

Thereafter, land action in America died out, though the war persisted in other theaters and on the high seas. Eventually Clinton was replaced by Sir Guy Carleton. While the peace treaties were under consideration and afterward, Carleton evacuated thousands of loyalists from America, including many from Savannah on July 11, 1782, and others from Charleston on December 14. The last British forces finally left New York on November 25, 1783. Washington then reentered the city in triumph.

Although the colonists ventured to challenge Britain's naval power from the outbreak of the conflict, the war at sea in its later stages was fought mainly between Britain and America's European allies, the American effort being reduced to privateering.

The importance of sea power was recognized early. In October 1775 the Continental Congress authorized the creation of the Continental Navy and established the Marine Corps in November. The navy, taking its direction from the naval and marine committees of the Congress, was only occasionally effective. In 1776 it had 27 ships against Britain's 270; by the end of the war, the British total had risen close to 500, and the American had dwindled to 20. Many of the best seamen available went off privateering, and both Continental Navy commanders and crews suffered from a lack of training and discipline.

The first significant blow by the navy was struck by Commodore Esek Hopkins, who captured New Providence (Nassau) in the Bahamas in 1776. Other captains, such as Lambert Wickes, Gustavus Conyngham, and John Barry, also enjoyed successes, but the Scottish-born John Paul Jones was especially notable. As captain of the *Ranger*, Jones scourged the British coasts in 1778, capturing the man-of-war *Drake*. As captain of the *Bonhomme Richard* in 1779, he intercepted a timber convoy and captured the British frigate *Serapis*.

More injurious to the British were the raids by American privateers on their shipping. American ships, furnished with letters of marque (an official commission) by the Congress or the states, swarmed about the British Isles. By the end of 1777 they had taken 560 British vessels, and by the end of the war they had probably seized 1,500. More than 12,000 British sailors also were captured. One result was that by 1781, British merchants were clamoring for an end to hostilities.

Most of the naval action occurred at sea. The significant exceptions were Arnold's battles against General Carleton's fleet on Lake Champlain at Valcour Island on October 11 and off Split Rock on October 13, 1776. Arnold lost both battles, but his construction of a fleet of tiny vessels, mostly gondolas (gundalows) and galleys, had forced the British to build a larger fleet and hence delayed their attack on Fort Ticonderoga until the following spring. This delay contributed significantly to Burgoyne's capitulation in October 1777.

The entrance of France into the war, followed by that of Spain in 1779 and the Netherlands in 1780, effected important changes in the naval aspect of the war. The Spanish and Dutch were not particularly active, but their role in keeping British naval forces tied down in Europe was significant. The British navy could not maintain an effective blockade of both the American coast and the enemies' ports. Owing to years of economy and neglect, Britain's ships of the line were neither modern nor sufficiently numerous. An immediate result was that France's Toulon fleet under d'Estaing got safely away to America, where it appeared off New York and later assisted General Sullivan in the unsuccessful siege of Newport. A fierce battle off Ushant, France, in July 1778 between the Channel fleet under Admiral Augustus Keppel and the Brest fleet under the comte d'Orvilliers proved inconclusive. Had Keppel won decisively, French aid to the Americans would have diminished and Rochambeau might never have been able to lead his expedition to America.

In the following year England was in real danger. Not only did it have to face the privateers of the United States, France, and Spain off its coasts, as well as the raids of John Paul Jones, but it also lived in fear of invasion. The combined fleets of France and Spain had acquired command of the Channel, and a French army of 50,000 waited for the propitious moment to board their transports. Luckily for the British, storms, sickness among the allied crews, and changes of plans terminated the threat.

Despite allied supremacy in the Channel in 1779, the threat of invasion, and the loss of islands in the West Indies, the British maintained control of the North American seaboard for most of 1779 and 1780, which made possible their southern land campaigns. They also reinforced Gibraltar, which the Spaniards had brought under siege in the fall of 1779, and sent a fleet under Admiral Sir George Rodney to the West Indies in early 1780. After fruitless maneuvering against the comte de Guichen, who had replaced d'Estaing, Rodney sailed for New York.

While Rodney had been in the West Indies, a French squadron slipped out of Brest and sailed to Newport with Rochambeau's army. Rodney, instead of trying to block the approach to Newport, returned to the West Indies, where, upon receiving instructions to attack Dutch possessions, he seized Sint Eustatius, the Dutch island that served as the principal depot for war materials shipped from Europe and transshipped into American vessels. He became so involved in the disposal of the enormous booty that he dallied at the island for six months.

In the meantime, a powerful British fleet relieved Gibraltar in 1781, but the price was the departure of the French fleet at Brest, part of it to India, the larger part under Admiral de Grasse to the West Indies. After maneuvering indecisively against Rodney, de Grasse received a request from Washington and Rochambeau to come to New York or the Chesapeake.

Earlier, in March, a French squadron had tried to bring troops from Newport to the Chesapeake but was forced to return by Admiral Marriot Arbuthnot, who had succeeded Lord Howe. Soon afterward Arbuthnot was replaced by Thomas Graves, a conventional-minded admiral.

Informed that a French squadron would shortly leave the West Indies, Rodney sent Samuel Hood north with a powerful force while he sailed for England, taking with him several formidable ships that might better have been left with Hood.

Soon after Hood dropped anchor in New York, de Grasse appeared in the Chesapeake, where he landed troops to help Lafayette contain Cornwallis until Washington and Rochambeau could arrive. Fearful that the comte de Barras, who was carrying Rochambeau's artillery train from Newport, might join de Grasse, and hoping to intercept him, Graves sailed with Hood to the Chesapeake. Graves had 19 ships of the line against de Grasse's 24. Though the battle that began on September 5 off the Virginia capes was not a skillfully managed affair, Graves had the worst of it and retired to New York. He ventured out again on October 17 with a strong contingent of troops and 25 ships of the line, while de Grasse, reinforced by Barras, now had 36 ships of the line. No battle occurred, however, when Graves learned that Cornwallis had surrendered.

Although Britain subsequently recouped some of its fortunes, by Rodney defeating and capturing de Grasse in the Battle of the Saints off Dominica in 1782 and British land and sea forces inflicting defeats in India, the turn of events did not significantly alter the situation in America as it existed after Yorktown. A new government under Lord Shelburne tried to get the American commissioners to agree to a separate peace, but, ultimately, the treaty negotiated with the Americans was not to go into effect until the formal conclusion of a peace with their European allies.

The Treaty of Paris (September 3, 1783) ended the U.S. War of Independence. Great Britain recognized the independence of the United States (with western boundaries to the Mississippi River) and ceded Florida to Spain. Other provisions called for payment of U.S. private debts to British citizens, American use of the Newfoundland fisheries, and fair treatment for American colonials loyal to Britain.

In explaining the outcome of the war, scholars have pointed out that the British never contrived an overall general strategy for winning it. Also, even if the war could have been terminated by British power in the early stages, the generals during that period, notably Howe, declined to make a prompt, vigorous, intelligent application of that power. They acted, to be sure, within the conventions of their age, but in choosing to take minimal risks (for example, Carleton at Ticonderoga and Howe at Brooklyn Heights and later in New Jersey and Pennsylvania) they lost the opportunity to deal potentially mortal blows to the rebellion. There was also a grave lack of understanding and cooperation at crucial moments (as with Burgoyne and Howe in 1777). Finally, the British counted too strongly on loyalist support they did not receive.

But British mistakes alone could not account for the success of the United States. Feeble as their war effort occasionally became, the Americans were able generally to take advantage of their enemies' mistakes. The Continental Army, moreover, was by no means an inept force even before Steuben's reforms. The militias, while usually unreliable, could perform admirably under the leadership of men who understood them, like Arnold, Greene, and Morgan, and often reinforced the Continentals in crises. Furthermore, Washington, a rock in adversity, learned slowly but reasonably well the art of generalship. The supplies and funds furnished by France from 1776 to 1778 were invaluable, while French military and naval support after 1778 was essential. The outcome, therefore, resulted from a combination of British blunders, American efforts, and French assistance.

Articles of Confederation

Serving as a bridge between the initial government by the Continental Congress of the Revolutionary period and the federal government provided under the U.S. Constitution of 1787, the Articles of Confederation was the first U.S. constitution (1781–89). Because the experience of overbearing British central authority was vivid in colonial minds, the drafters of the Articles deliberately established a confederation of sovereign states.

On paper, the Congress had power to regulate foreign affairs, war, and the postal service and to appoint military officers, control Indian affairs, borrow money, determine the value of coin, and issue bills of credit. In reality, however, the Articles gave the Congress no power to enforce its requests to the states for money or troops, and by the end of 1786 governmental effectiveness had broken down.

Nevertheless, some solid accomplishments had been achieved: certain state claims to western lands were settled, and the Northwest Ordinance of 1787 established the fundamental pattern of evolving government in the territories north of the Ohio River. Equally important, the Confederation provided the new nation with instructive experience in self-government under a written document. In revealing their own weaknesses, the Articles paved the way for the Constitutional Convention of 1787 and the present form of U.S. government.

Bill of Rights

The U.S. Bill of Rights are the first 10 amendments to the U.S. Constitution and were adopted as a single unit on December 15, 1791. They constitute a collection of mutually reinforcing guarantees of individual rights and of limitations on federal and state governments.

The Bill of Rights derives from the Magna Carta (1215), the English Bill of Rights (1689), the colonial struggle against king and Parliament, and a gradually broadening concept of equality among the American people. Virginia's 1776 Declaration of Rights, drafted chiefly by George Mason, was a notable forerunner. Besides being axioms of government, the guarantees in the Bill of Rights have binding legal force. Acts of Congress in conflict with them may be voided by the U.S. Supreme Court when the question of the constitutionality of such acts arises in litigation.

The Constitution in its main body forbids suspension of the writ of habeas corpus except in cases of rebellion or invasion (Article I, section 9); prohibits state or federal bills of attainder and ex post facto laws (I, 9, 10); requires that all crimes against the United States be tried by jury in the state where committed (III, 2); limits the definition, trial, and punishment of treason (III, 3); prohibits titles of nobility (I, 9) and religious tests for officeholding (VI); guarantees a republican form of government in every state (IV, 4); and assures each citizen the privileges and immunities of the citizens of the several states (IV, 2).

Popular dissatisfaction with the limited guarantees of the main body of the Constitution expressed in the state conventions called to ratify it led to demands and promises that the first Congress of the United States satisfied by submitting to the states 12 amendments. Ten were ratified. Individual states being subject to their own bills of rights, these amendments were limited to restraining the federal government. The Senate refused to submit James Madison's amendment (approved by the House of Representatives) protecting religious liberty, freedom of the press, and trial by jury against violation by the states.

Under the First Amendment, Congress can make no law respecting an establishment of religion or prohibiting its free exercise, or abridging freedom of speech or press or the right to assemble and petition for redress of grievances. Hostility to standing armies found expression in a guarantee of the people's right to bear arms and in limitation of the quartering of soldiers in private houses.

The Fourth Amendment secures the people against unreasonable searches and seizures and forbids the issuance of warrants except upon probable cause and directed to specific persons and places. The Fifth Amendment requires grand jury indictment in prosecutions for major crimes and prohibits double jeopardy for a single offense. It provides that no person shall be compelled to testify against himself and forbids the taking of life, liberty, or property without due process of law or the taking of private property for public use without just compensation. By the Sixth Amendment, an accused person is to have a speedy public trial by jury, to be informed of the nature of the accusation, to be confronted with prosecution witnesses, and to have the assistance of counsel. Excessive bail or fines and cruel or unusual punishment are forbidden by the Eighth Amendment. The Ninth Amendment protects unenumerated residual rights of the people, and by the Tenth, powers not delegated to the United States are reserved to the states or the people.

After the Civil War, slavery was abolished, and the Fourteenth Amendment (1868) declared that all persons born or naturalized in the United States and subject to its jurisdiction are citizens thereof. It forbids the states to abridge the privileges or immunities of citizens of the United States, or to deprive any person of life, liberty, or property without due process of law. After 1924, the due process clause was construed by the Supreme Court as guaranteeing that many of the same rights protected from federal violation were also protected from violation by the states. The clause finally made effective the major portion of Madison's unaccepted 1789 proposal.

Blair, John

An associate justice of the United States Supreme Court (1790–96), a member of one of Virginia's most prominent landed families, and a close friend of George Washington, John Blair (1732–1800) studied law at the Middle Temple in London and, in 1766, was elected to represent William and Mary College in the Virginia House of Burgesses. He served in the Burgesses until 1770, and then for five years he was clerk of the royal governor's Council.

In 1776 he took part in the convention to frame a constitution and plan of government for the new commonwealth of Virginia and was elected to the state Privy Council. In 1778 he was elected one of the judges of the state General Court and later became its chief justice. He subsequently served as a judge of the High Court of Chancery and was a judge of the Court of Appeals when it heard the case of *Commonwealth of Virginia* v. *Caton* in 1782. He sided with the majority when it laid down the principle that a court can annul a law deemed to conflict with the constitution. Blair took part in the Constitutional Convention of 1787 and, in 1789, was appointed by President Washington to the U.S. Supreme Court, taking his oath of office the following year. He was a judicial conservative and served on the court until his retirement in 1796.

▌Burr, Aaron

Aaron Burr (1756–1836) served as the third vice president of the United States (1801–05), but he had a turbulent political career that included killing his political rival, Alexander Hamilton, in a duel (1804) and ended with his arrest for treason in 1807.

Burr, the son of Aaron Burr and Esther Edwards, came from a prominent New Jersey family and was a grandson of the theologian Jonathan Edwards. He studied law and served on the staff of General George Washington during the American Revolution (1775–83) but was transferred after antagonizing him.

In 1782 Burr was admitted to the New York state bar, and his law practice in New York City soon flourished. In 1784 and 1785 he was elected to the state assembly, and in 1789 he was appointed attorney general by Governor George Clinton. By 1791 he had built a successful political coalition against General Philip Schuyler, father-in-law of Alexander Hamilton (then secretary of the treasury), and won election to the United States Senate, incurring the enmity of Hamilton. Burr failed to win reelection in 1797 and spent the next two years in state politics.

In 1800 Burr won the vice presidential nomination on the Jeffersonian Republican ticket. He carried New York state and thus helped bring about a national victory for his party. Under the electoral college procedures then prevailing, the electors had cast their votes for both Thomas Jefferson and Burr without indicating which should be president and which vice president. Both men had an equal number of electoral votes, and the Federalist-controlled House of Representatives had to break the tie. Although Burr maintained that he would not challenge Jefferson—an assertion that Jefferson did not wholly accept— Hamilton's determined opposition to Burr was a strong factor in Jefferson's election after 36 ballots. (In 1804 the Twelfth Amendment to the United States Constitution was adopted, requiring electors to cast separate ballots for president and vice president.)

In February 1804 Burr's friends in the New York legislature nominated him for the governorship. Hamilton helped to contribute to Burr's defeat by disseminating letters containing derogatory comments about Burr, and shortly thereafter Clinton replaced him as the Republican vice presidential candidate. Once again Burr felt himself to be the political victim of Hamilton's animosity, and he challenged him to a duel (July 11, 1804) at Weehawken, New Jersey, in which Hamilton was killed.

Arrest warrants were issued for Burr, whom many now viewed as a murderer, and he fled to Philadelphia, where he contacted his friend General James Wilkinson, a United States Army officer secretly in the pay of Spain. Expecting war to break out between the United States and Spain over boundary disputes, Wilkinson and Burr planned an invasion of Mexico in order to establish an independent government there. Possibly—the record is inconclusive—they also discussed a plan to foment a secessionist movement in the west and, joining it to Mexico, found an empire on the Napoleonic model. In any event, Wilkinson became alarmed and betrayed Burr to President Jefferson. Trying to escape to Spanish territory, Burr was arrested and returned for trial in the Circuit Court in Richmond, Virginia (May 1807), before Chief Justice John Marshall.

Although the evidence showed only that Burr had planned an illegal attack upon Spanish territory, he was tried for treason, and though he was acquitted, he remained under a cloud of suspicion and distrust. He soon left for Europe, where he tried in vain to enlist the aid of Napoleon in a plan to conquer Florida. Burr remained abroad for four years, living in customary indebtedness. He returned to New York in 1812 and practiced law. He married a wealthy widow, Elizabeth Brown Jumel, in 1833, though he frittered away much of her wealth within a year. Eventually she sued for divorce on grounds of adultery, and a divorce decree was granted on the day Burr died in 1836.

▌Carroll, Charles

Charles Carroll (1737–1832) was an American patriot leader, the longest surviving signer of the Declaration of Independence, and the only Roman Catholic to sign that document.

Until 1765 Carroll attended Jesuit colleges in Maryland and France and studied law in France and England. Before and during the American Revolution, he served on committees of correspondence and in the Continental Congress (1776–78), where he was an important member of the board of war. In 1776, with Benjamin Franklin, Samuel Chase, and his cousin the Reverend John Carroll, he was sent to Canada in a fruitless effort to persuade Canadians to join the cause of the 13 colonies.

Carroll was a state senator in Maryland (1777–1800) and concurrently a U.S. Senator (1789–92). When political parties were formed in the United States, he became a Federalist.

Chase, Samuel

A member of the Maryland assembly (1764–84) and the Continental Congress (1774–78, 1784–85), and a signer of the Declaration of Independence, Samuel Chase (1741–1811) served as chief judge of the Maryland General Court from 1791 to 1796, when President George Washington appointed him to the U.S. Supreme Court. In *Ware* v. *Hylton* (1796), an important early test of nationalism, he upheld the primacy of U.S. treaties over state statutes. In *Calder* v. *Bull* (1798), he asserted that legislative power over liberty and property is limited by "certain vital principles in our free Republican governments"; later courts read these principles into the "due process of law" clauses of the Fifth and Fourteenth Amendments to the Constitution.

During the struggle between the Federalist and Jeffersonian Republican parties, Chase, a Federalist, conducted his circuit court in a partisan manner. The House of Representatives, encouraged by Jefferson, charged Chase with improper actions in treason and sedition trials and with a political address to a grand jury. In March 1805 the Senate, acting as trial court, found him not guilty. His acquittal, by establishing the principle that federal judges could be removed only for indictable criminal acts, clarified the constitutional provision (Article III, section 1) that judges shall hold office during good behavior. Some scholars believe that if Chase had been found guilty, the Jefferson administration would have proceeded against other Federalist justices, particularly Chief Justice John Marshall, a leading opponent of Jefferson.

Checks and Balances

Checks and balances are a principle of government under which separate branches are empowered to prevent actions by other branches and are induced to share power. They are of fundamental importance in tripartite governments, such as that of the United States, which separate powers among legislative, executive, and judicial branches.

The framers of the U.S. Constitution, who were influenced by Montesquieu and William Blackstone among others, saw checks and balances as essential for the security of liberty under the Constitution: "It is by balancing each of these powers against the other two, that the efforts in human nature toward tyranny can alone be checked and restrained, and any degree of freedom preserved in the constitution" (John Adams). Though not expressly covered in the text of the Constitution, judicial review—the power of the courts to examine the actions of the legislative and the executive and administrative arms of government to ensure that they are constitutional—became an important part of government in the United States. Other checks and balances include the presidential veto of legislation (which Congress may override by a two-thirds vote) and executive and judicial impeachment by Congress. Only Congress can appropriate funds, and each house serves as a check on possible abuses of power or unwise action by the other. Congress, by initiating constitutional amendments, can in practice reverse decisions of the Supreme Court. The president appoints the members of the Supreme Court but only with the consent of the Senate, which also approves certain other executive appointments. The Senate also must approve treaties.

From 1932 the U.S. Congress exercised a so-called legislative veto. Clauses in certain laws qualified the authority of the executive branch to act by making specified acts subject to disapproval by the majority vote of one or both houses. In 1983, in a case concerning the deportation of an alien, the U.S. Supreme Court held that legislative vetoes were unconstitutional (the House of Representatives had overturned the Justice Department's suspension of the alien's deportation). The decision affected clauses in some 200 laws covering a wide range of subjects, including presidential war powers, foreign aid and arms sales, environmental protection, consumer interests, and others. Despite the court's decision, Congress continued to exercise this power, including the legislative veto in at least 11 of the bills it passed in 1984 alone.

Checks and balances that evolved from custom and Constitutional conventions include the congressional committee system and investigative powers, the role of political parties, and presidential influence in initiating legislation.

Clark, Abraham

Benefiting little from formal education, Abraham Clark (1726–94) became a surveyor and managed transfers of property. He had a gift for politics and served in many public offices in New Jersey. He championed the cause of the colonies and in 1776 was elected to the Continental Congress, where he voted for separation from Great Britain and signed the Declaration. He was reelected to the Continental Congress several times and was also a delegate to the Annapolis Convention (1786), an important rallying point in the movement toward a federal convention to revise the Articles of Confederation. He was chosen to be a delegate to the federal Constitutional Convention (1787) but was unable to attend because of illness. Clark opposed the adoption of the new U.S. Constitution until he was assured that a bill of rights would be added to it. He served in the U.S. House of Representatives from 1791 until his death.

Constitution of the United States of America

The Constitution of the United States is the fundamental law of the U.S. federal system of government and a landmark document of the Western world. It defines the principal organs of government and their jurisdictions and the basic rights of citizens and is the oldest written national constitution in use.

The Constitution was written during the summer of 1787 in Philadelphia, Pennsylvania, by 55 delegates to a Constitutional Convention that was called ostensibly to amend the Articles of Confederation (1781–89), the country's first written constitution. The Constitution was the product of political compromise after long and often rancorous debates over issues such as states' rights, representation, and slavery. Delegates from small and large states disagreed over whether the number of representatives in the new federal legislature should be the same for each state—as was the case under the Articles of Confederation—or different depending on a state's population. In addition, some delegates from northern states sought to abolish slavery or, failing that, to make representation dependent on the size of a state's free population. At the same time, some southern delegates threatened to abandon the convention if their demands to keep slavery and the slave trade legal and to count slaves for representation purposes were not met. Eventually the framers resolved their disputes by adopting a proposal put forward by the Connecticut delegation. The Great Compromise, as it came to be known, created a bicameral legislature with a Senate, in which all states would be equally represented, and a House of Representatives, in which representation would be apportioned on the basis of a state's free population plus three-fifths of its slave population. (The inclusion of the slave population was known separately as the three-fifths compromise.) A further compromise on slavery prohibited Congress from banning the importation of slaves until 1808 (Article I, Section 9). After all the disagreements were bridged, the new Constitution was submitted for ratification to the 13 states on September 28, 1787. In 1787–88, in an effort to persuade New York to ratify the Constitution, Alexander Hamilton, John Jay, and James Madison published a series of essays on the Constitution and republican government in New York newspapers. Their work, written under the pseudonym "Publius" and collected and published in book form as *The Federalist* (1788), became a classic exposition and defense of the Constitution. In June 1788, after the Constitution had been ratified by nine states (as required by Article VII), Congress set March 4, 1789, as the date for the new government to commence proceedings (the first elections under the Constitution were held late in 1788). Because ratification in many states was contingent on the promised addition of a Bill of Rights, Congress proposed 12 amendments in September 1789; 10 were ratified by the states, and their adoption was certified on December 15, 1791. (One of the original 12 proposed amendments, which prohibited midterm changes in compensation for members of Congress, was ratified in 1992 as the Twenty-seventh Amendment. The last one, concerning the ratio of citizens per member of the House of Representatives, has never been adopted.)

The authors of the Constitution were heavily influenced by the country's experience under the Articles of Confederation, which had attempted to retain as much independence and sovereignty for the states as possible and to assign to the central government only those nationally important functions that the states could not handle individually. But the events of the years 1781 to 1787, including the national government's inability to act during Shays's Rebellion (1786–87) in Massachusetts, showed that the Articles were unworkable because they deprived the national government of many essential powers, including direct taxation and the ability to regulate interstate commerce. It was hoped that the new Constitution would remedy this problem.

The framers of the Constitution were especially concerned with limiting the power of government and securing the liberty of citizens. The doctrine of legislative, executive, and judicial separation of powers, the checks and balances of each branch against the others, and the explicit guarantees of individual liberty were all designed to strike a balance between authority and liberty—the central purpose of American constitutional law.

The Constitution concisely organizes the country's basic political institutions. The main text comprises seven articles. Article I vests all legislative powers in the Congress—the House of Representatives and the Senate. The Great Compromise stipulated that representation in the House would be based on population, and each state is entitled to two senators. Members of the House serve terms of two years, senators terms of six. Among the powers delegated to Congress are the right to levy taxes, borrow money, regulate interstate commerce, provide for military forces, declare war, and determine member seating and rules of procedure. The House initiates impeachment proceedings, and the Senate adjudicates them.

Article II vests executive power in the office of the presidency of the United States. The president, selected by an electoral college to serve a four-year term, is given responsibilities common to chief executives, including serving as commander in chief of the armed forces, negotiating treaties (two-thirds of the Senate must concur), and granting pardons. The president's vast appointment powers, which include members of the federal judiciary and the cabinet, are subject to the "advice and consent" (majority approval) of the Senate (Article II, Section 2). Originally presidents were eligible for continual reelection, but the Twenty-second Amendment (1951) later prohibited any person from being elected president more than twice. Although the formal powers of the president are constitutionally quite limited and vague in comparison with those of the Congress, a variety of historical and technological factors—such as the centralization of power in the executive branch during war and the advent of television—have increased the informal responsibilities of the office extensively to embrace other aspects of political leadership, including proposing legislation to Congress.

Article III places judicial power in the hands of the courts. The Constitution is interpreted by the courts, and the Supreme Court of the United States is the final court of appeal from the state and lower federal courts. The power of American courts to rule on the constitutionality of laws, known as judicial review, is held by few other courts in the world and is not explicitly granted in the Constitution. The principle of judicial review was first asserted by Supreme Court Chief Justice John Marshall in *Marbury v. Madison* (1803), when the court ruled that it had the authority to void national or state laws.

Beyond the body of judicial rulings interpreting it, the Constitution acquires meaning in a broader sense at the hands of all who use it. Congress on innumerable occasions has given new scope to the document through statutes, such as those creating executive departments, the federal courts, territories, and states; controlling succession to the presidency; and setting up the executive budget system. The chief executive also has contributed to constitutional interpretation, as in the development of the executive agreement as an instrument of foreign policy. Practices outside the letter of the Constitution based on custom and usage are often recognized as constitutional elements; they include the system of political parties, presidential nomination procedures, and the conduct of election campaigns. The presidential cabinet is largely a constitutional "convention" based on custom, and the actual operation of the electoral college system is also a convention.

Article IV deals, in part, with relations between the states and privileges of the citizens of the states. These provisions include the full faith and credit clause, which requires states to recognize the official acts and judicial proceedings of other states; the requirement that each state provide citizens from other states with all the privileges and immunities afforded the citizens of that state; and the guarantee of a republican form of government for each state.

Article V stipulates the procedures for amending the Constitution. Amendments may be proposed by a two-thirds vote of both houses of Congress or by a convention called by Congress on the application of the legislatures of two-thirds of the states. Proposed amendments must be ratified by three-fourths of the state legislatures or by conventions in as many states, depending on the decision of Congress. All subsequent amendments have been proposed by Congress, and all but one—the Twenty-first Amendment, which repealed Prohibition—have been ratified by state legislatures.

Article VI, which prohibits religious tests for officeholders, also deals with public debts and the supremacy of the Constitution, citing the document as "the supreme Law of the Land; . . . any Thing in the Constitution or Laws of any State to the Contrary notwithstanding." Article VII stipulated that the Constitution would become operational after being ratified by nine states.

The national government has only those constitutional powers that are delegated to it either expressly or by implication; the states, unless otherwise restricted, possess all the remaining powers (Tenth Amendment). Thus, national powers are enumerated (Article I, Section 8, paragraphs 1–17), and state powers are not. The state powers are often called residual, or reserved, powers. The elastic, or necessary and proper, clause (Article I, Section 8, paragraph 18) states that Congress shall have the authority "To make all Laws which shall be necessary and proper for carrying into Execution" the various powers vested in the national government. Thus, it follows that, in addition to the delegated powers, Congress possesses implied powers, a proposition established by Chief Justice Marshall in *McCulloch* v. *Maryland* (1819). The issue of national versus state power was not fully resolved by this decision, however, and many political battles in American history—including debates on nullification, slavery, racial segregation, and abortion—often have been disputes over constitutional interpretations of implied and residual powers.

Competing concepts of federal supremacy and states' rights were brought into sharp relief in questions about commercial regulation. The commerce clause simply authorized Congress "To regulate Commerce with foreign Nations, and among the several States, and with the Indian Tribes." Particularly since a series of decisions in 1937, the court has interpreted Congress's regulatory power broadly under the commerce clause as new methods of interstate transportation and communication have come into use. States may not regulate any aspect of interstate commerce that Congress has preempted.

The federal government is obliged by many constitutional provisions to respect the individual citizen's basic rights. Some civil liberties were specified in the original document, notably in the provisions guaranteeing the writ of habeas corpus and trial by jury in criminal cases (Article III, Section 2) and forbidding bills of attainder and ex post facto laws (Article I, Section 9). But the most significant limitations to government's power over the individual were added in 1791 in the Bill of Rights. The Constitution's First Amendment guarantees the rights of conscience, such as freedom of religion, speech, and the press, and the right of peaceful assembly and petition. Other guarantees in the Bill of Rights require fair procedures for persons accused of a crime—such as protection against unreasonable search and seizure, compulsory self-incrimination, double jeopardy, and excessive bail—and guarantees of a speedy and public trial by a local, impartial jury before an impartial judge and representation by counsel. Rights of private property are also guaranteed. Although the Bill of Rights is a broad expression of individual civil liberties, the ambiguous wording of many of its provisions—such as the Second Amendment's right "to keep and bear arms" and the Eighth Amendment's prohibition of "cruel and unusual punishments"—has been a source of constitutional controversy and intense political debate. Further, the rights guaranteed are not absolute, and there has been considerable disagreement about the extent to which they limit governmental authority. The Bill of Rights originally protected citizens only from the national government. For example, although the Constitution prohibited the establishment of an official religion at the national level, the official state-supported religion of Massachusetts was Congregationalism until 1833. Thus, individual citizens had to look to state constitutions for protection of their rights against state governments.

Twenty-seven amendments have been added to the Constitution since 1789. In more than two centuries of operation, it has proved itself a dynamic document. It has served as a model for other countries, its provisions being widely imitated in national constitutions throughout the world. Although the Constitution's brevity and ambiguity have sometimes led to serious disputes about its meaning, they also have made it adaptable to changing historical circumstances and ensured its relevance in ages far removed from the one in which it was written.

Continental Congress

During the period of the American Revolution (1774–89) the Continental Congress served as the body of delegates who spoke and acted collectively for the people of the colony-states that later became the United States of America. The term most specifically refers to the bodies that met in 1774 and 1775–81 and are respectively designated as the First Continental Congress and the Second Continental Congress.

In the spring of 1774, the British Parliament's passage of the Intolerable (Coercive) Acts, including the closing of the port of Boston, provoked keen resentment in the colonies. The First Continental Congress, convened in response to the Acts by the colonial Committees of Correspondence, met in Philadelphia on September 5, 1774. Fifty-six deputies represented all the colonies except Georgia. Peyton Randolph of Virginia was unanimously elected president, thus establishing usage of that term as well as "Congress." Charles Thomson of Pennsylvania was elected secretary and served in that office during the 15-year life of the Congress.

To provide unity, delegates gave one vote to each state regardless of its size. The First Continental Congress included Patrick Henry, George Washington, John and Samuel Adams, John Jay, and John Dickinson. Meeting in secret session, the body rejected a plan for reconciling British authority with colonial freedom. Instead, it adopted a declaration of personal rights, including life, liberty, property, assembly, and trial by jury. The declaration also denounced taxation without representation and the maintenance of the British army in the colonies without their consent. Parliamentary regulation of American commerce, however, was willingly accepted.

In October 1774 the Congress petitioned the crown for a redress of grievances accumulated since 1763. In an effort to force compliance, it called for a general boycott of British goods and eventual nonexportation of American products, except rice, to Britain or the British West Indies. Its last act was to set a date for another Congress to meet on May 10, 1775, to consider further steps.

Before that Second Continental Congress assembled in the Pennsylvania State House, hostilities had already broken out between Americans and British troops at Lexington and Concord, Massachusetts. New members of the Second Congress included Benjamin Franklin and Thomas Jefferson. John Hancock and John Jay were among those who served as president. The Congress "adopted" the New England military forces that had converged upon Boston and appointed Washington commander in chief of the American army on June 15, 1775. It also acted as the provisional government of the 13 colony-states, issuing and borrowing money, establishing a postal service, and creating a navy. Although the Congress for some months maintained that the Americans were struggling for their rights within the British Empire, it gradually cut tie after tie with Britain until separation was complete. On July 2, 1776, with New York abstaining, the Congress "unanimously" resolved that "these United Colonies are, and of right ought to be, free and independent states." Two days later, it solemnly approved this Declaration of Independence. The Congress also prepared the Articles of Confederation, which, after being sanctioned by all the states, became the first U.S. constitution in March 1781.

The Articles placed Congress on a constitutional basis, legalizing the powers it had exercised since 1775. To underline this distinction, the Congress that met under the Articles of Confederation is often referred to as the Congress of the Confederation, or the Confederation Congress. This Congress continued to function until the new Congress, elected under the present Constitution, met in 1789.

Dayton, Jonathan

Jonathan Dayton (1760–1824) was the youngest member of the U.S. Constitutional Convention, served as speaker of the U.S. House of Representatives, and was a developer of large tracts in what later became the state of Ohio. The city of Dayton, Ohio, is named for him.

Immediately following graduation from the College of New Jersey (Princeton University) in 1776, Dayton enlisted in the New Jersey militia. He fought in the New York and New Jersey campaigns, rose to the rank of captain, was at Yorktown in 1781, and returned to civilian life two years later.

Dayton then studied law and was admitted to the bar, but his future lay more in public service than in private law practice.

He served in the New Jersey Assembly (1786–87) then—at age 27—became the youngest delegate at the Constitutional Convention. Dayton was a frequent participant in the debates and opposed several aspects of the Constitution. He nonetheless signed the final document.

Elected to a seat in the first Congress, Dayton instead served in the New Jersey Council (1789) and Assembly (1790). But when elected once again to the U.S. House in 1790, he joined that body and remained there through the end of the decade. As a congressman he backed Hamilton's financial program, pressed for suppression of the Whiskey Rebellion (1794; a challenge of Pennsylvania farmers to federal authority), and supported the Jay Treaty with Great Britain (1794). During his last two terms he was speaker of the House.

Dayton was elected to the Senate, where he served for the term of 1799–1805. He opposed Jefferson's administration by voting against the repeal of the Judiciary Act of 1801, against the Twelfth Amendment, and for the acquittal of Supreme Court Justice Samuel Chase. But he favored the Louisiana Purchase of 1803.

After Dayton left the Senate in 1805, he held public office just once more in his life—a term in the New Jersey legislature (1814–15). Most of his time he devoted to developing his large landholdings (250,000 acres) in Ohio. He apparently played some role in Aaron Burr's western conspiracy of 1807 but, though indicted for high treason, was never prosecuted.

Declaration of Independence

The Declaration of Independence was approved by the Continental Congress on July 4, 1776, and announced the separation of 13 North American British colonies from Great Britain. It explained why the Congress on July 2 "unanimously" by the votes of 12 colonies (with New York abstaining) had resolved that "these United Colonies are, and of right ought to be Free and Independent States." Accordingly, the day on which final separation was officially voted was July 2, although the 4th, the day on which the Declaration of Independence was adopted, has always been celebrated in the United States as the great national holiday—the Fourth of July, or Independence Day.

On April 19, 1775, when armed conflict began between Britain and the 13 colonies (the nucleus of the future United States), the Americans claimed that they sought only their rights within the British Empire. At that time few of the colonists consciously desired to separate from Britain. As the American Revolution proceeded during 1775–76 and Britain undertook to assert its sovereignty by means of large armed forces, making only a gesture toward conciliation, the majority of Americans increasingly came to believe that they must secure their rights outside the empire. The losses and restrictions that came from the war greatly widened the breach between the colonies and the mother country; moreover, it was necessary to assert independence in order to secure as much French aid as possible.

On April 12, 1776, the revolutionary convention of North Carolina specifically authorized its delegates in Congress to vote for independence. On May 15 the Virginia convention instructed its deputies to offer the motion, which was brought forward in the Congress by Richard Henry Lee on June 7. By that time the Congress had already taken long steps toward severing ties with Britain. It had denied Parliamentary sovereignty over the colonies as early as December 6, 1775, and it had declared on May 10, 1776, that the authority of the king ought to be "totally suppressed," advising all the several colonies to establish governments of their own choice.

The passage of Lee's resolution was delayed for several reasons. Some of the delegates had not yet received authorization to vote for separation; a few were opposed to taking the final step; and several men, among them John Dickinson, believed that the formation of a central government, together with attempts to secure foreign aid, should precede it. However, a committee consisting of Thomas Jefferson, John Adams, Benjamin Franklin, Roger Sherman, and Robert R. Livingston was promptly chosen on June 11 to prepare a statement justifying the decision to assert independence, should it be taken. The document was prepared, and on July 1 nine delegations voted for separation, despite warm opposition on the part of Dickinson. On the following day at the Pennsylvania State House (now Independence Hall) in Philadelphia, with the New York delegation abstaining only because it lacked permission to act, the Lee resolution was voted on and endorsed. (The convention of New York gave its consent on July 9, and the New York delegates voted affirmatively on July 15.) On July 19 the Congress ordered the document to be engrossed as "The Unanimous Declaration of the Thirteen United States of America." It was accordingly put on parchment, probably by Timothy Matlack of Philadelphia. Members of the Congress present on August 2 affixed their signatures to this parchment copy on that day, and others later. The last signer was Thomas McKean of Delaware, whose name was not placed on the document before 1777.

The Declaration of Independence was written largely by Jefferson, who had displayed talent as a political philosopher and polemicist in his *A Summary View of the Rights of British America*, published in 1774. At the request of his fellow committee members, he wrote the first draft. The members of the committee made a number of merely semantic changes, and they also expanded somewhat the list of charges against the king. The Congress made more substantial changes, deleting a condemnation of the British people, a reference to "Scotch & foreign mercenaries" (there were Scots in the Congress), and a denunciation of the African slave trade (this being offensive to some Southern and New England delegates).

It can be said, as John Adams did, that the declaration contained nothing really novel in its political philosophy, which was derived from John Locke, Algernon Sidney, and other English theorists. It may also be asserted that the argument offered was not without flaws in history and logic. Substantially abandoning contention on the basis of the rights of Englishmen, the declaration put forth the more fundamental doctrines of natural rights and of government under social contract. Claiming that Parliament never truly possessed sovereignty over the colonies and that the crown of right exercised it only under contract, the declaration contended that George III, with the support of a "pretended" legislature, had persistently violated the agreement between himself as governor and the Americans as the governed. A long list of accusations was offered toward proving this contention. The right and duty of revolution were then invoked.

Few will now claim that government arose among men as Locke and Jefferson said it did, and the social-contract theory has lost vogue among political scientists. It is likewise true, from a British viewpoint, that Parliament and crown could not be separated and that the history of the colonies after 1607 was not entirely consistent with the assertion that Parliament had never as of right possessed sovereignty over them. Furthermore, the specific charges brought against the king were partisan and not uniformly defensible, and the general accusation that he intended to establish an "absolute Despotism" is hardly warranted. It should be added that several of the heaviest specific complaints condemned actions of the British government taken after the beginning of hostilities.

The defects in the Declaration of Independence are not sufficient to force the conclusion that the document is unsound. On the contrary, it was in essence morally just and politically valid. If the right of revolution cannot be established on historical grounds, it nevertheless rests solidly upon ethical ones. The right of the colonists to government ultimately of their own choice is valid. Some of the phrases of the declaration have steadily exerted profound influence in the United States, especially the proclamation that "We hold these truths to be self-evident, that all men are created equal, that they are endowed by their Creator with certain unalienable Rights, that among these are Life, Liberty and the pursuit of Happiness." Although the meanings of these phrases, together with conclusions drawn from them, have been endlessly debated, the declaration has served to justify the extension of American political and social democracy.

The Declaration of Independence has also been a source of inspiration outside the United States. It encouraged Antonio de Nariño and Francisco de Miranda to strive toward overthrowing the Spanish empire in South America, and it was quoted with enthusiasm by the marquis de Mirabeau during the French Revolution. It remains a great historical landmark in that it contained the first formal assertion by a whole people of their right to a government of their own choice. What Locke had contended for as an individual, the Americans proclaimed as a body politic; moreover, they made good the argument by force of arms.

Since 1952 the original parchment document of the Declaration of Independence has resided in the National Archives exhibition hall in Washington, D.C.

A CLOSER LOOK

The Founding Fathers and Slavery

by Anthony Iaccarino

Although many of the Founding Fathers acknowledged that slavery violated the core American Revolutionary ideal of liberty, their simultaneous commitment to private property rights, principles of limited government, and intersectional harmony prevented them from making a bold move against slavery. The considerable investment of southern Founders in slave-based staple agriculture, combined with their deep-seated racial prejudice, posed additional obstacles to emancipation.

In his initial draft of the Declaration of Independence, Thomas Jefferson condemned the injustice of the slave trade and, by implication, slavery, but he also blamed the presence of enslaved Africans in North America on avaricious British colonial policies. Jefferson thus acknowledged that slavery violated the natural rights of the enslaved, while at the same time he absolved Americans of any responsibility for owning slaves themselves. The Continental Congress apparently rejected the tortured logic of this passage by deleting it from the final document, but this decision also signaled the Founders' commitment to subordinating the controversial issue of slavery to the larger goal of securing the unity and independence of the United States.

Nevertheless, the Founders, with the exception of those from South Carolina and Georgia, exhibited considerable aversion to slavery during the era of the Articles of Confederation (1781–89) by prohibiting the importation of foreign slaves to individual states and lending their support to a proposal by Jefferson to ban slavery in the Northwest Territory. Such antislavery policies, however, only went so far. The prohibition of foreign slave imports, by limiting the foreign supply, conveniently served the interests of Virginia and Maryland slaveholders, who could then sell their own surplus slaves southward and westward at higher prices. Furthermore, the ban on slavery in the northwest tacitly legitimated the expansion of slavery in the southwest.

Despite initial disagreements over slavery at the Constitutional Convention in 1787, the Founders once again demonstrated their commitment to maintaining the unity of the new United States by resolving to diffuse sectional tensions over slavery. To this end the Founders drafted a series of constitutional clauses acknowledging deep-seated regional differences over slavery while requiring all sections of the new country to make compromises as well. They granted slaveholding states the right to count three-fifths of their slave population when it came to apportioning the number of a state's representatives to Congress, thereby enhancing southern power in the House of Representatives. But they also used this same ratio to determine the federal tax contribution required of each state, thus increasing the direct federal tax burden of slaveholding states. Georgians and South Carolinians won a moratorium until 1808 on any Congressional ban against the importation of slaves, but in the meantime individual states remained free to prohibit slave imports if they so wished. Southerners also obtained the inclusion of a fugitive slave clause (Fugitive Slave Acts) designed to encourage the return of runaway slaves who sought refuge in free states, but the Constitution left enforcement of this clause to the cooperation of the states rather than to the coercion of Congress.

Although the Founders, consistent with their beliefs in limited government, opposed granting the new federal government significant authority over slavery, several individual northern Founders promoted antislavery causes at the state level. Benjamin Franklin in Pennsylvania, as well as John Jay and Alexander Hamilton in New York, served as officers in their respective state antislavery societies. The prestige they lent to these organizations ultimately contributed to the gradual abolition of slavery in each of the northern states.

Although slavery was legal in every northern state at the beginning of the American Revolution, its economic impact was marginal. As a result, northern Founders were freer to explore the libertarian dimensions of Revolutionary ideology. The experience of Franklin was in many ways typical of the evolving attitudes of northern Founders toward slavery. Although enmeshed in the slave system for much of his life, Franklin eventually came to believe that slavery ought to be abolished gradually and legally. Franklin himself had owned slaves, run ads in his *Pennsylvania Gazette* to secure the return of fugitive slaves, and defended the honor of slaveholding revolutionaries. By 1781, however, Franklin had divested himself of slaves, and shortly thereafter he became the president of the Pennsylvania Abolition Society. He also went further than most of his contemporaries by signing a petition to the First Federal Congress in 1790 for the abolition of slavery and the slave trade.

Unlike their northern counterparts, southern Founders generally steered clear of organized antislavery activities, primarily to maintain their legitimacy among slaveholding constituents. Furthermore, while a few northern and southern Founders manumitted a small number of slaves, no southern plantation-owning Founder, except George Washington, freed a sizeable body of enslaved laborers. Because his own slaves shared familial attachments with the dower slaves of his wife, Martha Custis Washington, he sought to convince her heirs to forego their inheritance rights in favor of a collective manumission so as to ensure that entire families, not just individual family members, might be freed. Washington failed to win the consent of the Custis heirs, but he nevertheless made sure, through his last will and testament, that his own slaves would enjoy the benefit of freedom.

Washington's act of manumission implied that he could envision a biracial United States where both blacks and whites might live together as free people. Jefferson, however, explicitly rejected this vision. He acknowledged that slavery violated the natural rights of slaves and that conflicts over slavery might one day lead to the dissolution of the union, but he also believed that, given alleged innate racial differences and deeply held prejudices, emancipation would inevitably degrade the character of the republic and unleash violent civil strife between blacks and whites. Jefferson thus advocated coupling emancipation with what he called "colonization," or removal, of the black population beyond the boundaries of the United States. His proposals won considerable support in the north, where racial prejudice was on the rise, but such schemes found little support among the majority of southern slaveholders.

When the last remaining Founders died in the 1830s, they

left behind an ambiguous legacy with regard to slavery. They had succeeded in gradually abolishing slavery in the northern states and northwestern territories but permitted its rapid expansion in the south and southwest. Although they eventually enacted a federal ban on the importation of foreign slaves in 1808, the enslaved population continued to expand through natural reproduction, while the growing internal domestic slave trade led to an increase in the tragic breakup of enslaved families.

Anthony Iaccarino is a professor of History and Humanities at Reed College.

Democratic-Republican Party

The Democratic-Republican Party, organized in 1792 as the Republican Party, was the first opposition political party in the United States. Its members held power nationally between 1801 and 1825. The party was the direct antecedent of the present Democratic Party.

During the two administrations of President George Washington (1789–97), many former Anti-Federalists—who had resisted adoption of the new federal Constitution (1787)—began to unite in opposition to the fiscal program of Alexander Hamilton, secretary of the treasury. After Hamilton and other proponents of a strong central government and a loose interpretation of the Constitution formed the Federalist Party in 1791, those who favored states' rights and a strict interpretation of the Constitution rallied under the leadership of Thomas Jefferson, who had served as Washington's first secretary of state. Jefferson's supporters, deeply influenced by the ideals of the French Revolution (1789), first adopted the name Republican to emphasize their antimonarchical views. The Republicans contended that the Federalists harbored aristocratic attitudes and that their policies placed too much power in the central government and tended to benefit the affluent at the expense of the common man. Although the Federalists soon branded Jefferson's followers "Democratic-Republicans," attempting to link them with the excesses of the French Revolution, the Republicans officially adopted the derisive label in 1798. The Republican coalition supported France in the European war that broke out in 1792, while the Federalists supported Britain. The Republicans' opposition to Britain unified the faction through the 1790s and inspired them to fight against the Federalist-sponsored Jay Treaty (1794) and the Alien and Sedition Acts (1798).

Notwithstanding the party's antielitist foundations, the first three Democratic-Republican presidents—Jefferson (1801–09), James Madison (1809–17), and James Monroe (1817–25)—were all wealthy, aristocratic Southern planters, though all three shared the same liberal political philosophy. Jefferson narrowly defeated the Federalist John Adams in the election of 1800; his victory demonstrated that power could be transferred peacefully between parties under the Constitution. Once in office, the Democratic-Republicans attempted to scale back Federalist programs but actually overturned few of the institutions they had criticized (for example, the Bank of the United States was retained until its charter expired in 1811). Nevertheless, Jefferson made a genuine effort to make his administration appear more democratic and egalitarian: he walked to the Capitol for his inauguration rather than ride in a coach-and-six, and he sent his annual message to Congress by messenger, rather than reading it personally. Federal excises were repealed, the national debt was retired, and the size of the armed forces was greatly reduced. However, the demands of foreign relations (such as the Louisiana Purchase in 1803) often forced Jefferson and his successors into a nationalistic stance reminiscent of the Federalists.

In the 20 years after 1808 the party existed less as a united political group than as a loose coalition of personal and sectional factions. The fissures in the party were fully exposed by the election of 1824, when the leaders of the two major factions, Andrew Jackson and John Quincy Adams, were both nominated for president. Meanwhile, William H. Crawford was nominated by the party's congressional caucus, and Henry Clay, another Democratic-Republican, was nominated by the Kentucky and Tennessee legislatures. Jackson carried the popular vote and a plurality in the electoral college, but because no candidate received a majority of the electoral vote, the presidency was decided by the House of Representatives. Clay, the speaker of the House of Representatives, finished fourth and was thus ineligible for consideration; he subsequently threw his support to Adams, who was elected president and promptly appointed Clay secretary of state. Following the election, the Democratic-Republicans split into two groups: the National Republicans, who became the nucleus of the Whig Party in the 1830s, were led by Adams and Clay, while the Democratic-Republicans were organized by Martin Van Buren, the future eighth president (1837–41), and led by Jackson. The Democratic-Republicans comprised diverse elements that emphasized local and humanitarian concerns, states' rights, agrarian interests, and democratic procedures. During Jackson's presidency (1829–37) they dropped the Republican label and called themselves simply Democrats or Jacksonian Democrats. The name Democratic Party was formally adopted in 1844.

▌ Dickinson, John

An American statesman often referred to as the "penman of the Revolution," John Dickinson (1732–1808) studied law in London at the Middle Temple and practiced law in Philadelphia (1757–60) before entering public life. He represented Pennsylvania in the Stamp Act Congress (1765) and drafted its declaration of rights and grievances. He won fame in 1767–68 as the author of the *Letters from a Farmer in Pennsylvania, to the Inhabitants of the British Colonies*, which appeared in many colonial newspapers. The letters helped turn opinion against the Townshend Acts (1767), under which new duties were collected to pay the salaries of royal officials in the Colonies. He also denounced the establishing of the American Board of Customs Commissioners at Boston to enforce the acts.

Dickinson was a delegate from Pennsylvania in the Continental Congress (1774–76) and was the principal author of the *Declaration . . . Setting Forth the Causes and Necessity of Their Taking Up Arms*. He helped prepare the first draft of the Articles of Confederation (1776–77) but voted against the Declaration of Independence (1776) because he still hoped for conciliation with the British. Although he was accused of being a loyalist, he later served in the patriot militia.

As a delegate from Delaware to the Federal Constitutional Convention (1787), Dickinson signed the U.S. Constitution and worked for its adoption. He later defended the document in a series of letters signed "Fabius."

Dickinson College at Carlisle, Pennsylvania, chartered in 1783, was named in his honor.

Federalist Papers

The Federalist papers were a series of 85 essays on the proposed new Constitution of the United States and on the nature of republican government, published between 1787 and 1788 by Alexander Hamilton, James Madison, and John Jay in an effort to persuade New York state voters to support ratification. Seventy-seven of the essays first appeared serially in New York newspapers, were reprinted in most other states, and were published in book form as *The Federalist* on May 28, 1788; the remaining eight papers appeared in New York newspapers between June 14 and August 16.

The authors of the Federalist papers presented a masterly defense of the new federal system and of the major departments in the proposed central government. They also argued that the existing government under the Articles of Confederation, the country's first constitution, was defective and that the proposed Constitution would remedy its weaknesses without endangering the liberties of the people.

As a general treatise on republican government, the Federalist papers are distinguished for their comprehensive analysis of the means by which the ideals of justice, the general welfare, and the rights of individuals could be realized. The authors assumed that the primary political motive of man was self-interest and that men—whether acting individually or collectively—were selfish and only imperfectly rational. The establishment of a republican form of government would not of itself provide protection against such characteristics: the representatives of the people might betray their trust; one segment of the population might oppress another; and both the representatives and the public might give way to passion or caprice. The possibility of good government, they argued, lay in man's capacity to devise political institutions that would compensate for deficiencies in both reason and virtue in the ordinary conduct of politics. This theme was predominant in late-18th-century political thought in America and accounts in part for the elaborate system of checks and balances that was devised in the Constitution.

In one of the most notable essays, *Federalist 10*, Madison rejected the then common belief that republican government was possible only for small states. He argued that stability, liberty, and justice were more likely to be achieved in a large area with a numerous and heterogeneous population. Although frequently interpreted as an attack on majority rule, the essay is in reality a defense of both social, economic, and cultural pluralism and of a composite majority formed by compromise and conciliation. Decision by such a majority, rather than by a monistic one, would be more likely to accord with the proper ends of government. This distinction between a proper and an improper majority typifies the fundamental philosophy of the Federalist papers; republican institutions, including the principle of majority rule, were not considered good in themselves but were good because they constituted the best means for the pursuit of justice and the preservation of liberty.

All the papers appeared over the signature "Publius," and the authorship of some of the papers was once a matter of scholarly dispute. However, computer analysis and historical evidence has led nearly all historians to assign authorship in the following manner: Hamilton wrote numbers 1, 6–9, 11–13, 15–17, 21–36, 59–61, and 65–85; Madison, numbers 10, 14, 18–20, 37–58, and 62–63; and Jay, numbers 2–5 and 64.

Federalist Party

The Federalist Party was the first party of government under the Constitution of the United States, holding power from 1789 to 1801 and advocating a strong central government. The term *federalist* was first used in 1787 to describe the supporters of the newly written Constitution, who emphasized the federal character of the proposed Union. Parties were generally deplored as inimical to republican government, and President George Washington was able to exercise nonpartisan leadership during the first few years of the new government (begun in 1789). Strong division, however, developed over the fiscal program of the secretary of the treasury, Alexander Hamilton, whom Washington supported. Differences were intensified by ideological attitudes toward the French Revolution, and by 1795 administration supporters had hardened into a regular party, which succeeded in electing John Adams to the presidency in 1796.

Over the decade of the 1790s, the Federalists stood for the following economic policies: funding of the old Revolutionary War debt and the assumption of state debts, passage of excise laws, creation of a central bank, maintenance of a tariff system, and favorable treatment of American shipping. In foreign affairs they observed neutrality in the war that broke out between France and Great Britain in 1793; approved the Jay Treaty of 1794, which terminated the difficulties with Britain; and sponsored strong defense and internal security legislation in the crisis of 1798–99, when French demands almost forced open war. These policies were strongly resisted, especially in the south; the opposition, organized by James Madison and Thomas Jefferson beginning in 1791, became the Republican Party.

The Federalists never held power again after 1801. Their failure is attributable to the Republicans' political skill and to the Federalists' own incapacity or unwillingness to organize politically, their internal divisions (especially between supporters of Adams and Hamilton), and their aversion to compromising principles for the sake of winning elections. Furthermore, New England Federalists adopted a divisive policy of sectionalism, moving dangerously near secession in 1808 and strenuously opposing the War of 1812. By 1817 the party was practically dead, though the opposing Republicans had adopted the Federalists' principles of nationality and had accepted many of their economic ideas.

The accomplishments of the Federalists were great: the party organized the enduring administrative machinery of national government; fixed the practice of a liberal interpretation of the Constitution; established traditions of federal fiscal integrity and credit worthiness; and initiated the important doctrine of neutrality in foreign affairs, allowing the infant nation to develop in peace for more than a century.

▌Franklin, Benjamin

Benjamin Franklin (1706–90), who wrote under the pseudonym Richard Saunders, was an American printer and publisher, author, inventor and scientist, and diplomat. One of the foremost of the Founding Fathers, Franklin helped draft the Declaration of Independence and was one of its signers, represented the United States in France during the American Revolution, and was a delegate to the Constitutional Convention. He made important contributions to science, especially in the understanding of electricity, and is remembered for the wit, wisdom, and elegance of his writing.

Franklin, a native of Boston, was born the 10th son of the 17 children of a man who made soap and candles, one of the lowliest of the artisan crafts. In an age that privileged the first-born son, Franklin was, as he tartly noted in his *Autobiography*, "the youngest Son of the youngest Son for five Generations back." He learned to read very early and had one year in grammar school and another under a private teacher, but his formal education ended at age 10. At 12 he was apprenticed to his brother James, a printer. His mastery of the printer's trade, of which he was proud to the end of his life, was achieved between 1718 and 1723. In the same period he read tirelessly and taught himself to write effectively.

His first enthusiasm was for poetry, but, discouraged with the quality of his own, he gave it up. Prose was another matter. Young Franklin discovered a volume of *The Spectator*—featuring Joseph Addison and Sir Richard Steele's famous periodical essays, which had appeared in England in 1711–12—and saw in it a means for improving his writing. He read these *Spectator* papers over and over, copied and recopied them, and then tried to recall them from memory. He even turned them into poetry and then back into prose. Franklin realized, as all the Founders did, that writing competently was such a rare talent in the 18th century that anyone who could do it well immediately attracted attention.

Benjamin Franklin, engraving, 1775.

"Prose writing" became, as he recalled in his *Autobiography*, "of great Use to me in the Course of my Life, and was a principal Means of my Advancement."

In 1721 James Franklin founded a weekly newspaper, the *New-England Courant*, to which readers were invited to contribute. Benjamin, now 16, read and perhaps set in type these contributions and decided that he could do as well himself. In 1722 he wrote a series of 14 essays signed "Silence Dogood" in which he lampooned everything from funeral eulogies to the students of Harvard College. For one so young to assume the persona of a middle-aged woman was a remarkable feat, and Franklin took "exquisite Pleasure" in the fact that his brother and others became convinced that only a learned and ingenious wit could have written these essays.

Late in 1722 James Franklin got into trouble with the provincial authorities and was forbidden to print or publish the *Courant*. To keep the paper going, he discharged his younger brother from his original apprenticeship and made him the paper's nominal publisher. New indentures were drawn up but not made public. Some months later, after a bitter quarrel, Benjamin secretly left home, sure that James would not "go to law" and reveal the subterfuge he had devised.

Failing to find work in New York City, Franklin at age 17 went on to Quaker-dominated Philadelphia, a much more open and religiously tolerant place than Puritan Boston. One of the most memorable scenes of the *Autobiography* is the description of his arrival on a Sunday morning, tired and hungry. Finding a bakery, he asked for three pennies' worth of bread and got "three great Puffy Rolls." Carrying one under each arm and munching on the third, he walked up Market Street past the door of the Read family, where stood Deborah, his future wife. She saw him and "thought I made, as I certainly did, a most awkward ridiculous Appearance."

A few weeks later he was rooming at the Reads' and employed as a printer. By the spring of 1724 he was enjoying the companionship of other young men with a taste for reading, and he was also being urged to set up in business for himself by the governor of Pennsylvania, Sir William Keith. At Keith's suggestion, Franklin returned to Boston to try to raise the necessary capital. His father thought him too young for such a venture, so Keith offered to foot the bill himself and arranged Franklin's passage to England so that he could choose his type and make connections with London stationers and booksellers. Franklin exchanged "some promises" about marriage with Deborah Read and with a young friend, James Ralph, as his companion, sailed for London in November 1724, just over a year after arriving in Philadelphia. Not until his ship was well out at sea did he realize that Governor Keith had not delivered the letters of credit and introduction he had promised.

In London Franklin quickly found employment in his trade and was able to lend money to Ralph, who was trying to establish himself as a writer. The two young men enjoyed the theater and the other pleasures of the city, including women. While in London, Franklin wrote *A Dissertation on Liberty and Necessity, Pleasure and Pain* (1725), a Deistical pamphlet inspired by his having set type for William Wollaston's moral tract, *The Religion of Nature Delineated*. Franklin argued in his essay that since human beings have no real freedom of choice, they are not morally responsible for their actions. This was perhaps a nice justification for his self-indulgent behavior in London and his ignoring of Deborah, to whom he had written only once. He later repudiated the pamphlet, burning all but one of the copies still in his possession.

By 1726 Franklin was tiring of London. He considered becoming an itinerant teacher of swimming, but when Thomas Denham, a Quaker merchant, offered him a clerkship in his store in Philadelphia with a prospect of fat commissions in the West Indian trade, he decided to return home.

Denham died, however, a few months after Franklin entered his store. The young man, now 20, returned to the printing trade and in 1728 was able to set up a partnership with a friend. Two years later he borrowed money to become sole proprietor.

His private life at this time was extremely complicated. Deborah Read had married, but her husband had deserted her and disappeared. One matchmaking venture failed because Franklin wanted a dowry of £100 to pay off his business debt. A strong sexual drive, "that hard-to-be-govern'd Passion of Youth," was sending him to "low Women," and he thought he very much needed to get married. His affection for Deborah having "revived," he "took her to Wife" on September 1, 1730. At this point Deborah may have been the only woman in Philadelphia who would have him, for he brought to the marriage an illegitimate son, William, just born of a woman who has never been identified. Franklin's common-law marriage lasted until Deborah's death in 1774. They had a son, Franky, who died at age four, and a daughter, Sarah, who survived them both. William was brought up in the household and apparently did not get along well with Deborah.

Franklin and his partner's first coup was securing the printing of Pennsylvania's paper currency. Franklin helped get this business by writing *A Modest Enquiry into the Nature and Necessity of a Paper Currency* (1729), and later he also became public printer of New Jersey, Delaware, and Maryland. Other moneymaking ventures included the *Pennsylvania Gazette*, published by Franklin from 1729 and generally acknowledged as among the best of the colonial newspapers, and *Poor Richard's* almanac, printed annually from 1732 to 1757. Despite some failures, Franklin prospered. Indeed, he made enough to lend money with interest and to invest in rental properties in Philadelphia and many coastal towns. He had franchises or partnerships with printers in the Carolinas, New York, and the British West Indies. By the late 1740s he had become one of the wealthiest colonists in the northern part of the North American continent.

As he made money, he concocted a variety of projects for social improvement. In 1727 he organized the Junto, or Leather Apron Club, to debate questions of morals, politics, and natural philosophy and to exchange knowledge of business affairs. The need of Junto members for easier access to books led in 1731 to the organization of the Library Company of Philadelphia. Through the Junto, Franklin proposed a paid city watch, or police force. A paper read to the same group resulted in the organization of a volunteer fire company. In 1743 he sought an intercolonial version of the Junto, which led to the formation of the American Philosophical Society. In 1749 he published *Proposals Relating to the Education of Youth in Pennsilvania*; in 1751 the Academy of Philadelphia, from which grew the University of Pennsylvania, was founded. He also became an enthusiastic member of the Freemasons and promoted their "enlightened" causes.

Although still a tradesman, he was picking up some political offices. He became clerk of the Pennsylvania legislature in 1736 and postmaster of Philadelphia in 1737. Prior to 1748, though, his most important political service was his part in organizing a militia for the defense of the colony against possible invasion by the French and the Spaniards, whose privateers were operating in the Delaware River.

In 1748 Franklin, at age 42, had become wealthy enough to retire from active business. He took off his leather apron and became a gentleman, a distinctive status in the 18th century. Since no busy artisan could be a gentleman, Franklin never again worked as a printer; instead, he became a silent partner in the printing firm of Franklin and Hall, realizing in the next 18 years an average profit of over £600 annually. He announced his new status as a gentleman by having his portrait painted in a velvet coat and a brown wig; he also acquired a coat of arms, bought several slaves, and moved to a new and more spacious house in "a more quiet Part of the Town." Most important, as a gentleman and "master of [his] own time," he decided to do what other gentlemen did—engage in what he termed "Philosophical Studies and Amusements."

In the 1740s electricity was one of these curious amusements. It was introduced to Philadelphians by an electrical machine sent to the Library Company by one of Franklin's English correspondents. In the winter of 1746–47, Franklin and three of his friends began to investigate electrical phenomena. Franklin sent piecemeal reports of his ideas and experiments to Peter Collinson, his Quaker correspondent in London. Since he did not know what European scientists might have already discovered, Franklin set forth his findings timidly. In 1751 Collinson had Franklin's papers published in an 86-page book titled *Experiments and Observations on Electricity*. In the 18th century the book went through five English editions, three in French, and one each in Italian and German.

Franklin's fame spread rapidly. The experiment he suggested to prove the identity of lightning and electricity was apparently first made in France before he tried the simpler but more dangerous expedient of flying a kite in a thunderstorm. But his other findings were original. He created the distinction between insulators and conductors. He invented a battery for storing electrical charges. He coined new English words for the new science of electricity—*conductor, charge, discharge, condense, armature, electrify*, and others. He showed that electricity was a single "fluid" with positive and negative or plus and minus charges and not, as traditionally thought, two kinds of fluids. And he demonstrated that the plus and minus charges, or states of electrification of bodies, had to occur in exactly equal amounts—a crucial scientific principle known today as the law of conservation of charge.

Despite the success of his electrical experiments, Franklin never thought science was as important as public service. As a leisured gentleman, he soon became involved in more high-powered public offices. He became a member of the Philadelphia City Council in 1748, justice of the peace in 1749, and in 1751 a city alderman and a member of the Pennsylvania Assembly. But he had his sights on being part of a larger arena, the British Empire, which he regarded as "the greatest Political Structure Human Wisdom ever yet erected." In 1753 Franklin became a royal officeholder, deputy postmaster general, in charge of mail in all the northern colonies. Thereafter he began to think in intercolonial terms. In 1754 his "Plan of Union" for the colonies was adopted by the Albany Congress, which was convened at the beginning of the French and Indian War and included representatives from the Iroquois Confederacy. The plan called for the establishment of a general council, with representatives from the several colonies, to organize a common defense against the French. Neither the colonial legislatures nor the king's advisers were ready for such union, however, and the plan failed. But Franklin had become acquainted with important imperial officials, and his ambition to succeed within the imperial hierarchy had been whetted.

In 1757 he went to England as the agent of the Pennsylvania Assembly in order to get the family of William Penn,

"Join, or Die," the first known American cartoon, published by Benjamin Franklin in his Pennsylvania Gazette, 1754, to support his plan for colonial union presented at the Albany Congress.

the proprietors under the colony's charter, to allow the colonial legislature to tax their ungranted lands. But Franklin and some of his allies in the assembly had a larger goal of persuading the British government to oust the Penn family as the proprietors of Pennsylvania and make that colony a royal province. Except for a two-year return to Philadelphia in 1762–64, Franklin spent the next 18 years living in London, most of the time in the apartment of Margaret Stevenson, a widow, and her daughter Polly at 36 Craven Street near Charing Cross. His son, William, now age 27, and two slaves accompanied him to London. Deborah and their daughter, Sally, age 14, remained in Philadelphia.

Before he left for London, Franklin decided to bring his *Poor Richard*'s almanac to an end. While at sea in 1757, he completed a 12-page preface for the final 1758 edition of the almanac titled "Father Abraham's Speech" and later known as the *The Way to Wealth*. In this preface Father Abraham cites only those proverbs that concern hard work, thrift, and financial prudence. *The Way to Wealth* eventually became the most widely reprinted of all Franklin's works, including the *Autobiography*.

This time Franklin's experience in London was very different from his sojourn in 1724–26. London was the largest city in Europe and the center of the burgeoning British Empire, and Franklin was famous; consequently, he met everyone else who was famous, including David Hume, Captain James Cook, Joseph Priestley, and John Pringle, who was physician to Lord Bute, the king's chief minister. In 1759 Franklin received an honorary degree from the University of Saint Andrews in Scotland, which led to his thereafter being called "Dr. Franklin." Another honorary degree followed in 1762 from the University of Oxford. Everyone wanted to paint his portrait and make mezzotints for sale to the public. Franklin fell in love with the sophistication of London and England; by contrast, he disparaged the provinciality and vulgarity of America. He was very much the royalist, and he bragged of his connection with Lord Bute, which enabled him in 1762 to get his son, William, then age 31, appointed royal governor of New Jersey.

Reluctantly, Franklin had to go back to Pennsylvania in 1762 in order to look after his post office, but he promised his friends in London that he would soon return and perhaps stay forever in England. After touring the post offices up and down North America, a trip of 1,780 miles (2,900 km), he had to deal with an uprising of some Scotch-Irish settlers in the Paxton region of western Pennsylvania who were angry at the Quaker assembly's unwillingness to finance military protection from the Indians on the frontier. After losing an election to the Pennsylvania Assembly in 1764, Franklin could hardly wait to get back to London. Deborah stayed in Philadelphia, and Franklin never saw her again.

He soon had to face the problems arising from the Stamp Act of 1765, which created a firestorm of opposition in America. Like other colonial agents, Franklin opposed Parliament's stamp tax, asserting that taxation ought to be the prerogative of the colonial legislatures. But once he saw that passage of the tax was inevitable, he sought to make the best of the situation. After all, he said, empires cost money. He ordered stamps for his printing firm in Philadelphia and procured for his friend John Hughes the stamp agency for Pennsylvania. In the process, he almost ruined his position in American public life and nearly cost Hughes his life.

Franklin was shocked by the mobs that effectively prevented enforcement of the Stamp Act everywhere in North America. He told Hughes to remain cool in the face of the mob. "A firm Loyalty to the Crown and faithful Adherence to the Government of this Nation . . . ," he said, "will always be the wisest Course for you and I to take, whatever may be the Madness of the Populace or their blind Leaders." Only Franklin's four-hour testimony before Parliament denouncing the act in 1766 saved his reputation in America. The experience shook Franklin, and his earlier confidence in the wisdom of British officials became punctuated by doubts and resentments. He began to feel what he called his "Americanness" as never before.

During the next four or five years Franklin sought to bridge the growing gulf between the colonies and the British government. Between 1765 and 1775 he wrote 126 newspaper pieces, most of which tried to explain each side to the other. But, as he said, the English thought him too American, while the Americans thought him too English. He had not, however, given up his ambition of acquiring a position in the imperial hierarchy. But in 1771 opposition by Lord Hillsborough, who had just been appointed head of the new American Department, left Franklin depressed and dispirited; in a mood of frustration, nostalgia, and defiance, he began writing his *Autobiography*, which eventually became one of the most widely read autobiographies ever published.

In recounting the first part of his life, up to age 25—the best part of the *Autobiography*, most critics agree—Franklin sought to soothe his wounds and justify his apparent failure in British politics. Most important, in this beginning part of his Autobiography, he in effect was telling the world (and his son) that as a free man who had established himself against overwhelming odds as an independent and industrious artisan, he did not have to kowtow to some patronizing, privileged aristocrat.

When the signals from the British government shifted and Hillsborough was dismissed from the cabinet, Franklin dropped the writing of the *Autobiography*, which he would not resume until 1784 in France following the successful negotiation of the treaty establishing American independence. Franklin still thought he might be able to acquire an imperial office and work to hold the empire together. But he became involved in the affair of the Hutchinson letters—an affair that ultimately destroyed his position in England. In 1772 Franklin had sent back to Boston some letters written in the 1760s by Thomas Hutchinson, then lieutenant governor of Massachusetts, in which Hutchinson had made some indiscreet remarks about the need to abridge American liberties. Franklin naively thought that these letters would somehow throw blame for the imperial crisis on native officials such as Hutchinson and thus absolve the ministry in London of responsibility. This, Franklin believed, would allow his friends in the ministry, such as Lord Dartmouth, to settle the differences between the mother country and her colonies, with Franklin's help.

The move backfired completely, and on January 29, 1774, Franklin stood silent in an amphitheater near Whitehall while being viciously attacked by the British solicitor-general before the Privy Council and the court, most of whom were hooting and laughing. Two days later he was fired as deputy postmaster. After some futile efforts at reconciliation, he sailed for America in March 1775.

Although upon his arrival in Philadelphia Franklin was immediately elected to the Second Continental Congress, some Americans remained suspicious of his real loyalties. He had been so long abroad that some thought he might be a British spy. He was delighted that the Congress in 1776 sent him back to Europe as the premier agent in a commission seeking military aid and diplomatic recognition from France. He played on the French aristocracy's liberal sympathies for the oppressed Americans and extracted not only diplomatic recognition of the new republic but also loan after loan from an increasingly impoverished French government. His image as the democratic folk genius from the wilderness of America preceded him, and he exploited it brilliantly for the American cause. His face appeared everywhere—on medallions, on snuffboxes, on candy boxes, in rings, in statues, in prints; women even did their hair à la Franklin. Franklin played his role to perfection. In violation of all protocol, he dressed in a simple brown-and-white linen suit and wore a fur cap, no wig, and no sword to the court of Versailles, the most formal and elaborate court in all of Europe. And the French aristocracy and court loved it, caught up as they were with the idea of America.

Dr. Franklin erhält, als Gesandter des Americanischen Frey Staats, seine erste Audienz in Frankreich, zu Versailles. am 20ten Märtz 1778.

Franklin's first audience with Louis XVI. Armed with news of the victory at Saratoga, Benjamin Franklin, America's commissioner to France, feigned interest in conciliation with the British. Instead, the French, who wanted the war to continue, offered an alliance and assistance with the American Revolutionary War.

Beset with the pain of gout and a kidney stone, and surrounded by spies and his sometimes clumsy fellow commissioners—especially Arthur Lee of Virginia and John Adams of Massachusetts, who disliked and mistrusted him—Franklin nonetheless succeeded marvelously. He first secured military and diplomatic alliances with France in 1778 and then played a crucial role in bringing about the final peace treaty with Britain in 1783. In violation of their instructions and the French alliance, the American peace commissioners signed a separate peace with Britain. It was left to Franklin to apologize to the comte de Vergennes, Louis XVI's chief minister, which he did in a beautifully wrought diplomatic letter.

No wonder the eight years in France were the happiest of Franklin's life. He was doing what he most yearned to do—shaping events on a world stage. At this point, in 1784, he resumed work on his *Autobiography*, writing the second part of it, which presumes human control over one's life.

In 1785 Franklin reluctantly had to come to America to die, even though all his friends were in France. Although he feared he would be "a stranger in my own country," he now knew that his destiny was linked to America.

His reception was not entirely welcoming. The family and friends of the Lees in Virginia and the Adamses in Massachusetts spread stories of his overweening love of France and his dissolute ways. The Congress treated him shabbily, ignoring his requests for some land in the West and a diplomatic appointment for his grandson. In 1788 he was reduced to petitioning the Congress with a pathetic "Sketch of the Services of B. Franklin to the United States," which the Congress never answered. Just before his death in 1790, Franklin retaliated by signing a memorial requesting that the Congress abolish slavery in the United States. This memorandum provoked some congressmen into angry defenses of slavery, which Franklin exquisitely mocked in a newspaper piece published a month before he died.

Upon his death the Senate refused to go along with the House in declaring a month of mourning for Franklin. In contrast to the many expressions of French affection for Franklin, his fellow Americans gave him one public eulogy—and that was delivered by his inveterate enemy the Rev. William Smith, who passed over Franklin's youth because it seemed embarrassing.

Following the publication of the *Autobiography* in 1794, Franklin's youth was no longer embarrassing. In the succeeding decades, he became the hero of countless early 19th-century artisans and self-made businessmen who were seeking a justification of their rise and their moneymaking. They were the creators of the modern folksy image of Franklin, the man who came to personify the American dream.

Franklin was not only the most famous American in the 18th century but also one of the most famous figures in the Western world of the 18th century; indeed, he is one of the most celebrated and influential Americans who has ever lived. Although one is apt to think of Franklin exclusively as an inventor, as an early version of Thomas Edison, which he was, his 18th-century fame came not simply from his many inventions but, more important, from his fundamental contributions to the science of electricity. If there had been a Nobel Prize for Physics in the 18th century, Franklin would have been a contender. Enhancing his fame was the fact that he was an American, a simple man from an obscure background who emerged from the wilds of America to dazzle the entire intellectual world. Most Europeans in the 18th century thought of America as a primitive, undeveloped place full of forests and savages and scarcely capable of producing enlightened thinkers. Yet Franklin's electrical discoveries in the mid-18th century had surpassed the achievements of the most sophisticated scientists of Europe. Franklin became a living example of the natural untutored genius of the New World that was free from the encumbrances of a decadent and tired Old World—an image that he later parlayed into French support for the American Revolution.

Despite his great scientific achievements, however, Franklin always believed that public service was more important than science, and his political contributions to the formation of the United States were substantial. He had a hand in the writing of the Declaration of Independence, contributed to the drafting of the Articles of Confederation—America's first national constitution—and was the oldest member of the Constitutional Convention of 1787 that wrote the Constitution of the United States of America in Philadelphia. More important, as diplomatic representative of the new American republic in France during the Revolution, he secured both diplomatic recognition and financial and military aid from the government of Louis XVI and was a crucial member of the commission that negotiated the treaty by which Great Britain recognized its former 13 colonies as a sovereign nation. Since no one else could have accomplished all that he did in France during the Revolution, he can quite plausibly be regarded as America's greatest diplomat.

Equally significant, perhaps, were Franklin's many contributions to the comfort and safety of daily life, especially in his adopted city of Philadelphia. No civic project was too large or too small for his interest. In addition to his lightning rod and his Franklin stove, he invented bifocal glasses, the odometer, and the glass harmonica (armonica). He had ideas about everything—from the nature of the Gulf Stream to the cause of the common cold. He suggested the notions of matching grants and Daylight Saving Time. Almost single-handedly he helped to create a civic society for the inhabitants of Philadelphia. Moreover, he helped to establish new institutions that people now take for granted: a fire company, a library, an insurance company, an academy, and a hospital.

Probably Franklin's most important invention was himself. He created so many personas in his newspaper writings and almanac and in his posthumously published *Autobiography* that it is difficult to know who he really was. Following his death in 1790, he became so identified during the 19th century with the persona of his *Autobiography* and the Poor Richard maxims of his almanac—for example, "Early to bed, early to rise, makes a man healthy, wealthy, and wise"—that he acquired the image of the self-made moralist obsessed with the getting and saving of money. Consequently, many imaginative writers, such as Edgar Allan Poe, Henry David Thoreau, Herman Melville, Mark Twain, and D. H. Lawrence, attacked Franklin as a symbol of America's middle-class moneymaking business values. Indeed, early in the 20th century the famous German sociologist Max Weber found Franklin to be the perfect exemplar of the "Protestant ethic" and the modern capitalistic spirit. Although Franklin did indeed become a wealthy tradesman by his early 40s, when he retired from his business, during his lifetime in the 18th century he was not identified as a self-made businessman or a budding capitalist. That image was a creation of the 19th century. But as long as America continues to be pictured as the land of enterprise and opportunity, where striving and hard work can lead to success, then that image of Franklin is the one that is likely to endure.

French and Indian War

The French and Indian War was the American phase of a world-wide, nine-years' war (1754–63) fought between France and Great Britain. (The more complex European phase was the Seven Years' War [1756–63].) It determined the control of the vast colonial territory of North America.

The French and Indian War began over the specific issue of whether the upper Ohio River valley was a part of the British Empire, and therefore open for trade and settlement by Virginians and Pennsylvanians, or part of the French Empire. Behind this issue loomed an infinitely larger one, however: which national culture was to dominate the heart of North America.

Settlers of English extraction were in a preponderance in the coveted area, but French exploration, trade, and Indian alliances predominated. As early as 1749, the governor-general of New France specifically ordered the area cleared of all British, with the aim of restricting their settlements to the territory east of the Appalachian Mountains. In the spring of 1754, the French ousted a Virginia force from the forks of the Ohio River, and a skirmish was precipitated by Colonel George Washington. Shortly, Washington's force was surrounded at Fort Necessity, Pennsylvania, and forced to surrender. Ultimately the war spread to every part of the world where either of the two nations had territorial interests.

The first four years saw nothing but severe reverses for the British regulars and American colonials, primarily because of superior French land forces in the New World. Lack of colonial assistance to the war effort compounded British problems. By the end of 1757, however, the course of the war began to be altered by three major influences. One was the dynamic leadership of the British prime minister, William Pitt the Elder, who saw that victory in North America was the supreme task in the worldwide struggle and who has been truly called the organizer of victory in the Great War for the Empire. The second was the increasing superiority of British financial and industrial resources, food supplies, and naval equipment, as opposed to growing national bankruptcy and economic paralysis faced by France. Finally, both the British and Americans were becoming seasoned wilderness fighters.

In 1758 and 1759, aided by effective blockades off the coast of France as well as in the Gulf of St. Lawrence, the British won important victories at Louisbourg, Fort Frontenac, Fort Carillon (later Ticonderoga), and Crown Point, and at Fort Duquesne (now Pittsburgh) and Fort Niagara. The climax came with the British victory on the Plains of Abraham (September 13, 1759), where Quebec was forced to surrender and where both commanders, James Wolfe and the marquis de Montcalm, were fatally wounded. A year later, Montreal and the whole of New France had fallen. By the Treaty of Paris (February 10, 1763), France ceded its territory on mainland North America east of the Mississippi River (including Canada) to Great Britain; Spain ceded Florida to Britain but in return received the Louisiana Territory (that is, the western half of the Mississippi River basin) and New Orleans from the French. Though unpopular with the British public, which would have preferred France's rich sugar-producing islands of the West Indies rather than Canada, the 1763 treaty is often thought to mark the beginning of Britain's imperial greatness. Ironically, Britain's problems arising from victory, such as war debts and the administration and settlement of an expanded colonial empire, contained the very seeds of the conflict that would lead to the American Revolution during the following decade.

Gerry, Elbridge

Elbridge Gerry (1744–1814) was the son of Thomas Gerry, a merchant, and Elizabeth Greenleaf. He graduated from Harvard in 1762 and entered his father's business. He was a member of the Massachusetts legislature and General Court (1772–73), served on a Committee of Correspondence, was a member of the Massachusetts Provincial Congress (1774–75), and was a delegate to the Continental Congress in Philadelphia (1776–81), where he was an early advocate of independence. He was also a member of Congress (1783–85) under the Articles of Confederation and a delegate to the Constitutional Convention in Philadelphia (1787). He was an outspoken opponent of ratification of the United States Constitution, fearing that it might give way to aristocratic or monarchical rule. However, he gave it his full support after its ratification, helping to draft the Bill of Rights and serving as a representative in Congress for two terms (1789–93).

In 1797 President John Adams sent Gerry, John Marshall, and Charles Cotesworth Pinckney to France on the mission that resulted in the XYZ Affair. The mission, an unsuccessful attempt to negotiate a treaty to settle several long-standing disputes, ended early because of the duplicitous treatment of the American negotiators by the French foreign minister, Charles-Maurice de Talleyrand, and his subordinates. After the French agents demanded bribes, Marshall and Pinckney departed in disgust; however, Gerry remained in Paris in the vain hope that Talleyrand might offer him, a known friend of France, terms that had been refused to Marshall and Pinckney. This action brought a storm of abuse and censure from Federalist partisans, from which Gerry never fully cleared himself.

After four attempts to win election as governor of Massachusetts, Gerry succeeded in 1810 and was reelected in 1811. His administration was notable for dividing electoral districts for partisan political advantage—a process now known as *gerrymandering*.

In 1812 Gerry, an ardent supporter of war with Great Britain in the War of 1812, was elected vice president of the United States on the Jeffersonian Republican ticket with Madison. In 1813, while presiding over the Senate, Gerry, who along with Madison was in ill health, refused to yield his chair at the close of the legislative session, thus preventing William Giles, a senator from Virginia and an advocate of peace with Britain, from becoming president pro tempore of the Senate and thereby second in line (after the vice president) to succeed the president under the Presidential Succession Act of 1792. Gerry suffered a hemorrhage of the lungs on his way to the Senate and died in 1814.

Gwinnett, Button

An American merchant, patriot, and signer of the Declaration of Independence, Button Gwinnett (1735–77) is known chiefly because his autographs are of extreme rarity and collectors have forced their value to a high figure. (In 2001 one of his 36 autographs sold at public auction for $110,000.)

Gwinnett emigrated from England to Georgia sometime before 1765. In January 1776 he was elected a delegate from that colony to the Continental Congress and, as such, signed the Declaration. Returning to Georgia, Gwinnett was a member of the convention to frame a new state constitution. He died from wounds received in a duel with Lachlan McIntosh, a Continental general, whose brother Gwinnett had arrested.

Hale, Nathan

A graduate of Yale University (1773) and a schoolteacher, Nathan Hale (1755–76) joined a Connecticut regiment in 1775, served in the siege of Boston, and was commissioned a captain (1776). He went to New York with William Heath's brigade and is said to have participated in the capture of a provision sloop from under the guns of a British man-of-war. Hale was captured by the British while attempting to return to his regiment, having penetrated the British lines on Long Island to obtain information. He was hanged without trial the next day.

An American Revolutionary officer who attempted to spy on the British and was hanged, Hale is regarded by American Revolutionary tradition as a hero and a martyr. He is supposed to have said before his death that his only regret was that he had but one life to lose for his country, a remark similar to one in Joseph Addison's play *Cato*.

Hamilton, Alexander

Alexander Hamilton (1755/57–1804) was a delegate to the Constitutional Convention (1787), a major author of the Federalist

Papers, published as *The Federalist* (which helped win ratification for the Constitution), and the first secretary of the treasury of the United States (1789–95).

His father was James Hamilton, a drifting trader and son of Alexander Hamilton, the laird of Cambuskeith, Ayrshire, Scotland; his mother was Rachel Fawcett Lavine, the daughter of a French Huguenot physician and the wife of John Michael Lavine, a German or Danish merchant who had settled on the island of St. Croix in the Danish West Indies. Rachel probably began living with James Hamilton in 1752, but Lavine did not divorce her until 1758.

In 1765 James Hamilton abandoned his family. Destitute, Rachel set up a small shop, and at the age of 11 Alexander went to work, becoming a clerk in the countinghouse of two New York merchants who had recently established themselves at St. Croix. When Rachel died in 1768, Alexander became a ward of his mother's relatives, and in 1772 his ability, industry, and engaging manners won him advancement from bookkeeper to manager. Later, friends sent him to a preparatory school in Elizabethtown, New Jersey, and in the autumn of 1773 he entered King's College (later Columbia) in New York. Intensely ambitious, he became a serious and successful student, but his studies were interrupted by the brewing revolt against Great Britain. He publicly defended the Boston Tea Party, in which Boston colonists destroyed several tea cargoes in defiance of the tea tax. In 1774–75 he wrote three influential pamphlets, which upheld the agreements of the Continental Congress on the nonimportation, nonconsumption, and nonexportation of British products and attacked British policy in Quebec. Those anonymous publications—one of them attributed to John Jay and John Adams, two of the ablest of American propagandists—gave the first solid evidence of Hamilton's precocity.

In March 1776, through the influence of friends in the New York legislature, Hamilton was commissioned a captain in the provincial artillery. He organized his own company and at the

Battle of Trenton, when he and his men prevented the British under Lord Cornwallis from crossing the Raritan River and attacking George Washington's main army, showed conspicuous bravery. In February 1777 Washington invited him to become an aide-de-camp with the rank of lieutenant colonel. In his four years on Washington's staff he grew close to the general and was entrusted with his correspondence. He was sent on important military missions and, thanks to his fluent command of French, became liaison officer between Washington and the French generals and admirals.

Eager to connect himself with wealth and influence, Hamilton married Elizabeth, the daughter of General Philip Schuyler, the head of one of New York's most distinguished families. Meantime, having tired of the routine duties at headquarters and yearning for glory, he pressed Washington for an active command in the field. Washington refused, and in early 1781 Hamilton seized upon a trivial quarrel to break with the general and leave his staff. Fortunately, he had not forfeited the general's friendship, for in July Washington gave him command of a battalion. At the siege of Cornwallis's army at Yorktown in October, Hamilton led an assault on a British stronghold.

In letters to a member of Congress and to Robert Morris, the superintendent of finance, Hamilton analyzed the financial and political weaknesses of the government. In November 1781, with the war virtually over, he moved to Albany, where he studied law and was admitted to practice in July 1782. A few months later the New York legislature elected him to the Continental Congress. He continued to argue in essays for a strong central government, and in Congress from November 1782 to July 1783 he worked for the same end, being convinced that the Articles of Confederation were the source of the country's weakness and disunion.

In 1783 Hamilton began to practice law in New York City. He defended unpopular loyalists who had remained faithful to the British during the Revolution in suits brought against them under a state law called the Trespass Act. Partly as a result of his efforts, state acts disbarring loyalist lawyers and disfranchising loyalist voters were repealed. In that year he also won election to the lower house of the New York legislature, taking his seat in January 1787. Meanwhile, the legislature had appointed him a delegate to the convention in Annapolis, Maryland, that met in September 1786 to consider the commercial plight of the Union. Hamilton suggested that the convention exceed its delegated powers and call for another meeting of representatives from all the states to discuss various problems confronting the nation. He drew up the draft of the address to the states from which emerged the Constitutional Convention that met in Philadelphia in May 1787. After persuading New York to send a delegation, Hamilton obtained a place for himself on the delegation.

Hamilton went to Philadelphia as an uncompromising nationalist who wished to replace the Articles of Confederation with a strong centralized government, but he did not take much part in the debates. He served on two important committees, one on rules in the beginning of the convention and the other on style at the end of the convention. In a long speech on June 18, he presented his own idea of what the national government should be. Under his plan, the national government would have had unlimited power over the states. Hamilton's plan had little impact on the convention; the delegates went ahead to frame a constitution that, while it gave strong power to a federal government, stood some chance of being accepted by the people. Since the other two delegates from New York, who were strong opponents of a Federalist constitution, had withdrawn from the convention, New York was not officially represented, and Hamilton had no power to sign for his state. Nonetheless, even though he knew that his state wished to go no further than a revision of the Articles of Confederation, he signed the new constitution as an individual.

Opponents in New York quickly attacked the Constitution, and Hamilton answered them in the newspapers under the signature Caesar. Since the Caesar letters seemed not influential, Hamilton turned to another classical pseudonym, Publius, and to two collaborators, James Madison, the delegate from Virginia, and John Jay, the secretary of foreign affairs, to write *The Federalist*, a series of 85 essays in defense of the Constitution and republican government that appeared in newspapers between October 1787 and May 1788. Hamilton wrote at least two-thirds of the essays, including some of the most important ones that interpreted the Constitution, explained the powers of the executive, the senate, and the judiciary, and expounded the theory of judicial review (that is, the power of the Supreme Court to declare legislative acts unconstitutional and, thus, void). Although written and published in haste, *The Federalist* was widely read, had a great influence on contemporaries, became one of the classics of political literature, and helped shape American political institutions. In 1788 Hamilton was reappointed a delegate to the Continental Congress from New York. At the ratifying convention in June, he became the chief champion of the Constitution and, against strong opposition, won approval for it.

When President Washington in 1789 appointed Hamilton the first secretary of the treasury, Congress asked him to draw up a plan for the "adequate support of the public credit." Envisaging himself as something of a prime minister in Washington's official family, Hamilton developed a bold and masterly program designed to build a strong union, one that would weave his political philosophy into the government. His immediate objectives were to establish credit at home and abroad and to strengthen the national government at the expense of the states. He outlined his program in four notable reports to Congress (1790–91).

In the first two, *Reports on the Public Credit*, which he submitted on January 14, 1790, and December 13, 1790, he urged the funding of the national debt at full value, the assumption in full by the federal government of debts incurred by the states during the Revolution, and a system of taxation to pay for the assumed debts. His motive was as much political as economic. Through payment by the central government of the states' debts, he hoped to bind the men of wealth and influence, who had acquired most of the domestically held bonds, to the national government. But such powerful opposition arose to the funding and assumption scheme that Hamilton was able to push it through Congress only after he had made a bargain with Thomas Jefferson, who was then secretary of state, whereby he gained southern votes in Congress for it in exchange for his own support in locating the future national capital on the banks of the Potomac.

Hamilton's third report, the *Report on a National Bank*, which he submitted on December 14, 1790, advocated a national bank called the Bank of the United States and modeled after the Bank of England. With the bank, he wished to solidify the partnership between the government and the business classes who would benefit most from it and further advance his program to strengthen the national government. After Congress passed the bank charter, Hamilton persuaded Washington to sign it into law. He advanced the argument that the Constitution was the source of implied as well as enumerated powers and that through implication the government had the right to charter a national bank as a proper means of regulating the currency. This doctrine of implied powers became the basis for interpreting and expanding the Constitution in later years. In the *Report on Manufactures*, the fourth, the longest, the most complex, and the most farsighted of his reports, submitted on December 5, 1791, he proposed to aid the growth of infant industries through various protective laws. Basic to it was his idea that the general welfare required the encouragement of manufacturers and that the federal government was obligated to direct the economy to that end. In writing his report, Hamilton had leaned heavily on *The Wealth of Nations*, written in 1776 by the Scottish political economist Adam Smith, but he revolted against Smith's laissez-faire idea that the state must keep hands off the economic processes, which meant that it could provide no bounties, tariffs, or other aid. The report had greater appeal to posterity than to Hamilton's contemporaries, for Congress did nothing with it.

A result of the struggle over Hamilton's program and over issues of foreign policy was the emergence of national political parties. Like Washington, Hamilton had deplored parties, equating them with disorder and instability. He had hoped to establish a government of superior persons who would be above party. Yet he became the leader of the Federalist Party, a political organization in large part dedicated to the support of his policies. Hamilton placed himself at the head of that party because he needed organized political support and strong leadership in the executive branch to get his program through Congress. The political organization that challenged the Hamiltonians was the Republican Party (later Democratic-Republican Party) created by James Madison, a member of the House of Representatives, and Secretary of State Thomas Jefferson. In foreign affairs the Federalists favored close ties with England, whereas the Republicans preferred to strengthen the old attachment to France. In attempting to carry out his program, Hamilton interfered in Jefferson's domain of foreign affairs. Detesting the French Revolution and the egalitarian doctrines it spawned, he tried to thwart Jefferson's policies that might aid France or injure England and to induce Washington to follow his own ideas in foreign policy. Hamilton went so far as to warn British officials of Jefferson's attachment to France and to suggest that they bypass the secretary of state and instead work through himself and the president in matters of foreign policy. This and other parts of Hamilton's program led to a feud with Jefferson in which the two men attempted to drive each other from the cabinet.

When war broke out between France and England in February 1793, Hamilton wished to use the war as an excuse for jettisoning the French alliance of 1778 and steering the United

States closer to England, whereas Jefferson insisted that the alliance was still binding. Washington essentially accepted Hamilton's advice and in April issued a proclamation of neutrality that was generally interpreted as pro-British.

At the same time, British seizure of U.S. ships trading with the French West Indies and other grievances led to popular demands for war against Great Britain, which Hamilton opposed. He believed that such a war would be national suicide, for his program was anchored on trade with Britain and on the import duties that supported his funding system. Usurping Jefferson's functions, Hamilton persuaded the president to send John Jay to London to negotiate a treaty. Hamilton wrote Jay's instructions, manipulated the negotiations, and defended the unpopular treaty Jay brought back in 1795, notably in a series of newspaper essays he wrote under the signature Camillus; the treaty kept the peace and saved his system.

Lashed by criticism, tired, and anxious to repair his private fortune, Hamilton left the cabinet on January 31, 1795. His influence as an unofficial adviser, however, continued as strong as ever. Washington and his cabinet consulted him on almost all matters of policy. When Washington decided to retire, he turned to Hamilton, asking his opinion as to the best time to publish his farewell. With his eye on the coming presidential election, Hamilton advised withholding the announcement until a few months before the meeting of the presidential electors. Following that advice, Washington gave his *Farewell Address* in September 1796. Hamilton drafted most of the address, and some of his ideas were prominent in it. In the election, Federalist leaders passed over Hamilton's claims and nominated John Adams for the presidency and Thomas Pinckney for the vice presidency. Because Adams did not appear devoted to Hamiltonian principles, Hamilton tried to manipulate the electoral college so as to make Pinckney president. Adams won the election, and Hamilton's intrigue succeeded only in sowing distrust within his own party. Hamilton's influence in the government continued, however, for Adams retained Washington's cabinet, and its members consulted Hamilton on all matters of policy, gave him confidential information, and in effect urged his policies on the president.

When France broke relations with the United States, Hamilton stood for firmness but agreed with the president's policy of trying to reestablish friendly relations. After the failure of a peace mission that President Adams had sent to Paris in 1798, followed by the publication of dispatches insulting to U.S. sovereignty, Hamilton wanted to place the country under arms. He even believed that the French, who had embarked on an undeclared naval war, might attempt to invade the country. Hamilton sought command of the new army, though Washington would be its titular head. Adams resisted Hamilton's desires, but in September 1798 Washington forced him to make Hamilton second in command of the army, the inspector general, with the rank of major general. Adams never forgave Hamilton for this humiliation. Hamilton wanted to lead his army into Spain's Louisiana and the Floridas and other points south but never did. Through independent diplomacy, Adams kept the quarrel from spreading and at the order of Congress disbanded the provisional army. Hamilton resigned his commission in June 1800. Meantime Adams had purged his cabinet of those he regarded as "Hamilton's spies."

In retaliation, Hamilton tried to prevent Adams's reelection. In October 1800 he privately circulated a personal attack on Adams, *The Public Conduct and Character of John Adams, Esq., President of the United States.* Aaron Burr of New York, the Republican candidate for vice president and Hamilton's political enemy, obtained a copy and had it published. Hamilton was then compelled to acknowledge his authorship and to bring his quarrel with Adams into the open, a feud that revealed an irreparable schism in the Federalist Party. Thomas Jefferson and Aaron Burr won the election, but because both had received the same number of electoral votes, the choice between them for president was cast into the House of Representatives. Hating Jefferson, the Federalists wanted to throw the election to Burr. Hamilton helped to persuade them to select Jefferson instead. By supporting his old Republican enemy, who won the presidency, Hamilton lost prestige within his own party and virtually ended his public career.

In 1801 Hamilton built a country house called the Grange on Manhattan island and helped found a Federalist newspaper, the *New York Evening Post*, the policies of which reflected his ideas. Through the *Post* he hailed the purchase of Louisiana in 1803, even though New England Federalists had opposed it. Some of them talked of secession and in 1804 began to negotiate with Burr for his support. Almost all the Federalists but Hamilton favored Burr's candidacy for the governorship of New York state. Hamilton urged the election of Burr's Republican opponent, who won by a close margin, but it is doubtful that Hamilton's influence decided the outcome. In any event, Hamilton and Burr had long been enemies, and Hamilton had several times thwarted Burr's ambitions. In June 1804, after the election, Burr demanded satisfaction for remarks Hamilton had allegedly made at a dinner party in April in which he said he held a "despicable opinion" of Burr. Hamilton held an aversion to dueling, but as a man of honor he felt compelled to accept Burr's challenge. The two antagonists met early in the morning of July 11 on the heights of Weehawken, New Jersey, where Hamilton's eldest son, Philip, had died in a duel three years before. Burr's bullet found its mark, and Hamilton fell. Hamilton left his wife and seven children heavily in debt, which friends helped to pay off.

Hamilton was a man both of action and of ideas, but all his ideas involved action and were directed toward some specific goal in statecraft. Unlike Benjamin Franklin or Thomas Jefferson, he did not have a broad inquisitive mind, nor was he speculative in his thinking in the philosophical sense of seeking intangible truths. He was ambitious, purposeful, a hard worker, and one of America's administrative geniuses. In foreign policy he was a realist, believing that self-interest should be the nation's polestar; questions of gratitude, benevolence, and moral principle, he held, were irrelevant.

Most of all, Hamilton was one of America's first great nationalists. He believed in an indivisible nation where the people would give their loyalty not to any state but to the nation. Although a conservative, he did not fear change or experimentation. The conservatism that led him to denounce democracy as hostile to liberty stemmed from his fear that democracy tended to invade the rights of property, which he held sacred. His concern for property was a means to an end. He wished to make private property sacred because upon it he planned to build a strong central government, one capable of suppressing internal disorders and assuring tranquility. His economic, political, military, and diplomatic schemes were all directed toward making the Union strong. Hamilton's most enduring monument was the Union, for much of it rested on his ideas.

Hancock, John

After graduating from Harvard (1754), John Hancock (1737–93) entered a mercantile house in Boston owned by his uncle Thomas Hancock, who later left him a large fortune. In 1765 he became a selectman of Boston and from 1769 to 1774 was a member of the Massachusetts General Court. He was chairman of the Boston town committee formed immediately after the Boston Massacre in 1770 to demand the removal of British troops from the city.

In 1774 and 1775 Hancock was president of the first and second provincial congresses, and he shared with Samuel Adams the leadership of the Massachusetts Patriots. With Adams he was forced to flee Lexington for Philadelphia when warned in April 1775 that he was being sought by General Thomas Gage's troops, approaching from Boston. Hancock was a member of the Continental Congress from 1775 to 1780; he served as its president from May 1775 to October 1777, and was the first signer of the Declaration of Independence. He hoped to become commander in chief of the Continental Army, but George Washington was selected instead.

John Hancock, undated engraving by J. B. Longacre from a painting by John Singleton Copley.

Hancock was a member of the Massachusetts Constitutional Convention of 1780 and in the same year was elected governor of the state. He served in Congress under the Articles of Confederation in 1785–86 and then returned to the governorship. He presided over the Massachusetts Convention of 1788 that ratified the federal Constitution, although he had been unfriendly at first toward the document. Hancock died while serving his ninth term as governor.

▋ Henry, Patrick

Patrick Henry (1736–99) was the son of John Henry, a well-educated Scotsman who served in the colony of Virginia as a surveyor, colonel, and justice of the Hanover County Court. Before he was 10, Patrick received some rudimentary education in a local school, later reinforced by tutoring from his father, who was trained in the classics. As a youth, he failed twice in seven years as a storekeeper and once as a farmer; and during this period he increased his responsibilities by marriage, in 1754, to Sarah Shelton. The demands of a growing family spurred him to study for the practice of law, and in this profession he soon displayed remarkable ability. Within a few years after his admission to the bar in 1760 he had a large and profitable clientele. He was especially successful in criminal cases, where he made good use of his quick wit, his knowledge of human nature, and his forensic gifts.

Meanwhile, his oratorical genius had been revealed in the trial known as the Parson's Cause (1763). This suit grew out of the Virginia law, disallowed by King George III, that permitted payment of the Anglican clergy in money instead of tobacco when the tobacco crop was poor. Henry astonished the audience in the courtroom with his eloquence in invoking the doctrine of

Print showing Patrick Henry making his "Give me liberty or give me death"
speech, Virginia Assembly, 1775.

natural rights, the political theory that man is born with certain inalienable rights. Two years later, at the capitol in Williamsburg, where he had just been seated as a member of the House of Burgesses (the lower house of the colonial legislature), he delivered a speech opposing the British Stamp Act. The act was a revenue law requiring certain colonial publications and documents to bear a legal stamp. Henry offered a series of resolutions asserting the right of the colonies to legislate independently of the English Parliament, and he supported these resolutions with great eloquence. "Caesar had his Brutus, Charles the First his Cromwell, and George III . . ." Here he was interrupted by cries of "Treason! treason!" But he concluded, according to a likely version, ". . . may profit by their example. If *this* be treason, make the most of it."

During the next decade Henry was an influential leader in the radical opposition to the British government. He was a member of the first Virginia Committee of Correspondence, which aided intercolonial cooperation, and a delegate to the Continental congresses of 1774 and 1775. At the second Virginia Convention, on March 23, 1775, in St. John's Church, Richmond, he delivered the speech that assured his fame as one of the great advocates of liberty. Convinced that war with Great Britain was inevitable, he presented strong resolutions for equipping the Virginia militia to fight against the British and defended them in a fiery speech with the famed peroration, "I know not what course others may take, but as for me, give me liberty or give me death."

The resolutions passed, and Henry was appointed commander of the Virginia forces, but his actions were curbed by the Committee of Safety; in reaction, he resigned on February 28, 1776. Henry served on the committee in the Virginia Convention of 1776 that drafted the first constitution for the state. He was elected governor the same year and was reelected in 1777 and 1778 for one-year terms, thereby serving continuously as long as the new constitution permitted. As wartime governor, he gave Gen. George Washington able support, and during his second term he authorized the expedition to invade the Illinois country under the leadership of George Rogers Clark.

After the death of his first wife, Henry married Dorothea Dandridge and retired to life on his estate in Henry County. He was recalled to public service as a leading member of the state legislature from 1780 to 1784 and again from 1787 to 1790. From 1784 to 1786 he served as governor. He declined to attend the Philadelphia Constitutional Convention of 1787 and in 1788 was the leading opponent of ratification of the U.S. Constitution at the Virginia Convention. This action, which has aroused much controversy ever since, resulted from his fear that the original document did not secure either the rights of the states or those of individuals, as well as from his suspicion that the north would abandon to Spain the vital right of navigation on the Mississippi River.

Henry was reconciled, however, to the new federal government, especially after the passage of the Bill of Rights, for which he was in great measure responsible. Because of family responsibilities and ill health, he declined a series of offers of high posts in the new federal government. In 1799, however, he consented to run again for the state legislature, where he wished to oppose the Kentucky and Virginia resolutions, which claimed that the states could determine the constitutionality of federal laws. During his successful electoral campaign, he made his last speech, a moving plea for American unity. He died at his home, Red Hill, before he was to have taken the seat.

Hopkinson, Francis

Francis Hopkinson (1737–91) was educated at the College of Philadelphia (later the University of Pennsylvania) and also studied law. After a brief business career, he launched a successful legal practice in New Jersey.

In 1774 Hopkinson was appointed to the governor's council, and in 1776 he represented New Jersey in the Continental Congress. He signed the Declaration of Independence and later served in several minor offices in the new American government. From 1779 to 1789 he was judge of the admiralty court for Pennsylvania, and from 1789 to his death he was U.S. district judge for eastern Pennsylvania. An ardent backer of the Constitution, he wrote several effective articles that contributed to the ratification effort in Pennsylvania.

Hopkinson was an accomplished player of the harpsichord and a composer of both religious and secular songs. In addition, he wrote poetry and literary essays. During the Revolution, he ridiculed the British and their loyalist sympathizers with pointed political satires. After the Revolution, he maintained a steady correspondence with Benjamin Franklin, George Washington, and Thomas Jefferson.

Among his varied pursuits, Hopkinson was also an artist. He designed the seal of the American Philosophical Society, the seal for the State of New Jersey, and seals for various departments of the U.S. government. There is strong evidence to support the view that he helped design the American flag; the U.S. Congress, however, turned down his petition for payment, asserting that others had contributed to the design.

Intolerable Acts

The Intolerable Acts (1774), also known as the Coercive Acts, were the four punitive measures enacted by the British Parliament in retaliation for acts of colonial defiance, together with the Quebec Act establishing a new administration for the territory ceded to Britain after the French and Indian War (1754–63).

Angered by the Boston Tea Party (1773), the British government passed the Boston Port Bill, closing that city's harbor until restitution was made for the destroyed tea. Second, the

Massachusetts Government Act abrogated the colony's charter of 1691, reducing it to the level of a crown colony, substituting a military government under General Thomas Gage, and forbidding town meetings without approval.

The third, the Administration of Justice Act, was aimed at protecting British officials charged with capital offenses during law enforcement by allowing them to go to England or another colony for trial. The fourth Coercive Act included new arrangements for housing British troops in occupied American dwellings, thus reviving the indignation that surrounded the earlier Quartering Act, which had been allowed to expire in 1770.

The Quebec Act, under consideration since 1773, removed all the territory and fur trade between the Ohio and Mississippi rivers from possible colonial jurisdiction and awarded it to the province of Quebec. By establishing French civil law and the Roman Catholic religion in the coveted area, the act raised the specter of popery before the mainly Protestant colonies.

The Intolerable Acts represented an attempt to reimpose strict British control over the American colonies, but after 10 years of vacillation, the decision to be firm had come too late. Rather than cowing Massachusetts and separating it from the other colonies, the oppressive measures became the justification for convening the First Continental Congress later in 1774.

▌Jay, John

A founding father of the United States who served the new nation in both law and diplomacy, John Jay (1745–1829) established important judicial precedents as first chief justice of the United States (1789–95) and negotiated the Jay Treaty of 1794, which settled major grievances with Great Britain and promoted commercial prosperity.

A successful New York attorney, Jay deplored the growing estrangement between the colonies and the mother country, fearing that independence might stir up violence and mob rule. Nevertheless, once the revolution was launched, he became one of its staunchest supporters. As a delegate to the First Continental Congress (1774) in Philadelphia, he drafted *The Address to the People of Great Britain*, stating the claims of colonists. He helped assure the approval of the Declaration of Independence (1776) in New York, where he was a member of the provincial congress. The following year he helped draft New York's first constitution, was elected the state's first chief justice, and in 1778 was chosen president of the Continental Congress.

In 1779 Jay was appointed minister plenipotentiary to Spain, which had joined France in openly supporting the revolutionaries against Britain. His mission—to borrow money and to gain access to the Mississippi River—proved abortive, and he was sent in May 1782 to join Benjamin Franklin in Paris as joint negotiator for peace with Great Britain. In undercover talks with the British he won surprisingly liberal terms, which were later included essentially intact in the Treaty of Paris (September 3, 1783), which concluded the war.

On his return from abroad, Jay found that Congress had elected him secretary for foreign affairs (1784–90). Frustrated by the limitations on his powers in that office, he became convinced that the nation needed a more strongly centralized government than was provided for by the Articles of Confederation, and he plunged into the fight for ratification of the new federal Constitution, framed in 1787. Using the pseudonym Publius, he collaborated with Alexander Hamilton and James Madison by writing five essays for *The Federalist*—the classic defense of the new governmental structure. In 1789 President George Washington appointed Jay the country's first chief justice, in which capacity he was instrumental in shaping Supreme Court procedures in its formative years. His most notable case was *Chisholm* v. *Georgia*, in which Jay and the court affirmed the subordination of the states to the federal government. Unfavorable reaction to the decision led to adoption of the Eleventh Amendment, denying federal courts authority in suits by citizens against a state.

In 1794 Washington sent Jay as a special envoy to Great Britain to help avert war over accumulated grievances. The commercial agreement, called the Jay Treaty (November 19), aroused a storm of protest among the Jeffersonian Republicans, who denounced it as a sellout by pro-British Federalists. Mobs burned Jay in effigy, and opponents denounced him as a traitor. Before the negotiations, Jay at one time had been considered a leading candidate to succeed Washington, but the unpopular treaty ruined whatever chances he had for the presidency. New York Federalists, however, elected him governor (1795–1801), an office from which he retired to spend the remainder of his life uneventfully on his farm.

Jay Treaty

The Jay Treaty (1794) was an agreement that assuaged antagonisms between the United States and Great Britain, established a base upon which America could build a sound national economy, and assured its commercial prosperity.

Negotiations were undertaken because of the fears of Federalist leaders that disputes with Great Britain would lead to war. In the treaty Britain, conceding to primary American grievances, agreed to evacuate the Northwest Territory by June 1, 1796; to compensate for its depredations against American shipping; to end discrimination against American commerce; and to grant the United States trading privileges in England and the British East Indies. Signed in London by Lord Grenville, the British foreign minister, and John Jay, U.S. chief justice and envoy extraordinary, the treaty also declared the Mississippi

River open to both countries; prohibited the outfitting of privateers by Britain's enemies in U.S. ports; provided for payment of debts incurred by Americans to British merchants before the American Revolution; and established joint commissions to determine the boundaries between the United States and British North America in the northwest and northeast.

By February 1796 the treaty, with the exception of an article dealing with West Indian trade, had been ratified by the United States and Great Britain. France, then at war with England, interpreted the treaty as a violation of its own commercial treaty of 1778 with the United States This resentment led to French maritime attacks on the United States and between 1798 and 1800 to an undeclared naval war. Finally, the commissions provided for by the Jay Treaty gave such an impetus to the principle of arbitration that modern international arbitration has been generally dated from the treaty's ratification.

Jefferson, Thomas

Long regarded as America's most distinguished "apostle of liberty"—the draftsman of the Declaration of Independence of the United States, an early advocate of total separation of church and state, and the most eloquent American proponent of individual freedom as the core meaning of the American Revolution—Thomas Jefferson (1743–1826) has come under increasingly critical scrutiny within the scholarly world. At the popular level, both in the United States and abroad, he remains an incandescent icon, an inspirational symbol for both major U.S. political parties, as well as for dissenters in communist China, liberal reformers in central and eastern Europe, and aspiring democrats in Africa and Latin America. His image within scholarly circles has suffered, however, as the focus on racial equality has prompted a more negative reappraisal of

Thomas Jefferson, oil on canvas by Rembrandt Peale, 1800 (in the White House Collection, Washington, D.C.).

his dependence upon slavery and his conviction that American society remain a white man's domain. The huge gap between his lyrical expression of liberal ideals and the more attenuated reality of his own life has transformed Jefferson into America's most problematic and paradoxical hero. The Jefferson Memorial in Washington, D.C., was dedicated to him on April 13, 1943, the 200th anniversary of his birth.

Albermarle County, where he was born, lay in the foothills of the Blue Ridge Mountains in what was then regarded as a western province of the Old Dominion. His father, Peter Jefferson, was a self-educated surveyor who amassed a tidy estate that included 60 slaves. According to family lore, Jefferson's earliest memory was as a three-year-old boy "being carried on a pillow by a mounted slave" when the family moved from Shadwell to Tuckahoe. His mother, Jane Randolph Jefferson, was descended from one of the most prominent families in Virginia. She raised two sons, of whom Jefferson was the eldest, and six daughters. There is reason to believe that Jefferson's relationship with his mother was strained, especially after his father died in 1757, because he did everything he could to escape her supervision and had almost nothing to say about her in his memoirs. He boarded with the local schoolmaster to learn his Latin and Greek until 1760, when he entered the College of William and Mary in Williamsburg.

By all accounts he was an obsessive student, often spending 15 hours of the day with his books, 3 hours practicing his violin, and the remaining 6 hours eating and sleeping. The two chief influences on his learning were William Small, a Scottish-born teacher of mathematics and science, and George Wythe, the leading legal scholar in Virginia. From them Jefferson learned a keen appreciation of supportive mentors, a concept he later institutionalized at the University of Virginia. He read law with Wythe from 1762 to 1767, then left Williamsburg to practice, mostly representing small-scale planters from the western counties in cases involving land claims and titles. Although he handled no landmark cases and came across as a nervous and somewhat indifferent speaker before the bench, he earned a reputation as a formidable legal scholar. He was a shy and extremely serious young man.

In 1768 he made two important decisions: first, to build his own home atop an 867-foot-high mountain near Shadwell that he eventually named Monticello and, second, to stand as a candidate for the House of Burgesses. These decisions nicely embodied the two competing impulses that would persist throughout his life—namely, to combine an active career in politics with periodic seclusion in his own private haven. His political timing was also impeccable, for he entered the Virginia legislature just as opposition to the taxation policies of the British Parliament was congealing. Although he made few speeches and tended to follow the lead of the Tidewater elite, his support for resolutions opposing Parliament's authority over the colonies was resolute.

In the early 1770s his own character was also congealing. In 1772 he married Martha Wayles Skelton, an attractive and delicate young widow whose dowry more than doubled his holdings in land and slaves. In 1774 he wrote *A Summary View of the Rights of British America*, which was quickly published, though without his permission, and catapulted him into visibility beyond Virginia as an early advocate of American independence from Parliament's authority; the American colonies were tied to Great Britain, he believed, only by wholly voluntary bonds of loyalty to the king.

His reputation thus enhanced, the Virginia legislature appointed him a delegate to the Second Continental Congress in the spring of 1775. He rode into Philadelphia—and into American history—on June 20, 1775, a tall (slightly above 6 feet 2 inches [1.88 metres]) and gangly young man with reddish-blond hair, hazel eyes, a burnished complexion, and rock-ribbed certainty about the American cause. In retrospect, the central paradox of his life was also on display, for the man who the following year was to craft the most famous manifesto for human equality in world history arrived in an ornate carriage drawn by four handsome horses and accompanied by three slaves.

Jefferson's inveterate shyness prevented him from playing a significant role in the debates within the Congress. John Adams, a leader in those debates, remembered that Jefferson was silent even in committee meetings, though consistently staunch in his support for independence. His chief role was as a draftsman of resolutions. In that capacity, on June 11, 1776, he was appointed to a five-person committee, which also included Adams and Benjamin Franklin, to draft a formal statement of the reasons why a break with Great Britain was justified. Adams asked him to prepare the first draft, which he did within a few days. He later claimed that he was not striving for "originality of principle or sentiment," only seeking to provide "an expression of the American mind," that is, putting into words those ideas already accepted by a majority of Americans. This accurately describes the longest section of the Declaration of Independence, which lists the grievances against George III. It does not, however, describe the following 55 words, which are generally regarded as the seminal statement of American political culture:

> We hold these truths to be self-evident; that all men are created equal; that they are endowed by their Creator with certain inalienable rights; that among these are life, liberty and the pursuit of happiness; that to secure these rights, governments are instituted among men, deriving their just powers from the consent of the governed.

On July 3–4 the Congress debated and edited Jefferson's draft, deleting and revising fully one-fifth of the text. But they made no changes whatsoever in this passage, which over succeeding generations became the lyrical sanction for every liberal movement in American history. At the time, Jefferson himself was disconsolate that the Congress had seen fit to make any changes in his language. Nevertheless, he was not regarded by his contemporaries as the author of the Declaration, which was seen as a collective effort by the entire Congress. Indeed, he was not known by most Americans as the principal author until the 1790s.

He returned to Virginia in October 1776 and immediately launched an extensive project for the reform of the state's legal code to bring it in line with the principles of the American Revolution. Three areas of reform suggest the arc of his political vision: first, he sought and secured abolition of primogeniture, entail, and all those remnants of feudalism that discouraged a broad distribution of property; second, he proposed a comprehensive plan of educational reform designed to assure access at the lowest level for all citizens and state support at the higher levels for the most talented; third, he advocated a law prohibiting any religious establishment and requiring complete separation of church and state. The last two proposals were bitterly contested, especially the statute for religious freedom, which was not enacted until 1786.

Taken together, these legal reforms capture the essence of Jefferson's political philosophy, which was less a comprehensive body of thought than a visionary prescription. He regarded the past as a "dead hand" of encrusted privileges and impediments that must be cast off to permit the natural energies of individual citizens to flow freely. The American Revolution, as he saw it, was the first shot in what would eventually became a global battle for human liberation from despotic institutions and all coercive versions of government.

At the end of what was probably the most creative phase of

his public career, personal misfortune struck in two successive episodes. Elected governor of Virginia in 1779, he was caught off-guard by a surprise British invasion in 1780 against which the state was defenseless. His flight from approaching British troops was described in the local press, somewhat unfairly, as a cowardly act of abdication. (Critics would recall this awkward moment throughout the remainder of his long career.) Then, in September 1782, his wife died after a difficult delivery in May of their third daughter. These two disasters caused him to vow that he would never again desert his family for his country.

The vow was sincere but short-lived. Jefferson agreed, albeit reluctantly, to serve as a delegate to the Continental Congress in December 1782, where his major contribution was to set forth the principle that territories in the west should not be treated as colonies but rather should enter the Union with status equal to the original states once certain conditions were met. Then, in 1784, recognizing the need to escape the memories of Martha that haunted the hallways at Monticello, he agreed to replace Franklin as American minister to France; or, as legend tells the story, he agreed to succeed Franklin, noting that no one could replace him.

During his five-year sojourn in Paris, Jefferson accomplished very little in any official sense. Several intractable conditions rendered his best diplomatic efforts futile: the United States was heavily in debt owing to the recent war, so few European nations were interested in signing treaties of amity and commerce with the infant American republic; the federal government created under the Articles of Confederation was notoriously weak, so clear foreign policy directives proved impossible; Great Britain already enjoyed a monopoly, controlling more than 80 percent of America's foreign trade, so it had no incentive to negotiate commercial treaties on less favorable terms; and France was drifting toward a cataclysmic political crisis of its own, so relations with the upstart new nation across the Atlantic were hardly a high priority.

As a result, Jefferson's diplomatic overtures to establish a market for American tobacco and to reopen French ports to whale oil produced meager results, his efforts to create an alliance of American and European powers to contest the terrorism of the Barbary pirates proved stillborn, and his vision of open markets for all nations, a world without tariffs, seemed excessively visionary. His only significant achievement was the negotiation of a $400,000 loan from Dutch bankers that allowed the American government to consolidate its European debts, but even that piece of diplomacy was conducted primarily by John Adams, then serving as American minister to the Court of St. James's in London.

But the Paris years were important to Jefferson for personal reasons and are important to biographers and historians for the new light they shed on his famously elusive personality. The dominant pattern would seem to be the capacity to live comfortably with contradiction. For example, he immersed himself wholeheartedly in the art, architecture, wine, and food of Parisian society but warned all prospective American tourists to remain in America so as to avoid the avarice, luxury, and sheer sinfulness of European fleshpots. He made a point of bringing along his elder daughter, Martha (called Patsy as a girl), and later sent for his younger daughter, Maria (called Polly), all as part of his genuine devotion as a single parent. But he then placed both daughters in a convent, wrote them stern lecture-like letters about proper female etiquette, and enforced a patriarchal distance that was in practice completely at odds with his theoretical commitment to intimacy.

With women in general his letters convey a message of conspicuous gallantry, playfully flirtatious in the manner of a male coquette. The most self-revealing letter he ever wrote, "a dialogue between the head and the heart," was sent to Maria Cosway, an Anglo-Italian beauty who left him utterly infatuated. Jefferson and Cosway, who was married to a prominent if somewhat degenerate English miniaturist, spent several months in a romantic haze, touring Parisian gardens, museums, and art shows together, but whether Jefferson's head or heart prevailed, either in the letter or in life, is impossible to know. Meanwhile, there is considerable evidence to suggest, but not to prove conclusively, that Jefferson initiated a sexual liaison with his attractive young mulatto slave Sally Hemings in 1788, about the time his torrid affair with Cosway cooled down—this despite his public statements denouncing blacks as biologically inferior and sexual relations between the races as taboo.

During the latter stages of Jefferson's stay in Paris, Louis XVI, the French king, was forced to convene the Assembly of Notables in Versailles to deal with France's deep financial crisis. Jefferson initially regarded the assembly as a French version of the Constitutional Convention, then meeting in Philadelphia. Much influenced by moderate leaders such as the marquis de Lafayette, he expected the French Revolution to remain a bloodless affair that would culminate in a revised French government, probably a constitutional monarchy along English lines. He remained oblivious to the resentments and volatile energies pent up within French society that were about to explode in the Reign of Terror, mostly because he thought the French Revolution would follow the American model. He was fortunate to depart France late in 1789, just at the onset of mob violence.

Even before his departure from France, Jefferson had overseen the publication of *Notes on the State of Virginia*. This book, the only one Jefferson ever published, was part travel guide, part scientific treatise, and part philosophical meditation. Jefferson had written it in the fall of 1781 and had agreed to a French edition only after learning that an unauthorized version was already in press. *Notes* contained an extensive discussion of slavery, including a graphic description of its horrific effects on both blacks and whites, a strong assertion that it violated the principles on which the American Revolution was based, and an apocalyptic prediction that failure to end slavery would lead to "convulsions which will probably never end but in the extermination of one or the other race." It also contained the most explicit assessment that Jefferson ever wrote of what he believed were the biological differences between blacks and whites, an assessment that exposed the deep-rooted racism that he, like most Americans and almost all Virginians of his day, harbored throughout his life.

To his critics in later generations, Jefferson's views on race seemed particularly virulent because of his purported relationship with Sally Hemings, who bore several children obviously fathered by a white man, some of whom had features resembling those of Jefferson. The public assertion of this relationship was originally made in 1802 by a disreputable journalist interested in injuring Jefferson's political career. His claim was corroborated, however, by one of Hemings's children in an 1873 newspaper interview and then again in a 1968 book by Winthrop Jordan revealing that Hemings became pregnant only when Jefferson was present at Monticello. Finally, in 1998, DNA samples were gathered from living descendants of Jefferson and Hemings. Tests revealed that Jefferson was almost certainly the father of some of Hemings's children. What remained unclear was the character of the relationship—consensual or coercive, a matter of love or rape, or a mutually satisfactory arrangement. Jefferson's admirers preferred to consider it a love affair and to see Jefferson and Hemings as America's preeminent biracial couple. His critics, on the other hand, considered Jefferson a sexual predator whose eloquent statements about human freedom and equality were hypocritical.

In any case, coming as it did at the midpoint of Jefferson's career, the publication of *Notes* affords the opportunity to review Jefferson's previous and subsequent positions on the most volatile and therefore most forbidden topic in the revolutionary era. Early in his career Jefferson had taken a leadership role in pushing slavery onto the political agenda in the Virginia assembly and the federal Congress. In the 1760s and 1770s, like most Virginia planters, he endorsed the end of the slave trade.

(Virginia's plantations were already well stocked with slaves, so ending the slave trade posed no economic threat and even enhanced the value of the existent slave population.) In his original draft of the Declaration of Independence, he included a passage, subsequently deleted by the Continental Congress, blaming both the slave trade and slavery itself on George III. Unlike most of his fellow Virginians, Jefferson was prepared to acknowledge that slavery was an anomaly in the American republic established in 1776. His two most practical proposals came in the early 1780s: a gradual emancipation scheme by which all slaves born after 1800 would be freed and their owners compensated, and a prohibition of slavery in all the territories of the west as a condition for admission to the Union. By the time of the publication of *Notes*, then, Jefferson's record on slavery placed him among the most progressive elements of southern society. Rather than ask how he could possibly tolerate the persistence of slavery, it is more historically correct to wonder how this member of Virginia's planter class had managed to develop such liberal convictions.

Dating the onset of a long silence is inevitably an imprecise business, but by the time of his return to the United States in 1789 Jefferson had backed away from a leadership position on slavery. The ringing denunciations of slavery presented in *Notes* had generated controversy, especially within the planter class of Virginia, and Jefferson's deep aversion to controversy made him withdraw from the cutting edge of the antislavery movement once he experienced the sharp feelings it aroused. Moreover, the very logic of his argument in *Notes* exposed the inherent intractability of his position. Although he believed that slavery was a gross violation of the principles celebrated in the Declaration of Independence, he also believed that people of African descent were biologically inferior to whites and could never live alongside whites in peace and harmony. They would have to be transported elsewhere, back to Africa or perhaps the Caribbean, after emancipation. Because such a massive deportation was a logistical and economic impossibility, the unavoidable conclusion was that though slavery was wrong, ending it, at least at present, was inconceivable. That became Jefferson's public position throughout the remainder of his life.

It also shaped his personal posture as a slave owner. Jefferson owned, on average, about 200 slaves at any point in time, and slightly over 600 over his lifetime. To protect himself from facing the reality of his problematic status as plantation master, he constructed a paternalistic self-image as a benevolent father caring for what he called "my family." Believing that he and his slaves were the victims of history's failure to proceed along the enlightened path, he saw himself as the steward for those entrusted to his care until a better future arrived for them all. In the meantime, his own lavish lifestyle and all the incessant and expensive renovations of his Monticello mansion were wholly dependent on slave labor. Whatever silent thoughts he might have harbored about freeing his slaves never found their way into the record. (He freed only five slaves, all members of the Hemings family.) His mounting indebtedness rendered all such thoughts superfluous toward the end, because his slaves, like all his possessions, were mortgaged to his creditors and therefore not really his to free.

Jefferson returned to the United States in 1789 to serve as the first secretary of state under President George Washington. He was entering the most uncharted waters in American history. There had never been an enduring republican government in a nation as large as the United States, and no one was sure if it was possible or how it would work. The Constitution ratified in 1788 was still a work-in-progress, less a blueprint that provided answers than a framework for arguing about the salient questions. And because Jefferson had been serving in France when the constitutional battles of 1787–88 were waged in Philadelphia and then in the state ratifying conventions, he entered the volatile debates of the 1790s without a clear track record of his constitutional convictions. In truth, unlike his friend and disciple James Madison, Jefferson did not think primarily in constitutional categories. His major concern about the new Constitution was the absence of any bill of rights. He was less interested in defining the powers of government than in identifying those regions where government could not intrude.

During his tenure as secretary of state (1790–93), foreign policy was his chief responsibility. Within the cabinet a three-pronged division soon emerged over American policy toward the European powers. While all parties embraced some version of the neutrality doctrine, the specific choices posed by the ongoing competition for supremacy in Europe between England and France produced a bitter conflict. Washington and Adams, who was serving as vice president, insisted on complete neutrality, which in practice meant tacking back and forth between the two dominant world powers of the moment. Alexander Hamilton pushed for a pro-English version of neutrality—chiefly commercial ties with the most potent mercantile power in the world. Jefferson favored a pro-French version of neutrality, arguing that the Franco-American treaty of 1778 obliged the United States to honor past French support during the war for independence, and that the French Revolution embodied the "spirit of '76" on European soil. Even when the French Revolution spun out of control and began to devour its own partisans, Jefferson insisted that these bloody convulsions were only temporary excesses justified by the larger ideological issues at stake.

This remained his unwavering position throughout the decade. Even after he retired from office late in 1793, he issued directives from Monticello opposing the Neutrality Act (1793) and the Jay Treaty (1795) as pacts with the British harlot and betrayals of our French brethren. Serving as vice president during the Adams presidency (1797–1801), Jefferson worked behind the scenes to undermine Adams's efforts to sustain strict neutrality and blamed the outbreak of the "quasi-war" with France in 1797–98 on what he called "our American

Anglophiles" rather than the French Directory. His foreign policy vision was resolutely moralistic and highly ideological, dominated by a dichotomous view of England as a corrupt and degenerate engine of despotism and France as the enlightened wave of the future.

Jefferson's position on domestic policy during the 1790s was a variation on the same ideological dichotomy. As Hamilton began to construct his extensive financial program—to include funding the national debt, assuming the state debts, and creating a national bank—Jefferson came to regard the consolidation of power at the federal level as a diabolical plot to subvert the true meaning of the American Revolution. As Jefferson saw it, the entire Federalist commitment to an energetic central government with broad powers over the domestic economy replicated the arbitrary policies of Parliament and George III, which the American Revolution had supposedly repudiated as monarchical and aristocratic practices, incompatible with the principles of republicanism. Jefferson sincerely believed that the "principles of '76" were being betrayed by a Federalist version of the "court party," whose covert scheme was to install monarchy and a pseudo-aristocracy of bankers and "monocrats" to rule over the American yeomanry.

All the major events of the decade—the creation of a national bank, the debate over the location of a national capital, the suppression of the Whiskey Rebellion in western Pennsylvania, the passage of the Jay Treaty, and, most notoriously, the enforcement of the Alien and Sedition Acts—were viewed through this ideological lens. By the middle years of the decade two distinctive political camps had emerged, calling themselves Federalists and Republicans (later Democratic-Republicans). Not that modern-day political parties, with their mechanisms for raising money, selecting candidates, and waging election campaigns, were fully formed at this stage. (Full-blooded political parties date from the 1830s and 1840s.) But an embryonic version of the party structure was congealing, and

Jefferson, assisted and advised by Madison, established the rudiments of the first opposition party in American politics under the Republican banner.

The partnership between Jefferson and Madison, labeled by subsequent historians as "the great collaboration," deserves special attention. John Quincy Adams put it nicely when he observed that "the mutual influence of these two mighty minds on each other is a phenomenon, like the invisible and mysterious movements of the magnet in the physical world." Because the notion of a legitimate opposition to the elected government did not yet exist, and because the term *party* remained an epithet that was synonymous with faction, meaning an organized effort to undermine the public interest, Jefferson and Madison were labeled as traitors by the Federalist press. They were, in effect, inventing a modern form of political behavior before there was any neutral vocabulary for talking about it. Jefferson's own capacity to live comfortably with contradictions served him well in this context, since he was creating and leading a political party while insisting that parties were evil agents. In 1796 he ran for the presidency against Adams, all the while claiming not to know that he was even a candidate. Most negative assessments of Jefferson's character date from this period, especially the charge of hypocrisy and duplicity.

The highly combustible political culture of the early republic reached a crescendo in the election of 1800, one of the most fiercely contested campaigns in American history. The Federalist press described Jefferson as a pagan and atheist, a treasonable conspirator against the duly elected administrations of Washington and Adams, a utopian dreamer with anarchistic tendencies toward the role of government, and a cunning behind-the-scenes manipulator of Republican propaganda. All these charges were gross exaggerations, save the last. Always operating through intermediaries, Jefferson paid several journalists to libel Adams, his old friend but current political enemy, and offered the vice presidency to Aaron Burr in return for delivering the electoral votes of New York. In the final tally the 12 New York votes made the difference, with the tandem of Jefferson and Burr winning 73 to 65. A quirk in the Constitution, subsequently corrected in the Twelfth Amendment, prevented electors from distinguishing between their choice of president and vice president, so Jefferson and Burr tied for the top spot, even though voter preference for Jefferson was incontestable. The decision was thrown into the House of Representatives where, after several weeks of debate and backroom wheeling and dealing, Jefferson was elected on the 36th ballot.

There was a good deal of nervous speculation whether the new American nation could survive a Jefferson presidency. The entire thrust of Jefferson's political position throughout the 1790s had been defiantly negative, rejecting as excessive the powers vested in the national government by the Federalists. In his Virginia Resolutions of 1798, written in protest of the Alien and Sedition Acts, he had described any projection of federal authority over the domestic policy of the states as a violation of "the spirit of '76" and therefore a justification for secession from the Union. (This became the position of the Confederacy in 1861.) His Federalist critics wondered how he could take an oath to preserve, protect, and defend the Constitution of the United States if his primary goal as president was to dismantle the federal institutions created by that very document. As he rose to deliver his inaugural address on March 4, 1801, in the still-unfinished Capitol of the equally unfinished national capital on the Potomac, the mood was apprehensive. The most rabid alarmists had already been proved wrong, since the first transfer of power from one political regime to another had occurred peacefully, even routinely. But it was still very much an open question whether, as Lincoln later put it, "any nation so conceived and so dedicated could long endure" in the absence of a central government along Federalist lines.

The major message of Jefferson's inaugural address was conciliatory. Its most famous line ("We are all republicans—we are all federalists") suggested that the scatological party battles of the previous decade must cease. He described his election as a recovery of the original intentions of the American Revolution, this after the hostile takeover of those "ancient and sacred truths" by the Federalists, who had erroneously assumed that a stable American nation required a powerful central government. In Jefferson's truly distinctive and original formulation, the coherence of the American republic did not require the mechanisms of a powerful state to survive or flourish. Indeed, the health of the emerging American nation was inversely proportional to the power of the federal government, for in the end the sovereign source of republican government was voluntary popular opinion, "the people," and the latent energies these liberated individuals released when unburdened by government restrictions.

In 1804 Jefferson was easily reelected over Federalist Charles Cotesworth Pinckney, winning 162 electoral votes to Pinckney's 14. Initially, at least, his policies as president reflected his desire for decentralization, which meant dismantling the embryonic federal government, the army and navy, and all federal taxation programs, as well as placing the national debt, which stood at $112 million, on the road to extinction. These reforms enjoyed considerable success for two reasons. First, the temporary cessation of the war between England and France for European supremacy permitted American merchants to trade with both sides and produced unprecedented national prosperity. Second, in selecting Albert Gallatin as secretary of the treasury, Jefferson placed one of the most capable managers of fiscal policy in the most strategic location. Gallatin, a Swiss-born prodigy with impeccable Republican credentials, dominated the cabinet discussions alongside Madison, the ever-loyal Jefferson disciple who served as secretary of state.

Actually there were very few cabinet discussions because Jefferson preferred to do the bulk of business within the executive branch in writing. Crafting language on the page was his most obvious talent, and he required all cabinet officers to submit drafts of their recommendations, which he then edited and returned for their comments. The same textual approach applied to his dealings with Congress. All of his annual messages were delivered in writing rather than in person. Indeed, apart from his two inaugural addresses, there is no record of Jefferson delivering any public speeches whatsoever. In part this was a function of his notoriously inadequate abilities as an orator, but it also reflected his desire to make the office of the presidency almost invisible. His one gesture at visibility was to schedule weekly dinners when Congress was in session, which became famous for the quality of the wine, the pell-mell seating arrangements, and the informal approach to etiquette—a clear defiance of European-style decorum.

The major achievement of his first term was also an act of defiance, though this time it involved defying his own principles. In 1803 Napoleon decided to consolidate his resources for a new round of the conflict with England by selling the vast Louisiana region, which stretched from the Mississippi Valley to the Rocky Mountains. Although the asking price, $15 million, was a stupendous bargain, assuming the cost meant substantially increasing the national debt. More significantly, what became known as the Louisiana Purchase violated Jefferson's constitutional scruples. Indeed, many historians regard it as the boldest executive action in American history. But Jefferson never wavered, reasoning that the opportunity to double the national domain was too good to miss. The American West always triggered Jefferson's most visionary energies, seeing it, as he did, as America's future, the place where the simple republican principles could be constantly renewed. In one fell swoop he removed the threat of a major European power from America's borders and extended the life span of the uncluttered agrarian values he so cherished. Even before news that the purchase was approved reached the United States in July 1803, Jefferson dispatched his private secretary, Meriwether Lewis, to lead an expedition to explore the new acquisition and the lands beyond, all the way to the Pacific.

If the Louisiana Purchase was the crowning achievement of

Jefferson's presidency, it also proved to be the high point from which events moved steadily in the other direction. Although the Federalist Party was dead as a national force, pockets of Federalist opposition still survived, especially in New England. Despite his eloquent testimonials to the need for a free press, Jefferson was outraged by the persistent attacks on his policies and character from those quarters, and he instructed the attorneys general in the recalcitrant states to seek indictments, in clear violation of his principled commitment to freedom of expression. He was equally heavy-handed in his treatment of Aaron Burr, who was tried for treason after leading a mysterious expedition into the American southwest allegedly designed to detach that region from the United States with Burr crowned as its benevolent dictator. The charges were never proved, but Jefferson demanded Burr's conviction despite the lack of evidence. He was overruled in the end by Chief Justice John Marshall, who sat as the judge in the trial.

But Jefferson's major disappointment had its origins in Europe with the resumption of the Napoleonic Wars, which resulted in naval blockades in the Atlantic and Caribbean that severely curtailed American trade and pressured the U.S. government to take sides in the conflict. Jefferson's response was the Embargo Act (1807), which essentially closed American ports to all foreign imports and American exports. The embargo assumed that the loss of American trade would force England and France to alter their policies, but this fond hope was always an illusion, since the embryonic American economy lacked the size to generate such influence and was itself wrecked by Jefferson's action. Moreover, the enforcement of the Embargo Act required the exercise of precisely those coercive powers by the federal government that Jefferson had previously opposed. By the time he left office in March 1809, Jefferson was a tired and beaten man, anxious to escape the consequences of his futile efforts to preserve American neutrality and eager to embrace the two-term precedent established by Washington.

During the last 17 years of his life Jefferson maintained a crowded and active schedule. He rose with the dawn each day, bathed his feet in cold water, then spent the morning on his correspondence (one year he counted writing 1,268 letters) and working in his garden. Each afternoon he took a two-hour ride around his grounds. Dinner, served in the late afternoon, was usually an occasion to gather his daughter Martha and her 12 children, along with the inevitable visitors. Monticello became a veritable hotel during these years, on occasion housing 50 guests. The lack of privacy caused Jefferson to build a separate house on his Bedford estate about 90 miles (140 km) from Monticello, where he periodically fled for seclusion.

Three architectural projects claimed a considerable share of his attention. Throughout his life Monticello remained a work-in-progress that had the appearance of a construction site. Even during his retirement years, Jefferson's intensive efforts at completing the renovations never quite produced the masterpiece of neoclassical design he wanted to achieve and that modern-day visitors to Monticello find so compelling. A smaller but more architecturally distinctive mansion at Bedford, called Poplar Forest, was completed on schedule. It, too, embodied neoclassical principles but was shaped as a perfect octagon. Finally, there was the campus of the University of Virginia at Charlottesville, which Jefferson called his "academical village." Jefferson surveyed the site, which he could view in the distance from his mountaintop, and chose the Pantheon of Rome as the model for the rotunda, the centerpiece flanked by two rows of living quarters for students and faculty. In 1976 the American Institute of Architects voted it "the proudest achievement of American architecture in the past 200 years." Even the "interior" design of the University of Virginia embodied Jeffersonian principles, in that he selected all the books for the library, defined the curriculum, picked the faculty, and chaired the Board of Visitors. Unlike every other American college at the time, "Mr. Jefferson's university" had no religious affiliation and imposed no religious requirement on its students. As befitted an institution shaped by a believer in wholly voluntary and consensual networks of governance, there were no curricular requirements, no mandatory code of conduct except the self-enforced honor system, no president or administration. Every aspect of life at the University of Virginia reflected Jefferson's belief that the only legitimate form of governance was self-governance.

In 1812 his vast correspondence began to include an exchange with his former friend and more recent rival John Adams. The reconciliation between the two patriarchs was arranged by their mutual friend Benjamin Rush, who described them as "the North and South poles of the American Revolution." That description suggested more than merely geographic symbolism, since Adams and Jefferson effectively, even dramatically, embodied the twin impulses of the revolutionary generation. As the "Sage of Monticello," Jefferson represented the Revolution as a clean break with the past, the rejection of all European versions of political discipline as feudal vestiges, the ingrained hostility toward all mechanisms of governmental authority that originated in faraway places. As the "Sage of Quincy (Massachusetts)," Adams resembled an American version of Edmund Burke, which meant that he attributed the success of the American Revolution to its linkage with past practices, most especially the tradition of representative government established in the colonial assemblies. He regarded the constitutional settlement of 1787–88 as a shrewd compromise with the political necessities of a nation–state exercising jurisdiction over an extensive, eventually continental, empire, not as a betrayal of the American Revolution but an evolutionary fulfillment of its promise.

These genuine differences of opinion made Adams and Jefferson the odd couple of the American Revolution and were the primary reasons why they had drifted to different sides of the divide during the party wars of the 1790s. The exchange of 158 letters between 1812 and 1826 permitted the two sages to pose

as philosopher-kings and create what is arguably the most intellectually impressive correspondence between statesmen in all of
American history. Beyond the elegiac tone and almost sculpted
serenity of the letters, the correspondence exposed the fundamental contradictions that the American Revolution managed
to contain. As Adams so poignantly put it, "You and I ought not
to die before we have explained ourselves to each other." And
because of Adams's incessant prodding, Jefferson was frequently forced to clarify his mature position on the most salient
issues of the era.

One issue that even Adams and Jefferson could not
discuss candidly was slavery. Jefferson's mature position on that
forbidden subject represented a further retreat from any leadership role in ending the "peculiar institution." In 1819, during
the debate in Congress over the Missouri Compromise, he
endorsed the expansion of slavery into all the western territories,
precisely the opposite of the position he had taken in the 1780s.
Though he continued to insist that slavery was a massive anomaly, he insisted even more strongly that it was wrong for the federal government to attempt any effort at emancipation. In fact,
he described any federal intrusion in the matter as a despotic act
analogous to George III's imperial interference in colonial
affairs or Hamilton's corrupt scheme to establish a disguised
form of monarchy in the early republic. His letters to fellow Virginians during his last years reflect a conspiratorial mentality
toward the national government and a clear preference for
secession if threatened with any mandatory plan for abolition.

Apart from slavery, the other shadow that darkened Monticello during Jefferson's twilight years was debt. Jefferson was
chronically in debt throughout most of his life, in part because
of obligations inherited from his father-in-law in his wife's
dowry, mostly because of his own lavish lifestyle, which never
came to terms with the proverbial bottom line despite careful
entries in his account books that provided him with only the
illusion of control. In truth, by the 1820s the interest on his debt

was compounding at a faster rate than any repayment schedule could meet. By the end, he was more than $100,000—in modern terms several million dollars—in debt. An exception was made in Virginia law to permit a lottery that Jefferson hoped would allow his heirs to retain at least a portion of his property. But the massiveness of his debt overwhelmed all such hopes. Monticello, including land, mansion, furnishings, and the vast bulk of the slave population, was auctioned off the year after his death, and his surviving daughter, Martha, was forced to accept charitable contributions to sustain her family.

Before that ignominious end, which Jefferson never lived to see, he managed to sound one last triumphant note that projected his most enduring and attractive message to posterity. In late June 1826 Jefferson was asked to join the Independence Day celebrations in Washington, D.C., on the 50th anniversary of the defining event in his and the nation's life. He declined, explaining that he was in no condition to leave his mountaintop. But he mustered up one final surge of energy to draft a statement that would be read in his absence at the ceremony. He clearly intended it as his final testament. Though some of the language, like the language of the Declaration itself, was borrowed from others, here was the vintage Jeffersonian vision:

> May it be to the world, what I believe it will be, (to some parts sooner, to others later, but finally to all,) the signal of arousing men to burst the chains under which monkish ignorance and superstition had persuaded them to bind themselves, and to assume the blessings and security of self-government. . . . All eyes are opened or opening to the rights of men. The general spread of the light of science has already laid open to every view the palpable truth, that the mass of mankind has not been born with saddles on their backs, nor a favored few, booted and spurred, ready to ride them legitimately by the grace of God. These are grounds of hope for others; for ourselves, let the annual return of this day forever refresh our recollections of these rights, and an undiminished devotion to them.

Even as these words were being read in Washington, Jefferson went to his maker in his bed at Monticello at about half past noon on July 4, 1826. His last conscious words, uttered the preceding evening, were "Is it the Fourth?" Always a man given to Herculean feats of self-control, he somehow managed to time his own death to coincide with history. More remarkably, up in Quincy on that same day his old rival and friend also managed to die on schedule. John Adams passed away later in the afternoon. His last words—"Thomas Jefferson still lives"—were wrong at the moment but right for the future, since Jefferson's complex legacy was destined to become the most resonant and controversial touchstone in all of American history.

A CLOSER LOOK

The Jefferson-Hemings Paternity Debate
by Joseph J. Ellis

Long before Americans learned about the sexual escapades of their 20th-century presidents—Warren Harding, John Kennedy, and Bill Clinton were the chief offenders—there was the story of Thomas Jefferson and Sally Hemings. Until recently, when newly developed techniques in genetic research made scientific evidence on long-dead figures available to historians, the claim that Jefferson and his mulatto slave were sexual partners could be neither proved nor disproved. One historian described the story as "the longest-running mini-series in American history." In January 2000 the Thomas Jefferson Memorial Foundation accepted the conclusion, supported by DNA evidence, that Jefferson and Hemings had at least one and probably six offspring between 1790 and 1808, though this conclusion was quickly and ardently contested by other individuals and groups.

The story has its origins in 1802, when a journalist of disreputable credentials, James Callender, published the initial accusation in *The Richmond Recorder*. Callender's motives were hardly pure. Jefferson had hired him to libel John Adams in the presidential campaign of 1800, and Callender had then turned on Jefferson when the payment for his services did not include a political appointment. Rumours about miscegenation at Monticello had been making the rounds in Virginia for several years. They were based on the fact that an attractive house slave named Sally Hemings had several children who were obviously fathered by a white man, some of whom had features that resembled those of Jefferson. Neither Callender nor the Federalist editors who quickly picked up the story were primarily concerned if it was true. They were interested in using the scandal as a weapon to wound Jefferson, whose political stature was nearing its zenith.

In terms of practical political consequences, the charges proved ineffectual. Jefferson was reelected by a landslide in 1804, and the party he had founded dominated national politics almost unopposed for decades. But throughout the 19th century the "Tom and Sally" story, as it was then known, persisted as a titillating piece of innuendo that cast a shadow of doubt over Jefferson's reputation in the history books.

Two new pieces of evidence surfaced in the 19th century, but they contradicted each another. In 1873 Madison Hemings, Sally's next-to-last child (born in 1805), gave an interview to *The Pike County* (Ohio) *Republican* in which he claimed that Jefferson was his father and, in fact, the father of all of Sally's five or six children. This claim was verified by Israel Jefferson, another ex-slave from Monticello and a longtime friend of Madison Hemings. The following year, James Parton published his *Life of Thomas Jefferson* and reported a story that had been circulating in the Jefferson and Randolph families for many years—namely, that Jefferson's nephew, Peter Carr, when confronted by Martha Jefferson, had admitted that he was the father of all or most of Sally's children.

There matters stood for nearly a century. The final piece of circumstantial evidence appeared in 1968 with the publication of Winthrop Jordan's *White Over Black: American Attitudes Toward the Negro, 1550–1812*. Jordan noticed that Sally Hemings had become pregnant only when Jefferson was present at Monticello, a significant revelation because he was away fully two-thirds of the time. Jordan's work also launched a new wave of scholarship that focused attention on Jefferson's highly problematic status as a slave owner who harbored decidedly negative views on African Americans and strong convictions about the impossibility of any biracial American society. The more critical assessment of Jefferson's character and legacy shed two different beams of light on the story of a sexual liaison with Sally Hemings. On one hand, it undercut the wholly reverential view of Jefferson, thereby making the charge even more plausible. On the other hand, it exposed the virulently racist values that Jefferson shared with other Virginia planters, thereby casting a new kind of doubt that he would engage in a long-term sexual relationship with a black woman. Over the next two decades scholarly opinion on the matter divided, though the majority of historians and biographers believed that the evidence remained inconclusive and unconvincing.

In November 1998 dramatic new scientific evidence became available. Several scholars had for many years advocated doing a DNA analysis of Jefferson's remains and comparing the results with the descendants of Sally Hemings. But the white descendants of the Jefferson family had resisted the thought of digging up their ancestor as a ghoulish suggestion. And the likelihood of obtaining a sufficient sample of genetic material after so many years seemed remote. However, new techniques for matching parts of the male Y-chromosome made it possible to perform the comparison without actually getting the sample from Jefferson himself.

Because the Y-chromosome is passed intact on the male side, statistically reliable results could be obtained from any male descendant in the Jefferson family. Dr. Eugene Foster, a retired pathologist at the University of Virginia, gathered DNA samples from a living descendant of Jefferson's paternal uncle, Field Jefferson, as well as from descendants of Sally's youngest and eldest sons. The results revealed a perfect match between specific portions of Jefferson's Y-chromosome and the Y-chromosome of Eston Hemings (born 1808). The chance of such a match occurring in a random sample is less than one in a thousand. The Foster study also included a comparison of the Hemings line with descendants of the Carr family, which showed no match, thereby undermining the explanation offered by Jefferson's white descendants that Carr had fathered Sally's children.

To be sure, the DNA evidence established probability rather than certainty. Several of Jefferson's male relatives had the same Y-chromosome, making them equally eligible genetically as fathers, though none of them was present at Monticello nine months before each of Sally's births, as Jefferson was. Nevertheless, those who most passionately contest Jefferson's paternity can correctly argue that it is not a matter of scientific certainty. Whether Jefferson's paternity has been proven beyond a reasonable doubt depends very much on who comprises the jury.

Where does that leave us? Perhaps the best way to put it is to say that the burden of proof has shifted rather dramatically. The new scholarly consensus is that Jefferson and Hemings were sexual partners. How long the liaison lasted is less clear, though the burden of proof now rests on those who wish to reject the claim of Madison Hemings that the relationship was long-standing. The character of the relationship is even more a matter of conjecture. Whether it was consensual or coercive, a matter of love or rape, or perhaps a mutual arrangement that provided Jefferson with physical gratification and Hemings with privileged status and the promise of freedom for her children, is a matter of lively debate. That debate is likely to persist for some time, in part because the historical evidence is virtually nonexistent and in part because the question of Jefferson's character has become a trophy in the culture wars. His admirers will be predisposed to interpret the liaison with Sally Hemings as a love affair, with Jefferson and Hemings cast in the role of America's most preeminent biracial couple. His critics will regard the relationship as symbolic of the predatory behavior of white slaveholders and clinching evidence of Jefferson's inveterate hypocrisy, which then expands to serve as a graphic illustration of the purely platitudinous character of his eloquent statements about human freedom and equality.

Joseph J. Ellis is a professor of History at Mount Holyoke College and the author of American Sphinx: The Character of Thomas Jefferson *(1997),* Founding Brothers: The Revolutionary Generation *(2000), and* His Excellency: George Washington *(2004), among other works.*

King, Rufus

A founding father of the United States who helped frame the federal Constitution and effect its ratification, Rufus King (1755–1827) was an active Federalist senator and able diplomat. He ran unsuccessfully for vice president (1804, 1808) and for president (1816).

Beginning his career in Massachusetts, King served in the state legislature (1783–84) and in the Continental Congress (1784–87), where he introduced the resolution (February 21, 1787) calling for a convention at Philadelphia to draft a new Constitution. An eloquent advocate of a strong central government, he signed the new document and contributed substantially to its acceptance in Massachusetts. In the Continental Congress he introduced a resolution (1785) that would prohibit slavery in the Northwest Territory—a provision included permanently in the Ordinance of 1787, which set the pattern for future standards in the territories.

In 1788 King moved to New York where, after a year in the state assembly, he was elected one of its first U.S. senators (1789–96) and became a recognized Federalist leader in Congress. Sharing the Anglophile sentiments of his party, King went on to represent the new nation with tact yet firmness as ambassador to Great Britain for eight years (1796–1803) and again in 1825–26. During the period of domination by the (Jeffersonian) Democratic-Republican Party, King served once more in the Senate (1813–25) but received only a modest proportion of electoral votes for the nation's highest offices on three different occasions.

Lee, Richard Henry

Educated in England, Richard Henry Lee (1732–94) served in the Virginia House of Burgesses (1758–75). He opposed arbitrary British policies at the time of the Stamp Act and the Townshend Acts, and, with Patrick Henry and Thomas Jefferson, he originated a plan for intercolonial committees of correspondence (March 1777).

Lee was an active member of the First Continental Congress, where admirers of his oratory compared him with Cicero. In the Second Continental Congress he introduced three resolutions: (1) for declaring independence; (2) for forming foreign alliances; and (3) for preparing a plan of confederation. His first resolution was adopted on July 2, 1776, and the Declaration of Independence followed two days later. He remained active in Congress until forced to resign in 1779 because of poor health. In 1777, 1780, and 1785 he served in the Virginia House of Delegates and in 1784 was back in Congress, where he remained until 1787, acting as its president in 1784. He opposed ratification of the federal Constitution because it created a "consolidated" government and lacked a bill of rights. He served, nonetheless, as senator from Virginia in the first Congress from 1789 to 1792, when he retired from public life.

▌Livingston, Robert R.

Robert R. Livingston (1746–1813) was an early American leader who served as a delegate to the Continental Congress, first secretary of the Department of Foreign Affairs (1781–83), and minister to France (1801–04).

Born into a wealthy and influential New York family, Livingston was admitted to the bar in 1770. Devoted to the idea of liberty, he worked on numerous committees of the Continental Congress at Philadelphia (1775–76, 1779–81, 1784–85), especially in the areas of finance and foreign and judicial affairs. He was a member of the committee that drafted the Declaration of Independence, and, after helping to draft New York state's first constitution (1777), he served as the state's first chancellor (1777–1801).

With the inauguration of the federal government under the Articles of Confederation (1781), Livingston was appointed secretary of the Department of Foreign Affairs, in which post he established vital administrative precedents and organized the conduct of foreign affairs on a businesslike basis. He insisted on greater independence for American delegates to the Paris Peace Conference (1782–83), but reprimanded them for negotiating without the full concurrence of France.

On April 30, 1789, under the new Constitution, Chancellor Livingston administered the oath of office in New York City to the nation's first president, George Washington. During the 1790s he gradually associated himself with the anti-Federalists and in 1801 was appointed by President Thomas Jefferson to represent the United States in France. In that capacity he rendered his most distinguished service by helping effect the Louisiana Purchase (1803)—one of the country's greatest diplomatic coups.

In retirement Livingston became enthusiastically involved with steam navigation experiments, and in partnership with the inventor Robert Fulton, he received a steamboat monopoly in

New York waters. Their first successful steam vessel, operating on the Hudson River in 1807, was named the *Clermont* after Livingston's ancestral home.

▌Louisiana Purchase

The Louisiana Purchase encompasses the western half of the Mississippi River basin purchased in 1803 from France by the United States. At less than three cents per acre for 828,000 square miles (2,144,520 square km), it was the greatest land bargain in U.S. history. The purchase doubled the size of the United States, greatly strengthened the country materially and strategically, provided a powerful impetus to westward expansion, and confirmed the doctrine of implied powers of the federal Constitution.

The Louisiana Territory had been the object of Old World interest for many years before 1803. Explorations and scattered settlements in the 17th and 18th centuries had given France control over the river and title to most of the Mississippi valley.

The first serious disruption of French control over Louisiana came during the Seven Years' War. In 1762 France ceded Louisiana west of the Mississippi River to Spain and in 1763 transferred virtually all of its remaining possessions in North America to Great Britain. This arrangement, however, proved temporary. French power rebounded under the subsequent military leadership of Napoleon Bonaparte, and on October 1, 1800, Napoleon induced a reluctant King Charles IV of Spain to agree, for a consideration, to cede Louisiana back to France. King Charles gave at least his verbal assent on the condition that France would never alienate the territory to a third power. With this treaty of retrocession, known as the Treaty of San Ildefonso (confirmed March 21, 1801), would go not only the growing and commercially significant port of New Orleans but the strategic mouth of the Mississippi River.

Reports of the supposed retrocession soon were received by the U.S. government with deep misgivings. During the preceding 12 years, Americans had streamed westward into the valleys of the Cumberland, Tennessee, and Ohio rivers. The very existence of these new settlers depended on their right to use the Mississippi River freely and to make transshipment of their exports at New Orleans. By terms of the Treaty of San Lorenzo, Spain, in 1795, had granted to the United States the right to ship goods originating in American ports through the mouth of the Mississippi without paying duty and also the right of deposit, or temporary storage, of American goods at New Orleans for transshipment. But in 1802 Spain in effect revoked the right of deposit, and so it was in an atmosphere of growing tension in the west that President Thomas Jefferson was confronted with the prospect of a new, wily, and more powerful keeper of the strategic window to the Gulf of Mexico.

Jefferson instructed Robert R. Livingston, the U.S. minister at Paris, to take two steps: (1) to approach Napoleon's minister, Charles Maurice de Talleyrand, with the object of preventing the retrocession in the event this act had not yet been completed; and (2) to try to purchase at least New Orleans if the property had actually been transferred from Spain to France. Direct negotiations with Talleyrand, however, appeared to be all but impossible. For months Livingston had to be content with tantalizing glimmerings of a possible deal between France and the United States. But even these faded as news of the Spanish governor's revocation of the right of deposit reached the U.S. minister. With this intelligence he had good reasons for thinking the worst: that Napoleon Bonaparte may have been responsible for this unfortunate act and that his next move might be to close the Mississippi River entirely to the Americans. Livingston had but one trump to play, and he played it with a flourish. He made it known that a rapprochement with Great Britain might, after all, best serve the interests of his country, and at that particular moment an Anglo-American rapprochement was about the least of Napoleon's desires.

There are good reasons to believe that French failure in Santo Domingo, the imminence of renewed war with Great Britain, and financial stringencies may all have prompted Napoleon in 1803 to offer for sale to the United States the entire Louisiana Territory. At this juncture, James Monroe arrived in Paris as Jefferson's minister plenipotentiary; and even though the two American ministers possessed neither instructions nor authority to purchase the whole of Louisiana, the negotiations that followed, with François, marquis de Barbé-Marbois, minister for the treasury, acting for Napoleon, moved swiftly to a conclusion.

A treaty was signed on May 2 but was antedated to April 30. By its terms the Louisiana Territory, in the form France had received it from Spain, was sold to the United States. For this vast domain the United States agreed to pay $11,250,000 outright and assumed claims of its citizens against France in the amount of $3,750,000. Interest payments incidental to the final settlement made the total price $27,267,622.

Precisely what the United States had purchased was unclear. The wording of the treaty was vague; it did not clearly describe the boundaries. It gave no assurances that West Florida was to be considered a part of Louisiana; neither did it delineate the southwest boundary. The American negotiators were fully aware of this.

But before the United States could establish fixed boundaries to Louisiana there arose a basic question concerning the constitutionality of the purchase. Did the Constitution of the United States provide for an act of this kind? The president, in principle a strict constructionist, thought that an amendment to the Constitution might be required to legalize the transaction;

but, after due consideration and considerable oratory, the Senate approved the treaty by a vote of 24 to 7.

The setting of fixed boundaries awaited negotiations with Spain and Great Britain. The exasperating dispute with Spain over the ownership of West Florida and Texas was finally settled by the purchase of the Floridas from Spain in 1819 and the establishment of a fixed southwest boundary line. This line followed the Sabine River from the Gulf of Mexico to the parallel of 32° N; ran thence due north to the Red River, following this stream to the meridian 100° W; thence north to the Arkansas River and along this stream to its source; thence north or south, as the case might be (the source of the Arkansas was not then known), to the parallel of 42° N and west along this line to the Pacific Ocean. The northern boundary was amicably established by an Anglo-American convention in 1818. It established the 49° parallel N between the Lake of the Woods and the Rocky Mountains as the American-Canadian border. The Rocky (then referred to as "Stony") Mountains were accepted as the western limit of the Louisiana Territory, and the Mississippi River was considered for all practical purposes the eastern boundary of the great purchase. Much of the territory turned out to contain rich mineral resources, productive soil, valuable grazing land, forests, and wildlife resources of inestimable value. Out of this empire were carved in their entirety the states of Louisiana, Missouri, Arkansas, Iowa, North Dakota, South Dakota, Nebraska, and Oklahoma; in addition, the area included most of the land in Kansas, Colorado, Wyoming, Montana, and Minnesota.

▌Madison, Dolley

American first lady (1809–17), the wife of James Madison, fourth president of the United States, Dolley Madison

Dolley Madison, engraving from an original picture by Gilbert Stuart.

(1768–1849) was raised in the plain style of her Quaker family and was renowned for her charm, warmth, and ingenuity. Her popularity as manager of the White House made that task a responsibility of every first lady who followed.

Dolley was one of eight children of John Payne, a merchant, and Mary Coles Payne. Soon after her birth, her father's business fell on hard times and the family moved to eastern Virginia, where they were active members of the Society of Friends. When she was 15 her family moved to Philadelphia, where Dolley married a young lawyer, John Todd, in 1790. The couple had two children, but in 1793 her youngest son and husband died during an epidemic of yellow fever, widowing Dolley at 25.

A few months later Aaron Burr, then a United States senator from New Jersey, introduced Dolley to James Madison, who was 17 years her senior; though a small man physically he was a towering political figure. There was a mutual, immediate, and strong attraction between James and Dolley, and they wed on September 15, 1794, at her sister's home in Virginia. Because her husband was Episcopalian, however, the Quakers disowned her. Soon after their marriage, accompanied by her son, the Madisons moved to Philadelphia, then the nation's capital, where James served as a member of the House of Representatives. During the presidency of John Adams (1797–1801), the Madisons lived on James's estate, Montpellier (now Montpelier), in Virginia. Soon after the election of Thomas Jefferson in 1800, they relocated to Washington, D.C., where James served as secretary of state and Dolley assisted the widowed Jefferson as hostess at official events, giving her ample preparation for her future role as first lady.

The first president's wife to preside over the White House for any significant amount of time, Dolley Madison set many precedents. She established the tradition that the mansion would reflect the first lady's tastes and ideas about entertaining. With the help of Benjamin Latrobe, architect and surveyor of public buildings, she decorated and furnished the house so that it was both elegant and comfortable. Unfortunately, not many Americans had the chance to see it before the British burned the mansion in August 1814 during the War of 1812. Dolley underscored the first lady's responsibility for caring for the mansion and its contents when she directed the removal and safe storage of precious holdings, including the famous Gilbert Stuart portrait of George Washington that still hangs in the East Room.

As hostess, Dolley Madison carefully balanced two competing traditions in the new nation: the democratic emphasis on equal treatment and the elitist notion that the president's house was the province of the privileged few. At weekly receptions she opened the doors to virtually anyone who wanted to come and then moved among the guests, greeting all with charming ease. In her stylish turbans and imported clothes, she became enormously popular and much imitated. Although most Americans approved, she did have her critics, including Elijah Mills, a senator from Massachusetts, who complained that she mixed "all classes of people . . . greasy boots and silk stockings."

Although she eschewed taking public stands on controversial issues, Dolley had a shrewd political sense and cultivated her husband's enemies as carefully as his friends. When President Madison dismissed his secretary of state, Robert Smith, she invited him to dinner; when he failed to accept she went to call on him personally. In the election of 1812, when many Americans complained that Madison had led them into an unnecessary war, she used her invitation lists to win him favor and a second term, according to some historians.

She insisted on visiting the household of every new representative or senator, a task that proved very time-consuming as the nation grew and the number of congressmen increased. Since many representatives chose to bring their families to Washington, dozens of households expected a call from the president's wife. Her successors found the practice too burdensome and stopped it.

Dolley Madison enjoyed a happy marriage; different as she and her husband were in personality, they doted on each other. However, her relationship with her son, John Payne Todd, was a different matter. He spent money recklessly and expected his mother to cover his debts and losses.

When James's second term ended in 1817, he and Dolley moved back to Montpellier, where they lived until his death in 1836. James's last decades were not prosperous, and the debts of young Payne Todd depleted the family's resources. To supplement Dolley's income after James's death, a sympathetic and grateful Congress appropriated $30,000 to purchase the Madison papers.

In 1837 Dolley moved back to Washington. Living in a home opposite the White House, she was the nation's most prestigious hostess. Presidents and social leaders called on her, and she was a frequent White House guest. But her profligate son continued to try her patience and deplete her purse. In 1842 she traveled to New York City to arrange a loan from the wealthy fur magnate John Jacob Astor, and Congress came to her aid once more by agreeing to buy the remaining Madison papers for $25,000, but only on the condition that the money be placed in trust so that her son could not get it.

When Dolley Madison died in 1849 she was one of the most popular figures in Washington and the nation's favorite first lady. At her funeral President Zachary Taylor, his cabinet, the diplomatic corps, and members of Congress lined up to pay their respects. She was buried beside James Madison at a family plot near Montpelier.

Madison, James

James Madison (1751–1836) was the fourth president of the United States (1809–17) and one of the founding fathers of his country. At the Constitutional Convention (1787) he influenced the planning and ratification of the U.S. Constitution and collaborated with Alexander Hamilton and John Jay in the publication of the Federalist Papers. As a member of the new House of Representatives, he sponsored the first 10 amendments to the Constitution, commonly called the Bill of Rights. He was secretary of state under President Thomas Jefferson when the Louisiana Territory was purchased from France. The War of 1812 was fought during his presidency. Madison was born at the home of his maternal grandmother. The son and namesake of a leading Orange County landowner and squire, he maintained his lifelong home in Virginia at Montpelier, near the Blue Ridge Mountains. In 1769 he rode horseback to the College of New Jersey (Princeton University), selected for its hostility to episcopacy. He completed the four-year course in two years, finding time also to demonstrate against England and to lampoon members of a rival literary society in ribald verse. Overwork produced several years of epileptoid hysteria and premonitions of early death, which thwarted military training but did not prevent home study of public law, mixed with early advocacy of independence (1774) and furious denunciation of the imprisonment of nearby dissenters from the established Anglican Church. Madison never became a church member, but in maturity he expressed a preference for Unitarianism.

His health improved, and he was elected to Virginia's 1776 Revolutionary convention, where he drafted the state's

James Madison, lithograph after a portrait by Gilbert Stuart, c. 1828.

guarantee of religious freedom. In the convention-turned-legislature he helped Thomas Jefferson disestablish the church but lost reelection by refusing to furnish the electors with free whiskey. After two years on the governor's council, he was sent to the Continental Congress in March 1780.

Five feet four inches tall and weighing about 100 pounds, small-boned, boyish in appearance, and weak of voice, he waited six months before taking the floor, but strong actions belied his mild demeanor. He rose quickly to leadership against the devotees of state sovereignty and enemies of Franco–U.S. collaboration in peace negotiations, contending also for the establishment of the Mississippi as a western territorial boundary and the right to navigate that river through its Spanish-held delta. Defending Virginia's charter title to the vast northwest against states that had no claim to western territories and whose major motive was to validate barrel-of-rum purchases from Indian tribes, Madison defeated the land speculators by persuading Virginia to cede the western lands to Congress as a national heritage.

Following the ratification of the Articles of Confederation in 1781, Madison undertook to strengthen the Union by asserting implied power in Congress to enforce financial requisitions upon the states by military coercion. This move failing, he worked unceasingly for an amendment conferring power to raise revenue and wrote an eloquent address adjuring the states to avert national disintegration by ratifying the submitted article. The chevalier de la Luzerne, French minister to the United States, wrote that Madison was "regarded as the man of the soundest judgment in Congress."

Reentering the Virginia legislature in 1784, Madison defeated Patrick Henry's bill to give financial support to "teachers of the Christian religion." To avoid the political effect of his extreme nationalism, he persuaded the states rights advocate John Tyler to sponsor the calling of the Annapolis Convention of 1786, which, aided by Madison's influence, produced the Constitutional Convention of 1787.

There his Virginia, or large-state, Plan, put forward through Governor Edmund Randolph, furnished the basic framework and guiding principles of the Constitution, earning him the title of father of the Constitution. Madison believed keenly in the value of a strong government in which power was well controlled because it was well balanced among the branches. Delegate William Pierce of Georgia wrote that, in the management of every great question, Madison "always comes forward the best informed Man of any point in debate." Pierce called him "a Gentleman of great modesty—with a remarkable sweet temper. He is easy and unreserved among his acquaintances, and has a most agreeable style of conversation."

Madison took day-by-day notes of debates at the Constitutional Convention, which furnish the only comprehensive history of the proceedings. To promote ratification he collaborated with Alexander Hamilton and John Jay in newspaper publication of the Federalist Papers (Madison wrote 29 out of 85), which became the standard commentary on the Constitution. His influence produced ratification by Virginia and led John Marshall to say that if eloquence included "persuasion by convincing, Mr. Madison was the most eloquent man I ever heard."

Elected to the new House of Representatives, Madison sponsored the first 10 amendments to the Constitution—the Bill of Rights—placing emphasis in debate on freedom of religion, speech, and press. His leadership in the House, which caused the Massachusetts congressman Fisher Ames to call him "our first man," came to an end when he split with Secretary of the Treasury Hamilton over methods of funding the war debts. Hamilton's aim was to strengthen the national government by cementing men of wealth to it; Madison sought to protect the interests of Revolutionary veterans.

Hamilton's victory turned Madison into a strict constructionist of the congressional power to appropriate for the general welfare. He denied the existence of implied power to establish a national bank to aid the Treasury. Later, as president, he asked for and obtained a bank as "almost [a] necessity" for that purpose, but he contended that it was constitutional only because Hamilton's bank had gone without constitutional challenge. Unwillingness to admit error was a lifelong characteristic. The break over funding split Congress into Madisonian and Hamiltonian factions, with Fisher Ames now calling Madison a "desperate party leader" who enforced a discipline "as severe as the Prussian." (Madisonians turned into Jeffersonians after Jefferson, having returned from France, became secretary of state.)

In 1794 Madison married a widow, Dolley Payne Todd (Dolley Madison), a handsome, buxom, vivacious Quaker 17 years his junior, who rejected church discipline and loved social activities. Her first husband had died in the yellow fever epidemic the previous year. She periodically served as official hostess for President Jefferson, who was a widower. As Madison's wife, she became a fixture at soirées, usually wearing a colorful feathered turban and an elegant dress ornamented with jewelry and furs. She may be said to have created the role of First Lady as a political partner of the president, although that label did not come into use until much later. An unpretentious woman, she ate heartily, gambled, rouged her face lavishly, and took snuff. The "Wednesday drawing rooms" that she instituted for the public added to her popularity. She earned the nation's undying gratitude for rescuing a Gilbert Stuart portrait of

George Washington in 1814 just ahead of the British troops who put the torch to the White House in the War of 1812.

Madison left Congress in 1797, disgusted by John Jay's treaty with England, which frustrated his program of commercial retaliation against the wartime oppression of U.S. maritime commerce. The Alien and Sedition Acts of 1798 inspired him to draft the Virginia Resolutions of that year, denouncing those statutes as violations of the First Amendment of the Constitution and affirming the right and duty of the states "to interpose for arresting the progress of the evil." Carefully worded to mean less legally than they seemed to threaten, they forced him to spend his octogenarian years combating South Carolina's interpretation of them as a sanction of state power to nullify federal law.

During eight years as Jefferson's secretary of state (1801–09), Madison used the words "The President has decided" so regularly that his own role can be discovered only in foreign archives. British diplomats dealing with Madison encountered "asperity of temper and fluency of expression." Senators John Adair and Nicholas Gilman agreed in 1806 that he "governed the President," an opinion held also by French minister Louis-Marie Turreau.

Although he was accused of weakness in dealing with France and England, Madison won the presidency in 1808 by publishing his vigorous diplomatic dispatches. Faced with a senatorial cabal on taking office, he made a senator's lackluster brother, Robert Smith, secretary of state and wrote all important diplomatic letters for two years before replacing him with James Monroe. Although he had fully supported Jefferson's wartime shipping embargo, Madison reversed his predecessor's policy two weeks after assuming the presidency by secretly notifying both Great Britain and France, then at war, that, in his opinion, if the country addressed should stop interfering with U.S. commerce and the other belligerent continued to do so, "Congress will, at the next ensuing session, authorize acts of hostility . . . against the other."

An agreement with England providing for repeal of its Orders in Council, which limited trade by neutral nations with France, collapsed because the British minister violated his instructions; he concealed the requirements that the United States continue its trade embargo against France, renounce wartime trade with Britain's enemies, and authorize England to capture any U.S. vessel attempting to trade with France. Madison expelled the minister's successor for charging, falsely, that the president had been aware of the violation.

Believing that England was bent on permanent suppression of American commerce, Madison proclaimed nonintercourse with England on November 2, 1810, and notified France on the same day that this would "necessarily lead to war" unless England stopped its impressment of American seamen and seizure of American goods and vessels. One week earlier, unknown to Congress (in recess) or the public, he had taken armed possession of the Spanish province of West Florida, claimed as part of the Louisiana Purchase. He was reelected in 1812, despite strong opposition and the vigorous candidacy of DeWitt Clinton.

With his actions buried in secrecy, Federalists and politicians pictured Madison as a timorous pacifist dragged into the War of 1812 (1812–15) by congressional war hawks, and they denounced the conflict as "Mr. Madison's War." In fact, the president had sought peace but accepted war as inevitable. As wartime commander in chief he was hampered by the refusal of Congress to heed pleas for naval and military development and made the initial error of entrusting army command to aging veterans of the Revolution. The small U.S. Navy sparkled, but on land defeat followed defeat.

By 1814, however, Madison had lowered the average age of generals from 60 to 36 years; victories resulted, ending a war the principal cause of which had been removed by revocation of the Orders in Council the day before the conflict began. Contemporary public opinion in the United States, Canada, England, and continental Europe proclaimed the result a U.S. triumph. Still, the country would never forget the ignominy of the president and his wife having to flee in the face of advancing British troops bent on laying waste Washington, D.C., including setting afire the executive mansion, the Capitol, and other public buildings.

The Federalist Party was killed by its opposition to the war, and the president was lifted to a pinnacle of popularity. Madison's greatest fault was delay in discharging incompetent subordinates, including Secretary of War John Armstrong, who had scoffed at the president's repeated warnings of a coming British attack on Washington and ignored presidential orders for its defense.

On leaving the presidency, Madison was eulogized at a Washington mass meeting for having won national power and glory "without infringing a political, civil, or religious right." Even in the face of sabotage of war operations by New England Federalists, he had lived up to the maxim he laid down in 1793 when he had said:

> If we advert to the nature of republican government we shall find that the censorial power is in the people over the government, and not in the government over the people.

Never again leaving Virginia, Madison managed his 5,000-acre farm for 19 years, cultivating the land by methods regarded today as modern innovations. As president of the Albemarle Agricultural Society, he warned that human life might be wiped out by upsetting the balance of nature, including invisible organisms. He hated slavery, which held him in its economic chains, and worked to abolish it through government purchase of slaves and their resettlement in Liberia, financed by sale of public lands. When his personal valet ran away in 1792 and was recaptured—a situation that usually meant sale into the yellow-fever-infested West Indies—Madison set him free and hired him. Another slave managed one-third of the Montpelier farmlands during Madison's years in federal office.

Madison participated in Jefferson's creation of the University of Virginia (1819) and later served as its rector. Excessive hospitality, chronic agricultural depression, the care of aged slaves, and the squandering of $40,000 by and on a wayward stepson made him land-poor in old age. His last years were spent in bed; he was barely able to bend his rheumatic fingers, which nevertheless turned out an endless succession of letters and articles combating nullification and secession—the theme of his final "Advice to My Country." Henry Clay called him, after George Washington, "our greatest statesman."

Marshall, John

John Marshall (1755–1835) was the fourth chief justice of the United States and principal founder of the U.S. system of constitutional law, including the doctrine of judicial review. The first of Marshall's great cases in more than 30 years of service was *Marbury* v. *Madison* (1803), which established the Supreme Court's right to state and expound constitutional law. His most important decision in exercising this authority was in *McCulloch* v. *Maryland* (1819), which upheld the authority of Congress to create the Bank of the United States. During his tenure Marshall participated in more than 1,000 decisions, writing 519 of them himself.

John Marshall was the eldest of 15 children of Thomas Marshall and Mary Keith Marshall. His childhood and youth were spent in the near-frontier region that in 1759 became Fauquier County, Virginia, and he later lived in the more extensive properties his father acquired in the Blue Ridge mountain area. His education appears to have been largely the product of his parents' efforts, supplemented only by the instruction afforded by a visiting clergyman who lived with the family for about a year and by a few months of slightly more formal training at an academy in Westmoreland County.

When political debate with England was followed by armed clashes in 1775, John Marshall, as lieutenant, joined his father in a Virginia regiment of minutemen and participated in the first fighting in that colony. Joining the Continental Army in 1776, he served under Washington for three years in New Jersey, New York, and Pennsylvania, including in this service the harsh winter of 1777–78 at Valley Forge. When the term of service of his Virginia troops expired in 1779, Marshall returned to Virginia and thereafter saw little active service prior to his discharge in 1781.

Marshall's career in law dates from 1780. His only formal training was a brief course of lectures given by George Wythe that he attended at William and Mary College early in that year. Licensed to practice in August 1780, he returned to Fauquier County and was elected to the Virginia House of Delegates in 1782 and 1784. Attending the sessions of the legislature in the capitol at Richmond, he established there both a law practice and a home, after marriage to Mary Ambler in January 1783.

For the next 15 years Marshall's career was marked by increasing stature at the brilliant bar of Virginia. He had not, in 1787, achieved a public position that would have sent him as a delegate to the Constitutional Convention in Philadelphia, but he was an active, if junior, proponent of the Constitution in the closely contested fight for ratification. Marshall was elected to the legislature that took the first step toward ratification by issuing a call for a convention to consider ratifying; he was also elected a delegate to the convention. His principal effort on the floor of the convention was, perhaps prophetically, a defense of the judiciary article. He then used his acknowledged popularity to gain or hold the narrow margin by which Virginia's ratification of the Constitution was won.

With the new government under the Constitution installed, President George Washington offered Marshall appointment as United States attorney for Virginia. Marshall declined. In 1789, however, he sought and obtained a further term in Virginia's House of Delegates as a supporter of the national government. As party lines emerged and became defined in the 1790s, Marshall became recognized as one of the leaders of the Federalist Party in Virginia. In 1795 Washington tendered him an appointment as attorney general. This, too, was declined, but Marshall returned to the state legislature as a Federalist leader.

His first federal service came when President John Adams appointed him member of a commission, with Elbridge Gerry and Charles C. Pinckney, to seek improved relations with the government of the French Republic. The mission was unsuccessful. But reports then were published disclosing that certain intermediaries, some shadowy figures known as X, Y, and Z, had approached the commissioners and informed them that they would not be received by the French government unless they first paid large bribes; the reports further revealed that these advances had been rebuffed in a memorial prepared by Marshall. Marshall thereupon became a popular figure, and the conduct of his mission was applauded by one of the earliest American patriotic slogans, "Millions for defense, but not one cent for tribute."

Returned from France, Marshall declined appointment to the Supreme Court to succeed Justice James Wilson but was persuaded by Washington to run for Congress. He was elected in 1799 as a Federalist from the Richmond district, though his service in the House of Representatives was brief. His chief accomplishment there appears to have been the effective defense of the president against a Republican attack for having honored a British request under the extradition treaty for the surrender of a seaman charged with murder on a British warship on the high seas. In May 1800 President Adams requested the resignation of his secretary of war and offered the post to Marshall. Marshall declined. The president next dismissed his secretary of state and tendered the vacant place in his Cabinet to Marshall.

In an administration harassed by dissension and with uncertain prospects in the forthcoming election, the appeal of the invitation must have been addressed principally to Marshall's loyalty. After some hesitation he accepted and almost immediately became the effective head of government when the president retired to his home in Massachusetts for a stay of a few months. In the autumn of 1800, Chief Justice Oliver Ellsworth resigned because of ill health. Adams, defeated in the election of November, tendered reappointment to John Jay, the first chief justice. Jay declined. The president then turned to his secretary of state and in January 1801 sent to the Senate the nomination of John Marshall to be chief justice. The last Federalist Senate confirmed the nomination on Jan. 27, 1801. On February 4, Marshall accepted the appointment but, at the president's request, continued to act as secretary of state for the last month of the Adams administration.

It fell to Marshall, and to the Supreme Court under and beginning with Marshall, to set forth the main structural lines of the government. Whether the Constitution had created a federation or a nation was not a matter on which agreement could have been won at the beginning of the 19th century. Though judicial decisions could not alone dispel differences of opinion, they could create a body of coherent, authoritative, and disinterested doctrine around which opinion could mass and become effective. To the task of creating such a core of agreement Marshall brought qualities that were admirably adapted for its accomplishment. His own mind had apparently a clear and well-organized concept of the effective government that he believed was needed and was provided by the Constitution. He wrote with a lucidity, a persuasiveness, and a vigor that gave to his judicial opinions a quality of reasoned inevitability that more than offset an occasional lack in precision of analysis. The 35 years of his magistracy gave opportunity for the development of a unified body of constitutional doctrine. It was the first aspect of Marshall's accomplishment that he and the court he headed did not permit this opportunity to pass unrecognized.

Prior to Marshall's appointment, it had been the custom of the Supreme Court, as it was in England, for each justice to deliver an opinion in each significant case. This method may be effective where a court is dealing with an organized and existing body of law, but with a new court and a largely unexplored body of law, it created an impression of tentativeness, if not of contradiction, which lent authority neither to the court nor to the law it expounded. With Marshall's appointment, and presumably at Marshall's instance, this practice changed. Thereafter, for some years, it became the general rule that there was only a single opinion from the Supreme Court. This change of practice alone would have contributed to making the court a more effective institution. And when the opinions were cast in the mold of Marshall's clear and compelling statement, the growth of the court's authority was assured.

Marbury v. *Madison* (1803) was the first of Marshall's great cases and the case that established for the court its power to state and expound constitutional law in disregard of federal statutes that it found in conflict with the Constitution. President Adams had appointed a number of justices of the peace for the District of Columbia shortly before his term expired. Their commissions had been signed and the seal of the United States affixed in the office of the secretary of state, but some of them, including that of William Marbury, remained undelivered. President Thomas Jefferson is believed to have ordered that some of them not be delivered.

After unsuccessful application at the Department of State, Marbury instituted suit in the Supreme Court against James Madison, the new secretary. Though the matter was not beyond question, the Court found that Congress had by statute authorized that such suits be started in the Supreme Court rather than in a lower court. But the Supreme Court, speaking through

Marshall, held that Article III of the Constitution did not permit this and that the court could not follow a statute that was in conflict with the Constitution. It thereby confirmed for itself its most controversial power, the function of judicial review, of finding and expounding the law of the Constitution.

Once the power of judicial review had been established, Marshall and the court followed with decisions that assured that it would be exercised, and the whole body of federal law determined, in a unified judicial system with the Supreme Court at its head. *Martin* v. *Hunter's Lessee* (1816) and *Cohens* v. *Virginia* (1821) affirmed the Supreme Court's right to review and overrule a state court on a federal question. *McCulloch* v. *Maryland* (1819) asserted the doctrine of "implied powers" granted Congress by the Constitution (in this instance, that Congress could create a bank of the United States, even though such a power was not expressly given by the Constitution).

McCulloch v. *Maryland* well illustrated that judicial review could have an affirmative aspect as well as a negative; it may accord an authoritative legitimacy to contested government action no less significant than its restraint of prohibited or unauthorized action. *Fletcher* v. *Peck* (1810) and *Dartmouth College* v. *Woodward* (1819) established the inviolability of a state's contracts. *Gibbons* v. *Ogden* (1824) established the federal government's right to regulate interstate commerce and to override state law in doing so. It must be clearly noted, however, that many of Marshall's decisions dealing with specific restraints upon government have turned out to be his less enduring ones, particularly in later eras of increasing governmental activity and control. It is in this area, indeed, that judicial review has evoked its most vigorous critics.

There was only one term of the Supreme Court each year, generally lasting about seven or eight weeks (a little longer after 1827). Each justice, however, also conducted a circuit court—Marshall in Richmond, Virginia, and Raleigh, North Carolina. It was in Richmond in 1807 that he presided at the treason trial of former Vice President Aaron Burr, during which he successfully frustrated President Jefferson's efforts toward a runaway conviction; Burr was freed. With hardly more than three months annually engaged in judicial duties, Marshall had much time to devote to private life. He early completed a five-volume *Life of George Washington* (1804–07). He cared for an invalid wife, who bore him 10 children, 4 of whom died in early life. He enjoyed companionship, drinking, and debating with fellow lights in Richmond. In general, for the first 30 years of his service as chief justice, his life was largely one of contentment.

In the autumn of 1831, at the age of 76, he underwent the rigors of surgery for the removal of kidney stones and appeared to make a rapid and complete recovery. But the death of his wife on Christmas of that year was a blow from which his spirits did not so readily recover. In 1835 his health declined rapidly, and on July 6 he died in Philadelphia. He was buried in Richmond.

Mason, George

George Mason (1725–92) was an American patriot and statesman who insisted on the protection of individual liberties in the composition of both the Virginia and U.S. Constitutions (1776, 1787); he was ahead of his time in opposing slavery and in rejecting the constitutional compromise that perpetuated it.

As a landowner and near neighbor of George Washington, Mason took a leading part in local affairs. He also became deeply interested in Western expansion and was active in the Ohio Company, organized in 1749 to develop trade and sell land on the upper Ohio River. At about the same time, Mason helped to found the town of Alexandria, Virginia. Because of ill health and family problems, he generally eschewed public office, though he accepted election to the House of Burgesses in

1759. Except for his membership in the Constitutional Convention at Philadelphia, this was the highest office he ever held—yet few men did more to shape U.S. political institutions.

A leader of the Virginia patriots on the eve of the American Revolution (1775–83), Mason served on the Committee of Safety and in 1776 drafted the state constitution, his declaration of rights being the first authoritative formulation of the doctrine of inalienable rights. Mason's work was known to Thomas Jefferson and influenced his drafting of the Declaration of Independence. The model was soon followed by most of the states and was also incorporated in diluted form in the federal Constitution. He served as a member of the Virginia House of Delegates from 1776 to 1788.

As a member of the Constitutional Convention, Mason strenuously opposed the compromise permitting the continuation of the slave trade until 1808. Although he was a Southerner, Mason castigated the trade as "disgraceful to mankind"; he favored manumission and education for bondsmen and supported a system of free labor. Because he also objected to the large and indefinite powers vested in the new government, he joined several other Virginians in opposing adoption of the new document. A Jeffersonian Republican, he believed that local government should be kept strong and central government weak. His criticism helped bring about the adoption of the Bill of Rights to the Constitution.

Soon after the Convention, Mason retired to his home, Gunston Hall.

George Mason, detail of an oil painting by L. Guillaume after a portrait by J. Hesselius (in the collection of the Virginia Historical Society).

Middleton, Arthur

British American planter, legislator, and signer of the Declaration of Independence, Arthur Middleton (1742–87) was one of the leaders in the controversies leading up to the American Revolution (1775–83).

After completing his education in England, Middleton returned to South Carolina in 1763 and was elected to the colonial legislature. In 1775–76 he was a member of the Council of Safety, a committee that directed leadership for the colony's preparations for revolution. He served on the legislative committee that drafted the South Carolina state constitution and was a delegate to the Continental Congress (1776–78).

At the siege of Charleston (1780) he served in the militia, was taken prisoner when the city fell to the British, and was sent to St. Augustine, Florida, as a prisoner of war. After being exchanged in July 1781, he was a member of the Continental Congress (1781–83), the South Carolina legislature (1785–86), and on the original board of trustees of the College of Charleston.

Monroe, James

James Monroe served as the fifth president of the United States (1817–25), and he issued an important contribution to U.S. foreign policy in the Monroe Doctrine, a warning to European nations against intervening in the Western Hemisphere. The period of his administration has been called the Era of Good Feelings.

Monroe's father, Spence Monroe, was of Scottish descent, and his mother, Elizabeth Jones Monroe, of Welsh descent. The family were owners of a modest 600 acres in Virginia. At age 16 Monroe entered the College of William and Mary but in 1776 left to fight in the American Revolution. As a lieutenant he crossed the Delaware with General George Washington for what became the Battle of Trenton. Suffering a near fatal wound in the shoulder, Monroe was carried from the field. Upon recovering, he was promoted to captain for heroism, and he took part in the Battles of Brandywine and Germantown. Advanced to major, he became aide-de-camp to General William Alexander (Lord Stirling) and with him shared the suffering of the troops at Valley Forge in the cruel winter of 1777–78. Monroe was a scout for Washington at the Battle of Monmouth and served as Lord Stirling's adjutant general.

In 1780, having resigned his commission in the army, he began the study of law under Thomas Jefferson, then governor of Virginia, and between the two men there developed an intimacy and a sympathy that had a powerful influence upon Monroe's later career. Jefferson also fostered a friendship between Monroe and James Madison.

Monroe was elected to the Virginia House of Delegates in 1782 and was chosen a member of the governor's council. From 1783 to 1786 he served in the Congress under the Articles of Confederation, the first constitution of the new nation. During his term he vigorously insisted on the right of the United States to navigate the Mississippi River, then controlled by the Spanish, and attempted, in 1785, to secure for the weak Congress the power to regulate commerce, thereby removing one of the great defects in the existing central government. In 1786 Monroe, 27 years old, and Elizabeth Kortright of New York,

James Monroe, oil sketch by E. O. Sully, 1836, after a contemporary portrait by Thomas Sully (in Independence National Historical Park, Philadelphia).

17 years old, were married. They had two daughters, Eliza Kort-right and Maria Hester, and a son who died in infancy. Eliza often was at her father's side as official hostess when he was president, substituting for her ailing mother. Maria's marriage to a cousin, Samuel L. Gouverneur, in 1820 was the first wedding performed in the President's House, as the White House was then called.

Retiring from Congress in 1786, Monroe began practicing law at Fredericksburg, Virginia. He was chosen a member of the Virginia House of Delegates in 1787 and in 1788 a member of the state convention at which Virginia ratified the new federal Constitution. In 1790 he was elected to the U.S. Senate, where he vigorously opposed President George Washington's adminis-tration; nevertheless, in 1794 Washington nominated him as minister to France.

It was the hope of the administration that Monroe's well-known French sympathies would secure for him a favorable reception and that his appointment would also conciliate France's friends in the United States. His warm welcome in France and his enthusiasm for the French Revolution, which he regarded as a natural successor to the American Revolution, dis-pleased the Federalists (the party of Alexander Hamilton, which encouraged close ties not to France but to England) at home. Monroe did nothing, moreover, to reconcile the French to the Jay Treaty, which regulated commerce and navigation between the United States and Great Britain during the French Revolu-tionary wars.

Without real justification, the French regarded the treaty as a violation of the French-American treaty of commerce and amity of 1778 and as a possible cause for war. Monroe led the French government to believe that the Jay Treaty would never be ratified by the United States, that the administration of George Washington would be overthrown as a result of the obnoxious treaty, and that better things might be expected after the election in 1796 of a new president, perhaps Thomas

Jefferson. Washington, though he did not know of this intrigue, sensed that Monroe was unable to represent his government properly and, late in 1796, recalled him.

Monroe returned to America in the spring of 1797 and in the following December published a defense of his course in a pamphlet of 500 pages entitled *A View of the Conduct of the Executive, in the Foreign Affairs of the United States*. Washington seems never to have forgiven Monroe for this stratagem, though Monroe's opinion of Washington and Jay underwent a change in his later years. In 1799 Monroe was chosen governor of Virginia and was twice reelected, serving until 1802.

There was much uneasiness in the United States when Spain restored Louisiana to France by the Treaty of San Ildefonso in October 1800 (confirmed March 1801). The Spanish district administrator's subsequent withdrawal of the United States' "right of deposit" at New Orleans—the privilege of storing goods there for later reshipment—greatly increased this feeling and led to much talk of war. Resolved to settle the matter by peaceful measures, President Jefferson in January 1803 appointed Monroe envoy extraordinary and minister plenipotentiary to France to aid Robert R. Livingston, the resident minister, in purchasing the territory at the mouth of the Mississippi—including the island of New Orleans—authorizing him at the same time to cooperate with Charles Pinckney, the minister at Madrid, in securing from Spain the cession of East and West Florida. On April 18 Monroe was further commissioned as the regular minister to Great Britain.

Monroe joined Livingston in Paris on April 12, after the latter's negotiations were well under way, and the two ministers, on finding Napoleon willing to dispose of the entire province of Louisiana, decided to exceed their instructions and effect its purchase. Accordingly, on May 2, 1803, they signed a treaty and two conventions (antedated to April 30) whereby France sold Louisiana to the United States. The fact that Monroe signed the treaty along with Livingston did not hurt his political career at home, but he is not entitled to much credit for the diplomatic achievement.

In July 1803 Monroe left Paris and entered upon his duties in London, and in the autumn of 1804 he proceeded to Madrid to assist Pinckney in his efforts to define the Louisiana boundaries and acquire the Floridas. After negotiating until May 1805 without success, Monroe returned to London and resumed his negotiations concerning the impressment of American seamen and the seizure of American vessels. As the British ministry was reluctant to discuss these vexing questions, little progress was made, and in May 1806 Jefferson ordered William Pinkney of Maryland to assist Monroe.

The result of the deliberations was a treaty signed on December 31, 1806, which contained no provision against impressments and provided no indemnity for the seizure of goods and vessels. Accompanying its signature was a British reservation maintaining freedom of action to retaliate against imminent French maritime decrees. In passing over these matters Monroe and Pinkney had disregarded their instructions, and Jefferson was so displeased with the treaty that he returned it to England for revision.

Monroe returned to the United States in December 1807. He was elected to the Virginia House of Delegates in the spring of 1810. In the following winter he was again chosen governor, serving from January to November 1811, when he resigned to become secretary of state under James Madison, a position he held until March 1817. The direction of foreign affairs in the troubled period immediately preceding and during the War of 1812, with Great Britain, thus fell upon him. On September 27, 1814, after the capture of Washington, D.C., by the British, he was appointed secretary of war and discharged the duties of this office, in addition to those of the Department of State, until March 1815.

In 1816 Monroe was elected president of the United States as the Republican candidate, defeating Rufus King, the

Federalist candidate; Monroe received 183 electoral votes and King, 34. By 1820, when he was reelected, receiving all the electoral votes but one, the Federalists had ceased to function as a party. The chief events of his calm and prosperous administration, which has been called the Era of Good Feelings, were the First Seminole War (1817–18); the acquisition of the Floridas from Spain (1819–21); the Missouri Compromise (1820), by which the first conflict over slavery under the Constitution was peacefully settled; recognition of the new Latin American states, former Spanish colonies, in Central and South America (1822); and—most intimately connected with Monroe's name—the enunciation, in the presidential message of December 2, 1823, of the Monroe Doctrine, which has profoundly influenced the foreign policy of the United States.

Not until 1848 when James K. Polk was president did the first reference to Monroe's statement as a "Doctrine" appear. The phrase "Monroe Doctrine" came into common use in the 1850s. The "principles of President Monroe," as the message was referred to in Congress, consisted of three openly proclaimed dicta: no further European colonization in the New World, abstention of the United States from the political affairs of Europe, and nonintervention of Europe in the governments of the American hemisphere. In the diplomatic correspondence preceding the proclamation of these principles in the president's message was a fourth dictum not publicly associated with the doctrine until 1869: the United States opposed the transfer of any existing European colonies from one European sovereign to another.

It is generally concluded that Secretary of State John Quincy Adams was the sole author of the noncolonization principle of the doctrine; the principle of abstention from European wars and politics was common to all the fathers of American independence, inherited and expressed by the younger Adams all his professional life; in cabinet meetings, Adams also urged the dictum of nonintervention in the affairs of the nations of the

Western Hemisphere. But Adams had no idea of proclaiming these dicta to the world. Monroe took responsibility for embodying them in a presidential message that he drafted himself. Modern historical judgment considers the Monroe Doctrine to be appropriately named.

President Monroe and his wife remained smitten by France after their sojourn there and with their daughters often spoke French together when they were in the White House. Elizabeth Monroe clothed herself in Paris creations and insisted on French etiquette and French cuisine at her table. Given the opportunity to refurnish the executive mansion when it was rebuilt after its destruction in 1814, the Monroes spent lavishly on gilded furniture, silverware, and various objets d'art imported from France. Some items that the president had purchased from impoverished French noble families while he was minister he now lent or sold to the government for use in the President's House at prices some considered suspiciously high, although Monroe was later cleared of impropriety.

The first lady, who was always in fragile health, suffered from an unidentified malady. She was often away from Washington for months at a time visiting her married daughters. To the considerable irritation of Washington society, she discontinued Dolley Madison's practice of paying courtesy calls on Washington hostesses. Still, Elizabeth Monroe was not without ardor; shortly after her arrival in France, during the Reign of Terror, she had helped to rescue Madame Lafayette, wife of the marquis de Lafayette, from prison and perhaps save her from the guillotine.

On the expiration of his second term Monroe retired to his home at Oak Hill, Virginia. In 1826 he became a regent of the University of Virginia and in 1829 was a member of the convention called to amend the state constitution. Having neglected his private affairs and incurred large expenditures during his missions to Europe and his presidency, he was deeply in debt and felt compelled to ask Congress to reimburse him. In 1826

Congress finally authorized the payment to him of $30,000. Almost immediately, adding additional claims, he went back to Congress seeking more money. Congress paid him another $30,000 in 1831, but he still did not feel satisfied. After his death Congress appropriated a small amount for the purchase of his papers from his heirs. Monroe died in 1831—like Jefferson and Adams before him on the Fourth of July—in New York City at the home of his daughter, Maria, with whom he was living after the death of his wife the year before. In 1858, the centennial year of his birth, his remains were reinterred with impressive ceremonies at Richmond, Virginia. After Liberia was created in 1821 as a haven for freed slaves, its capital city was named Monrovia in honor of the American president, who had supported the repatriation of blacks to Africa.

Thomas Jefferson, James Madison, John Quincy Adams, and many other prominent statesmen of Monroe's time all spoke loudly in his praise, but he suffers by comparison with the greater men of his time. Possessing none of their brilliance, he had, nevertheless, to use the words of John Quincy Adams, "a mindsound in its ultimate judgments, and firm in its final conclusions." Some of Monroe's popularity undoubtedly stemmed from the fact that he was the last of the Revolutionary War generation, and he reminded people of those heady times when the struggle for independence was in the balance. Tall and stately in appearance, he still wore the knee britches, silk stockings, and cocked hat of those days, and many of his admirers said that he resembled George Washington.

Morris, Gouverneur

Gouverneur Morris (1752–1816) was an American statesman, diplomat, and financial expert who helped plan the U.S. decimal coinage system.

Morris graduated from King's College (later Columbia University) in 1768, studied law, and was admitted to the bar in 1771. An extreme conservative in his political views, he distrusted the democratic tendencies of colonists who wanted to break with England, but his belief in independence led him to join their ranks. He served in the New York Provincial Congress (1775–77), where he led a successful fight to include a provision for religious toleration in the first state constitution. He then sat in the Continental Congress (1778–79).

Following his defeat for reelection to Congress in 1779, Morris settled in Philadelphia as a lawyer. His series of essays on finance (published in the *Pennsylvania Packet*, 1780) led to his appointment, under the Articles of Confederation, as assistant to the superintendent of finance, Robert Morris (to whom he was not related). During his tenure (1781–85) he proposed the decimal coinage system that, with some modifications by Thomas Jefferson, forms the basis of the present U.S. monetary system. During the Constitutional Convention (1787), Morris advocated a strong central government, with life tenure for the president and presidential appointment of senators. He was largely responsible for the final wording of the Constitution.

Morris was appointed minister to France in 1792; he openly disapproved of the French Revolution and sought to aid King Louis XVI in fleeing the country. His hostility led the French Revolutionary government to request his recall in 1794. After a brief term in the U.S. Senate (1800–03), he ended his public career. Unsympathetic to the forces of republicanism, he allied himself with the extreme Federalists, who hoped to create a northern confederation during the War of 1812. From 1810 he was chairman of the commission in charge of the construction of the Erie Canal.

Morris, Robert

Robert Morris (1734–1806) was an American merchant and banker who came to be known as the financier of the American Revolution (1775–83).

Morris left England to join his father in Maryland in 1747 and then entered a mercantile house in Philadelphia. During the war, Morris was vice president of the Pennsylvania Committee of Safety (1775–76) and was a member of both the Continental Congress (1775–78) and the Pennsylvania legislature (1778–79, 1780–81, 1785–86). Because he was hoping for reconciliation with Britain, he did not sign the Declaration of Independence until several weeks after its adoption.

As chairman or member of various committees of the Continental Congress, Morris practically controlled the financial operations of the war from 1776 to 1778. He raised the funds that made it possible for General George Washington to move his army from the New York area to Yorktown, where Lord Cornwallis surrendered (1781). Morris had borrowed from the French, requisitioned from the states, and also advanced money from his own pocket. That same year, in Philadelphia, Morris established the Bank of North America. After the war he served as superintendent of finance under the Articles of Confederation (1781–84). He was a delegate to the Constitutional Convention (1787) and served in the U.S. Senate (1789–95). Meanwhile, he had disposed of his mercantile and banking investments and had plunged heavily into land speculation. When returns from his lands slowed, he fell into bankruptcy and was confined in a debtors' prison for more than three years before his release in 1801.

Paine, Robert Treat

Robert Treat Paine (1731–1814) was an American politician, jurist, member of the Continental Congress (1774–78), and signer of the Declaration of Independence.

Paine graduated from Harvard in 1749 and, after trying teaching and the ministry, turned to the study of law and was admitted to the Massachusetts bar in 1757. An early champion of the patriot cause, he gained recognition throughout the colonies in 1770 when he was chosen as a prosecuting attorney in the murder trial of British soldiers involved in the Boston Massacre of March 5, 1770. He was elected several times to the Massachusetts legislature in the 1770s and became the state's first attorney general in 1777. He helped draft the state constitution in 1780 and from 1790 to 1804 served as a judge of the state supreme court. Long interested in astronomy, Paine was a founder of the American Academy of Arts and Sciences in 1780.

Paine, Thomas

Thomas Paine (1737–1809) was an English-American writer and political pamphleteer whose "Common Sense" and "Crisis" papers were important influences on the American Revolution. Other works that contributed to his reputation as one of the greatest political propagandists in history were *Rights of Man*, a defense of the French Revolution and of republican principles; and *The Age of Reason*, an exposition of the place of religion in society.

Paine was born of a Quaker father and an Anglican mother. His formal education was meager, just enough to enable him to master reading, writing, and arithmetic. At 13 he began work with his father as a corset maker and then tried various other occupations unsuccessfully, finally becoming an officer of the excise. His duties were to hunt for smugglers and collect the excise taxes on liquor and tobacco. The pay was insufficient to cover living costs, but he used part of his earnings to purchase books and scientific apparatus.

Paine's life in England was marked by repeated failures. He had two brief marriages. He was unsuccessful or unhappy in every job he tried. He was dismissed from the excise office after he published a strong argument in 1772 for a raise in pay as the only way to end corruption in the service. Just when his situation appeared hopeless, he met Benjamin Franklin in London, who advised him to seek his fortune in America and gave him letters of introduction.

Paine arrived in Philadelphia on November 30, 1774. His first regular employment was helping to edit the *Pennsylvania Magazine*. In addition Paine published numerous articles and some poetry, anonymously or under pseudonyms. One such article was "African Slavery in America," a scathing denunciation of the African slave trade, which he signed "Justice and Humanity."

Paine had arrived in America when the conflict between the colonists and England was reaching its height. After blood was spilled at the Battle of Lexington and Concord, April 19, 1775, Paine argued that the cause of America should not be just a revolt against taxation but a demand for independence. He put this idea into "Common Sense," which came off the press on January 10, 1776. The 50-page pamphlet sold more than 500,000 copies within a few months. More than any other single publication, "Common Sense" paved the way for the Declaration of Independence, unanimously ratified on July 4, 1776.

During the war that followed, Paine served as volunteer aide-de-camp to General Nathanael Greene. His great contribution to the patriot cause was the 16 "Crisis" papers issued between 1776 and 1783, each one signed "Common Sense." "The American Crisis. Number I," published on December 19,

1776, when George Washington's army was on the verge of disintegration, opened with the flaming words: "These are the times that try men's souls." Washington ordered the pamphlet read to all the troops at Valley Forge.

In 1777 Congress appointed Paine secretary to the Committee for Foreign Affairs. He held the post until early in 1779, when he became involved in a controversy with Silas Deane, a member of the Continental Congress, whom Paine accused of seeking to profit personally from French aid to the United States. But in revealing Deane's machinations, Paine was forced to quote from secret documents to which he had access as secretary of the Committee for Foreign Affairs. As a result, despite the truth of his accusations, he was forced to resign his post.

Paine's desperate need of employment was relieved when he was appointed clerk of the General Assembly of Pennsylvania on November 2, 1779. In this capacity he had frequent opportunity to observe that American troops were at the end of their patience because of lack of pay and scarcity of supplies. Paine took $500 from his salary and started a subscription for the relief of the soldiers. In 1781, pursuing the same goal, he accompanied John Laurens to France. The money, clothing, and ammunition they brought back with them were important to the final success of the Revolution. Paine also appealed to the separate states to cooperate for the well-being of the entire nation. In "Public Good" (1780) he included a call for a national convention to remedy the ineffectual Articles of Confederation and establish a strong central government under "a continental constitution."

At the end of the American Revolution, Paine again found himself poverty-stricken. His patriotic writings had sold by the hundreds of thousands, but he had refused to accept any profits in order that cheap editions might be widely circulated. In a petition to Congress endorsed by Washington, he pleaded for financial assistance. It was buried by Paine's opponents in Congress, but Pennsylvania gave him £500 and New York a farm in New Rochelle. Here Paine devoted his time to inventions, concentrating on an iron bridge without piers and a smokeless candle.

In April 1787 Paine left for Europe to promote his plan to build a single-arch bridge across the wide Schuylkill River near Philadelphia. But in England he was soon diverted from his engineering project. In December 1789 he published anonymously a warning against the attempt of Prime Minister William Pitt to involve England in a war with France over Holland, reminding the British people that war had "but one thing certain and that is increase of taxes." But it was the French Revolution that now filled Paine's thoughts. He was enraged by Edmund Burke's attack on the uprising of the French people in his *Reflections on the Revolution in France*, and though Paine admired Burke's stand in favor of the American Revolution, he rushed into print with his celebrated answer, *Rights of Man* (March 13, 1791). The book immediately created a sensation. At least eight editions were published in 1791, and the work was quickly reprinted in the United States, where it was widely distributed by the Jeffersonian societies. When Burke replied, Paine came back with *Rights of Man, Part II*, published on February 17, 1792.

What began as a defense of the French Revolution evolved into an analysis of the basic reasons for discontent in European society and a remedy for the evils of arbitrary government, poverty, illiteracy, unemployment, and war. Paine spoke out effectively in favor of republicanism as against monarchy and went on to outline a plan for popular education, relief of the poor, pensions for aged people, and public works for the unemployed, all to be financed by the levying of a progressive income tax. To the ruling class Paine's proposals spelled "bloody revolution," and the government ordered the book banned and the publisher jailed. Paine himself was indicted for treason, and an order went out for his arrest. But he was en route to France, having been elected to a seat in the National Convention, before the order for his arrest could be delivered. Paine was tried in absentia, found guilty of seditious libel, and declared an outlaw, and *Rights of Man* was ordered permanently suppressed.

In France Paine hailed the abolition of the monarchy but deplored the terror against the royalists and fought unsuccessfully to save the life of King Louis XVI, favoring banishment rather than execution. He was to pay for his efforts to save the king's life when the radicals under Robespierre took power. Paine was imprisoned from December 28, 1793, to November 4, 1794, when, with the fall of Robespierre, he was released and, though seriously ill, readmitted to the National Convention.

While in prison Part I of Paine's *Age of Reason* was published (1794), and it was followed by Part II after his release (1796). Although Paine made it clear that he believed in a Supreme Being and as a deist opposed only organized religion, the work won him a reputation as an atheist among the orthodox. The publication of his last great pamphlet, "Agrarian Justice" (1797), with its attack on inequalities in property ownership, added to his many enemies in establishment circles.

Paine remained in France until September 1, 1802, when he sailed for the United States. He quickly discovered that his services to the country had been all but forgotten and that he was widely regarded only as the world's greatest infidel. Despite his poverty and his physical condition, worsened by occasional drunkenness, Paine continued his attacks on privilege and religious superstitions. He died in New York City in 1809 and was buried in New Rochelle on the farm given to him by the state of New York as a reward for his Revolutionary writings. Ten years later, William Cobbett, the political journalist, exhumed the bones and took them to England, where he hoped to give Paine a funeral worthy of his great contributions to humanity. But the plan misfired, and the bones were lost, never to be recovered.

At Paine's death most U.S. newspapers reprinted the obituary notice from the *New York Citizen*, which read in part: "He had lived long, did some good and much harm." This remained the verdict of history for more than a century following his death, but in recent years the tide has turned: on January 30, 1937, *The Times of London* referred to him as "the English Voltaire," and on May 18, 1952, Paine's bust was placed in the New York University Hall of Fame.

A CLOSER LOOK

The Founding Fathers, Deism, and Christianity

by David L. Holmes

For some time the question of the religious faith of the Founding Fathers has generated a culture war in the United States. Scholars trained in research universities have generally argued that the majority of the Founders were religious rationalists or Unitarians. Pastors and other writers who identify themselves as Evangelicals have claimed not only that most of the Founders held orthodox beliefs but also that some were born-again Christians.

Whatever their beliefs, the Founders came from similar religious backgrounds. Most were Protestants. The largest number were raised in the three largest Christian traditions of colonial America—Anglicanism (as in the cases of John Jay, George Washington, and Edward Rutledge), Presbyterianism (as in the cases of Richard Stockton and the Rev. John Witherspoon), and Congregationalism (as in the cases of John Adams and Samuel Adams). Other Protestant groups included the Society of Friends (Quakers), the Lutherans, and the Dutch Reformed. Three Founders—Charles Carroll and Daniel Carroll of Maryland and Thomas Fitzsimmons of Pennsylvania—were of Roman Catholic heritage.

The sweeping disagreement over the religious faiths of the

Founders arises from a question of discrepancy. Did their private beliefs differ from the orthodox teachings of their churches? On the surface, most Founders appear to have been orthodox (or "right-believing") Christians. Most were baptized, listed on church rolls, married to practicing Christians, and frequent or at least sporadic attenders of services of Christian worship. In public statements, most invoked divine assistance.

But the widespread existence in 18th-century America of a school of religious thought called Deism complicates the actual beliefs of the Founders. Drawing from the scientific and philosophical work of such figures as Jean-Jacques Rousseau, Isaac Newton, and John Locke, Deists argued that human experience and rationality—rather than religious dogma and mystery—determine the validity of human beliefs. In his widely read *The Age of Reason*, Thomas Paine, the principal American exponent of Deism, called Christianity "a fable." Paine, the protégé of Benjamin Franklin, denied "that the Almighty ever did communicate anything to man, by . . . speech, . . . language, or . . . vision." Postulating a distant deity whom he called "Nature's God" (a term also used in the Declaration of Independence), Paine declared in a "profession of faith":

> I believe in one God, and no more; and I hope for happiness beyond this life. I believe in the equality of man; and I believe that religious duties consist in doing justice, loving mercy, and in endeavoring to make our fellow-creatures happy.

Thus, Deism inevitably subverted orthodox Christianity. Persons influenced by the movement had little reason to read the Bible, to pray, to attend church, or to participate in such rites as baptism, Holy Communion, and the laying on of hands (confirmation) by bishops. With the notable exceptions of Abigail Adams and Dolley Madison, Deism seems to have had little effect on women. For example, Martha Washington, the daughters of Thomas Jefferson, and Elizabeth Kortright Monroe and her daughters seem to have held orthodox Christian beliefs.

But Deistic thought was immensely popular in colleges from the middle of the 18th into the 19th century. Thus, it influenced many educated (as well as uneducated) males of the Revolutionary generation. Although such men would generally continue their public affiliation with Christianity after college, they might inwardly hold unorthodox religious views. Depending on the extent to which Americans of Christian background were influenced by Deism, their religious beliefs would fall into three categories: non-Christian Deism, Christian Deism, and orthodox Christianity.

One can differentiate a Founding Father influenced by Deism from an orthodox Christian believer by following certain criteria. Anyone seeking the answer should consider at least the following four points. First, an inquirer should examine the Founder's church involvement. However, because a colonial church served not only religious but also social and political functions, church attendance or service in a governing body (such as an Anglican vestry, which was a state office in colonies such as Maryland, Virginia, and South Carolina) fails to guarantee a Founder's orthodoxy. But Founders who were believing Christians would nevertheless be more likely to go to church than those influenced by Deism.

The second consideration is an evaluation of the participation of a Founder in the ordinances or sacraments of his church. Most had no choice about being baptized as children, but as adults they did have a choice about participating in communion or (if Episcopalian or Roman Catholic) in confirmation. And few Founders who were Deists would have participated in either rite. George Washington's refusal to receive communion in his adult life indicated Deistic belief to many of his pastors and peers.

Third, one should note the religious language a Founder used. Non-Christian Deists such as Paine refused to use Judeo-Christian terminology and described God with such expressions as "Providence," "the Creator," "the Ruler of Great

Events," and "Nature's God." Founders who fall into the category of Christian Deists used Deistic terms for God but sometimes added a Christian dimension—such as "Merciful Providence" or "Divine Goodness." Yet these Founders did not move further into orthodoxy and employ the traditional language of Christian piety. Founders who remained unaffected by Deism or who (like John Adams) became conservative Unitarians used terms that clearly conveyed their orthodoxy ("Savior," "Redeemer," "Resurrected Christ").

Finally, one should consider what friends, family, and, above all, clergy said about a Founder's religious faith. That Washington's pastors in Philadelphia clearly viewed him as significantly influenced by Deism says more about Washington's faith than do the opposite views of later writers or the cloudy memories of a few Revolutionary veterans who avowed Washington's orthodoxy decades after his death.

Although no examination of history can capture the inner faith of any person, these four indicators can help locate the Founders on the religious spectrum. Ethan Allen, for example, appears clearly to have been a non-Christian Deist. James Monroe, a close friend of Paine, remained officially an Episcopalian but may have stood closer to non-Christian Deism than to Christian Deism. Founders who fall into the category of Christian Deists include Washington (whose dedication to Christianity was clear in his own mind), John Adams, and, with some qualifications, Thomas Jefferson. Jefferson was more influenced by the reason-centered Enlightenment than either Adams or Washington. Orthodox Christians among the Founders include the staunchly Calvinistic Samuel Adams. John Jay (who served as president of the American Bible Society), Elias Boudinot (who wrote a book on the imminent Second Coming of Jesus), and Patrick Henry (who distributed religious tracts while riding circuit as a lawyer) clearly believed in Evangelical Christianity.

Although orthodox Christians participated at every stage of the new republic, Deism influenced a majority of the Founders.

The movement opposed barriers to moral improvement and to social justice. It stood for rational inquiry, for skepticism about dogma and mystery, and for religious toleration. Many of its adherents advocated universal education, freedom of the press, and separation of church and state. If the nation owes much to the Judeo-Christian tradition, it is also indebted to Deism, a movement of reason and equality that influenced the Founding Fathers' embrace of liberal political ideals remarkable for their time.

David L. Holmes is Walter G. Mason Professor of Religious Studies at the College of William and Mary and the author of The Faiths of the Founding Fathers *(2006).*

Paris, Treaty of

The Treaty of Paris (1783) was a collection of treaties concluding the American Revolution and signed by representatives of Great Britain on one side and the United States, France, and Spain on the other. Preliminary articles (often called the Preliminary Treaty of Paris) were signed at Paris between Britain and the United States on November 30, 1782. On September 3, 1783, three definitive treaties were signed—between Britain and the United States in Paris (the Treaty of Paris) and between Britain and France and Spain, respectively, at Versailles. The Netherlands and Britain also signed a preliminary treaty on September 2, 1783, and a final separate peace on May 20, 1784.

By the terms of the U.S.–Britain treaty, Britain recognized the independence of the United States with generous boundaries to the Mississippi River but retained Canada. Access to the Newfoundland fisheries was guaranteed to Americans, and navigation of the Mississippi was to be open to both Great Britain and the United States. Creditors of neither country were to be impeded in the collection of their debts, and Congress was to recommend to the states that American loyalists be treated fairly and their confiscated property restored. (Some of these provisions were to cause later difficulties and disputes.)

To France, Britain surrendered Tobago and Senegal. Spain retained Minorca and East and West Florida. The Netherlands came off poorly, ceding the port city of Nagappattinam in India to Britain and allowing the British free navigation rights in the Dutch-held Moluccas.

Paterson, William

William Paterson (1745–1806) was an Irish-born jurist who was one of the framers of the U.S. Constitution, a U.S. senator (1789–90), and governor of New Jersey (1790–93). He also served as an associate justice of the U.S. Supreme Court from 1793 to 1806.

Paterson emigrated to New Jersey with his family in 1747. He graduated in 1763 from the College of New Jersey (now Princeton University), studied law, and began to practice in 1769. He served twice in the provincial congress (1775–76), was a delegate to the state constitutional convention (1776), and from 1776 to 1783 was attorney general of New Jersey. In 1787 Paterson headed the New Jersey delegation to the federal Constitutional Convention, where he played a leading role in the opposition of the small states to representation according to population in the federal legislature. As an alternative to the Virginia (or large-state) Plan, Paterson submitted the New Jersey (or small-state) Plan, also called the Paterson Plan, which advocated an equal vote for all states. The issue was finally resolved with the compromise embodied in the bicameral legislature.

Paterson was instrumental in securing ratification of the final document in New Jersey and was elected one of the state's first two U.S. senators. Resigning his seat in 1790, he served as governor of New Jersey until 1793, when he was named an associate justice of the U.S. Supreme Court. The city of Paterson, New Jersey, was named for him.

Pinckney, Charles

American Founding Father and diplomat Charles Pinckney (1757–1824) was a political leader whose proposals for a new government—called the Pinckney plan—were largely incorporated into the Federal Constitution drawn up in 1787.

During the American Revolution, Pinckney was captured and held prisoner by the British. Serving in the Continental Congress for three years (1784–87), he played a leading role in calling a national convention to revise and strengthen the Articles of Confederation.

As a South Carolina delegate to the Constitutional Convention at Philadelphia, he submitted a detailed plan of government, which, although the original draft was not preserved, is known to have contained a number of provisions that were incorporated into the new Constitution. Pinckney possibly had as large a share in determining the style, form, and content of the document as any other individual. At home he supported ratification, presided over the convention that remodeled the South Carolina Constitution in 1790, and as governor (1789–92) guided the adjustment between the state and federal governments.

Pinckney began his political career as a Federalist but in 1791 transferred his allegiance to the Jeffersonian Republican

Party. He served in the state legislature (1792–96, 1810–14) and as governor (1796–98, 1806–08), U.S. senator (1798–1801), and representative (1819–21). He supported amendments to the state constitution that gave greater representation to the back country and extended suffrage to all white men. By opposing Federalist policies, especially in 1798, he estranged his two politically active cousins, Charles Cotesworth Pinckney and Thomas Pinckney. Reflecting his Southern background, he bitterly assailed the proposed restrictions on slavery contained in the Missouri Compromise of 1820.

His fidelity to his party was rewarded by appointment as U.S. minister to Spain (1801–05), where he negotiated an agreement providing for a joint tribunal to settle spoliation claims (arising from the seizure of a ship's papers when confiscated for suspected smuggling, carrying contraband of war, or being an enemy ship) and the restoration to U.S. shippers of the right of deposit (temporary storage of goods) at the port of New Orleans. He also won Spain's reluctant consent to Napoleon's sale of Louisiana to the United States, but failed to achieve the U.S. acquisition of Florida.

Pinckney, Charles Cotesworth

American soldier and statesman Charles Cotesworth Pinckney (1746–1825) was a diplomat who participated in the XYZ Affair, an unsavory diplomatic incident with France in 1798.

Pinckney entered public service in 1769 as a member of the South Carolina Assembly. He served in the first South Carolina Provincial Congress (1775) and later in both houses of the South Carolina legislature. During the American Revolution he was an aide to General George Washington at Brandywine and Germantown, Pennsylvania (both 1777), and later commanded a regiment at Savannah, Georgia; he was promoted to brigadier general in 1783. He took part in the Constitutional Convention of 1787, along with his cousin Charles Pinckney.

Pinckney was appointed minister to France (1796) but was refused recognition by the French Directory and left Paris for Amsterdam. He returned to Paris the following year as a member of a commission that included John Marshall and Elbridge Gerry. When one of the group of French negotiators (later referred to in the correspondence as "X, Y, and Z") suggested that the U.S. representatives offer a gift, Pinckney is said to have replied, "No! No! Not a sixpence!" No treaty was negotiated, and an undeclared war with France ensued. Upon his return home Pinckney was made a major general. An unsuccessful Federalist candidate for vice president in 1800 and for president in 1804 and 1808, Pinckney spent his later years in law practice.

Rodney, Caesar

Caesar Rodney (1728–84) was a delegate to the Continental Congress (1774–76, 1777–78), "president" of Delaware (1778–81), and a key signer of the Declaration of Independence. He had earlier served as high sheriff of Kent County, Delaware (1755) and as a delegate to the Stamp Act Congress (1765). One of Delaware's three delegates to the Continental Congress, Rodney had been away in Delaware when he got word of the impending vote on the resolution for independence. Hurrying back to Philadelphia on horseback, he arrived in time to break the tie in his delegation and cast Delaware's deciding vote for independence.

In 1777 he was made commander of the Delaware militia with the rank of brigadier general. In 1783, after his term as "president," he was elected to the legislature but died the next year.

▌Rush, Benjamin

Benjamin Rush (1746–1813) was born into a pious Presbyterian family. He was sent to a private academy and on to the College of New Jersey at Princeton, from which he was graduated in 1760. After a medical apprenticeship of six years, he sailed for Europe. He took a medical degree at the University of Edinburgh in 1768 and then worked in London hospitals and briefly visited Paris.

Returning home to begin medical practice in 1769, he was appointed professor of chemistry in the College of Philadelphia, and in the following year he published his *Syllabus of a Course of Lectures on Chemistry*, the first American textbook in this field. Despite war and political upheavals, Rush's practice grew to substantial proportions, partly owing to his literary output. The standard checklist of early American medical imprints lists 65 publications under his name, not counting scores of communications to newspapers and magazines. Another source of Rush's professional prestige was the large number of his private apprentices and students from all over the country. He taught some 3,000 students during his tenure as professor of, successively, chemistry, the theory and practice of medicine, and the institutes of medicine and clinical medicine in the College of Philadelphia and the University of Pennsylvania. After 1790 his lectures were among the leading cultural attractions of the city.

As a physician, Rush was a theorist, and a dogmatic one, rather than a scientific pathologist. Striving for a simple, unitary explanation of disease, he conjectured that all diseases are really one—a fever brought on by overstimulation of the blood vessels—and hence subject to a simple remedy—"depletion" by bloodletting and purges. The worse the fever, he believed, the more "heroic" the treatment it called for; in the epidemics of yellow fever that afflicted Philadelphia in the 1790s his cures were more dreaded by some than the disease.

In psychiatry Rush's contributions were more enduring. For many years he labored among the insane patients at the Pennsylvania Hospital, advocating humane treatment for them on the ground that mental disorders were as subject to healing arts as physical ones; indeed, he held that insanity often proceeded from physical causes, an idea that was a long step forward from the old notion that lunatics are possessed by devils. His *Medical Inquiries and Observations upon the Diseases of the Mind,*

Benjamin Rush, oil painting by Charles Willson Peale, after a painting by Thomas Sully (in the Independence National Historical Park, Philadelphia).

published in 1812, was the first and for many years the only American treatise on early psychiatry.

Rush was an early and active American patriot. As a member of the radical provincial conference in June 1776, he drafted a resolution urging independence and was soon elected to the Continental Congress, signing the Declaration of Independence with other members on August 2. For a year he served in the field as surgeon general and physician general of the Middle Department of the Continental Army, but early in 1778 he resigned because he considered the military hospitals mismanaged by his superior, who was supported by General Washington. Rush went on to question Washington's military judgment, a step that he was to regret and one that clouded his reputation until recent times. He resumed the practice and teaching of medicine and in 1797, by appointment of President John Adams, took on the duties of treasurer of the U.S. Mint. He held this office until his death.

Rutledge, John

John Rutledge (1739–1800) was an American legislator who, as a delegate to the Constitutional Convention of 1787, strongly supported the protection of slavery and the concept of a strong central government.

After studying in England, Rutledge returned to Charleston to practice law. Reflecting views acceptable to both planters and merchants in his area, he was chosen as a delegate to the Stamp Act Congress (1765) and to the Continental Congress (1774–77, 1782–83). After chairing the committee that framed the South Carolina constitution (1776), he was elected president of the state's General Assembly, but he resigned in 1778 when the constitution was amended to include provisions he considered too democratic. In 1779 he was elected South Carolina's governor, and after the state was invaded by the British in that year, he held the skeleton colonial government together until the end of the war.

At the Constitutional Convention in 1787, Rutledge spoke for Southern planters by supporting slavery. He argued in favor of dividing society into classes as a basis for representation and also postulated high property qualifications for holding office. As chairman of the Committee on Detail, he recommended the granting of indefinite powers of legislation to the national government for the purpose of promoting the general welfare.

John Rutledge, Associate Justice of the U.S. Supreme Court. Photograph of a painting.

From 1789 to 1791 he served as an associate justice of the U.S. Supreme Court and for the next four years as chief justice of the South Carolina Supreme Court. Nominated Chief Justice of the United States in 1795, he failed to win Senate confirmation because of his outspoken opposition to the Jay Treaty of the previous year.

His brother Edward Rutledge was a signer of the Declaration of Independence (1776), fought against the British in South Carolina during the American Revolution, and served in the South Carolina legislature (1782–98) and as governor (1798–1800) of the state.

▌Separation of Powers

The separation of powers is the division of the legislative, executive, and judicial functions of government among separate and independent bodies. Such a separation, it has been argued, limits the possibility of arbitrary excesses by government, since the sanction of all three branches is required for the making, executing, and administering of laws.

The doctrine may be traced to ancient and medieval theories of mixed government, which argued that the processes of government should involve the different elements in society such as monarchic, aristocratic, and democratic interests. The first modern formulation of the doctrine was that of the French writer Montesquieu in *De l'esprit des lois* (1748), although the English philosopher John Locke had earlier argued that legislative power should be divided between king and Parliament.

Montesquieu's argument that liberty is most effectively safeguarded by the separation of powers was inspired by the English constitution, although his interpretation of English political realities has since been disputed. His work was widely influential, most notably in America, where it profoundly influenced the framing of the Constitution. The U.S. Constitution further precluded the concentration of political power by providing staggered terms of office in the key governmental bodies.

Modern constitutional systems show a great variety of arrangements of the legislative, executive, and judicial processes, and the doctrine has consequently lost much of its rigidity and dogmatic purity. In the 20th century, and especially since World War II, governmental involvement in numerous aspects of social and economic life has resulted in an enlargement of the scope of executive power. Some who fear the consequences of this for individual liberty have favored establishing means of appeal against executive and administrative decisions (for example, through an ombudsman), rather than attempting to reassert the doctrine of the separation of powers.

Shays's Rebellion

Shays's Rebellion (August 1786–February 1787) was an uprising in western Massachusetts in opposition to high taxes and stringent economic conditions. Armed bands forced the closing of several courts to prevent execution of foreclosures and debt processes. In September 1786 Daniel Shays and other local leaders led several hundred men in forcing the Supreme Court in Springfield to adjourn. Shays led a force of about 1,200 men in an attack (January 1787) on the federal arsenal at Springfield, which was repulsed. Pursued by the militia, on February 4 he was decisively defeated at Petersham and fled to Vermont. As a result of the rebellion, the Massachusetts legislature enacted laws easing the economic condition of debtors.

Sherman, Roger

Active in both trade and law, Roger Sherman (1721–93) held numerous public offices, including several terms in the Connecticut legislature between 1755 and 1766, judge of the superior court (1766–85), and mayor of New Haven (1784–93). Although a staunch conservative, he was an early supporter of American independence from Britain. As a delegate to the Second Continental Congress at Philadelphia, he signed the Declaration of Independence (1776) and helped draft the Articles of Confederation.

Sherman's greatest service was rendered at the Constitutional Convention called to remedy the deficiencies of the Articles of Confederation. A critical difference appeared between larger states advocating congressional representation on the basis of population and smaller states desiring equal representation regardless of size. Sherman promoted what came to be known as the Connecticut (or Great) Compromise, providing for a bicameral legislature using a dual system of representation. His plan helped save the convention from disintegrating and established the basis of the present system of federal government.

Sherman served in Congress under the new Constitution, first as a representative (1789–91) and then as a senator (1791–93), supporting Alexander Hamilton's program for assumption of state debts, establishment of a national bank, and enactment of a tariff.

Stamp Act

The Stamp Act (1765) was the first British parliamentary attempt to raise revenue through direct taxation of all colonial commercial and legal papers, newspapers, pamphlets, cards, almanacs, and dice. The devastating effect of Pontiac's War (1763–64) on colonial frontier settlements added to the enormous new defense burdens resulting from Great Britain's victory (1763) in the French and Indian War. The British chancellor of the Exchequer, Sir George Grenville, hoped to meet at least half of these costs by the combined revenues of the Sugar

Act (1764) and the Stamp Act, a common revenue device in England. Completely unexpected was the avalanche of protest from the colonists, who effectively nullified the Stamp Act by outright refusal to use the stamps as well as by riots, stamp burning, and intimidation of colonial stamp distributors. Colonists passionately upheld their rights as Englishmen to be taxed only by their own consent through their own representative assemblies, as had been the practice for a century and a half. In addition to nonimportation agreements among colonial merchants, the Stamp Act Congress was convened in New York (October 1765) by moderate representatives of nine colonies to frame resolutions of "rights and grievances" and to petition the king and Parliament for repeal of the objectionable measures. Bowing chiefly to pressure (in the form of a flood of petitions to repeal) from British merchants and manufacturers whose colonial exports had been curtailed, Parliament, largely against the wishes of the House of Lords, repealed the act in early 1766. Simultaneously, however, Parliament issued the Declaratory Act, which reasserted its right of direct taxation anywhere within the empire, "in all cases whatsoever." The protest throughout the colonies against the Stamp Act contributed much to the spirit and organization of unity that was a necessary prelude to the struggle for independence a decade later.

▌Townshend Acts

The Townshend Acts were a series of four acts passed in June–July 1767 by the British Parliament in an attempt to assert what it considered to be its historic right of colonial authority through suspension of a recalcitrant representative assembly and through strict collection provisions of additional revenue duties. The British-American colonists named the acts after Charles Townshend, who sponsored them.

The Suspending Act prohibited the New York Assembly from conducting any further business until it complied with the financial requirements of the Quartering Act (1765) for the expenses of British troops stationed there. The second act, often called the Townshend duties, imposed direct revenue duties, payable at colonial ports, on lead, glass, paper, paint, and tea. It was the second time in the history of the colonies that a tax had been levied solely for the purpose of raising revenue. The third act established strict and often arbitrary machinery of customs collection in the American Colonies, including additional officers, searchers, spies, coast guard vessels, search warrants, writs of assistance, and a Board of Customs Commissioners at Boston, all to be financed out of customs revenues. The fourth Townshend Act lifted commercial duties on tea, allowing it to be exported to the Colonies free of all British taxes.

The acts posed an immediate threat to established traditions of colonial self-government, especially the practice of taxation through representative provincial assemblies. They were resisted everywhere with verbal agitation and physical violence, deliberate evasion of duties, renewed nonimportation agreements among merchants, and overt acts of hostility toward British enforcement agents, especially in Boston. Such colonial tumult, coupled with the instability of frequently changing British ministries, resulted, on March 5, 1770 (the same day as the Boston Massacre), in repeal of all revenue duties except that on tea, lifting of the Quartering Act requirements, and removal of troops from Boston, which thus temporarily averted hostilities.

▌Washington, George

George Washington (1732–99) was an American general and commander in chief of the colonial armies in the American

Revolution who subsequently served as first president of the United States (1789–97).

Washington's father, Augustine Washington, had gone to school in England, had tasted seafaring life, and then settled down to manage his growing Virginia estates. His mother was Mary Ball, whom Augustine, a widower, had married early the previous year. Washington's paternal lineage had some distinction; an early forebear was described as a "gentleman," Henry VIII later gave the family lands, and its members held various offices. But family fortunes fell with the Puritan revolution in England, and John Washington, grandfather of Augustine, migrated in 1657 to Virginia. The ancestral home at Sulgrave, Northamptonshire, is maintained as a Washington memorial. Little definite information exists on any of the line until Augustine. He was an energetic, ambitious man who acquired much land, built mills, took an interest in opening iron mines, and sent his two oldest sons to England for schooling. By his first wife, Jane

Engraving of George Washington, 1780.

Butler, he had four children; by his second wife, Mary Ball, he had six. Augustine died on April 12, 1743.

Little is known of George Washington's early childhood, spent largely on the Ferry Farm on the Rappahannock River, opposite Fredericksburg, Virginia. Mason L. Weems's stories of the hatchet and cherry tree and of young Washington's repugnance to fighting are apocryphal efforts to fill a manifest gap. He attended school irregularly from his 7th to his 15th year, first with the local church sexton and later with a schoolmaster named Williams. Some of his schoolboy papers survive. He was fairly well trained in practical mathematics—gauging, several types of mensuration, and such trigonometry as was useful in surveying. He studied geography, possibly had a little Latin, and certainly read some of *The Spectator* and other English classics. The copybook in which he transcribed at 14 a set of moral precepts, or *Rules of Civility and Decent Behavior in Company and Conversation*, was carefully preserved. His best training, however, was given him by practical men and outdoor occupations, not by books. He mastered tobacco growing and stock raising, and early in his teens he was sufficiently familiar with surveying to plot the fields about him.

At his father's death, the 11-year-old boy became the ward of his eldest half brother, Lawrence, a man of fine character who gave him wise and affectionate care. Lawrence inherited the beautiful estate of Little Hunting Creek, which had been granted to the original settler, John Washington, and which Augustine had done much since 1738 to develop. Lawrence married Anne (Nancy) Fairfax, daughter of Colonel William Fairfax, a cousin and agent of Lord Fairfax and one of the chief proprietors of the region. Lawrence also built a house and named the 2,500-acre holding Mount Vernon in honor of the admiral under whom he had served in the siege of Cartagena. Living there chiefly with Lawrence (though he spent some time near Fredericksburg with his other half-brother, Augustine, called Austin), George entered a more spacious and polite world. Anne Fairfax Washington was a woman of charm, grace, and culture; Lawrence had brought from his English school and naval service much knowledge and experience. A valued neighbor and relative, George William Fairfax, whose large estate, Belvoir, was about 4 miles (6 km) distant, and other relatives by marriage, the Carlyles of Alexandria, helped form George's mind and manners.

The youth turned first to surveying as a profession. Lord Fairfax, a middle-aged bachelor who owned more than

5,000,000 acres in northern Virginia and the Shenandoah Valley, came to America in 1746 to live with his cousin George William at Belvoir and to look after his properties. Two years later he sent to the Shenandoah Valley a party to survey and plot his lands to make regular tenants of the squatters moving in from Pennsylvania. With the official surveyor of Prince William County in charge, Washington went along as assistant. The 16-year-old lad kept a disjointed diary of the trip, which shows skill in observation. He describes the discomfort of sleeping under "one thread Bear blanket with double its Weight of Vermin such as Lice Fleas & c"; an encounter with an Indian war party bearing a scalp; the Pennsylvania-German emigrants, "as ignorant a set of people as the Indians they would never speak English but when spoken to they speak all Dutch"; and the serving of roast wild turkey on "a Large Chip," for "as for dishes we had none."

The following year (1749), aided by Lord Fairfax, Washington received an appointment as official surveyor of Culpeper County, and for more than two years he was kept almost constantly busy. Surveying not only in Culpeper but also in Frederick and Augusta counties, he made journeys far beyond the Tidewater region into the western wilderness. The experience taught him resourcefulness and endurance and toughened him in both body and mind. Coupled with Lawrence's ventures in land, it also gave him an interest in western development that endured throughout his life. He was always disposed to speculate in western holdings and to view favorably projects for colonizing the west, and he greatly resented the limitations that the crown in time laid on the westward movement. In 1752 Lord Fairfax determined to take up his final residence in the Shenandoah Valley and settled there in a log hunting lodge, which he called Greenway Court after a Kentish manor of his family's. There Washington was sometimes entertained and had access to a small library that Fairfax had begun accumulating at Oxford.

The years 1751–52 marked a turning point in Washington's life, for they placed him in control of Mount Vernon. Lawrence, stricken by tuberculosis, went to Barbados in 1751 for his health, taking George along. From this sole journey beyond the present borders of the United States, Washington returned with the light scars of an attack of smallpox. In July of the next year, Lawrence died, making George executor and residuary heir of his estate should his daughter, Sarah, die without issue. As she died within two months, Washington at age 20 became head of one of the best Virginia estates. He always thought farming the "most delectable" of pursuits. "It is honorable," he wrote, "it is amusing, and, with superior judgment, it is profitable." And, of all the spots for farming, he thought Mount Vernon the best. "No estate in United America," he assured an English correspondent, "is more pleasantly situated than this." His greatest pride in later days was to be regarded as the first farmer of the land.

He gradually increased the estate until it exceeded 8,000 acres. He enlarged the house in 1760 and made further enlargements and improvements on the house and its landscaping in 1784–86. He also tried to keep abreast of the latest scientific advances.

For the next 20 years the main background of Washington's life was the work and society of Mount Vernon. He gave assiduous attention to the rotation of crops, fertilization of the soil, and management of livestock. He had to manage the 18 slaves that came with the estate and others he bought later; by 1760 he paid taxes on 49 slaves—though he strongly disapproved of the institution and hoped for some mode of abolishing it. At the time of his death, more than 300 slaves were housed in the quarters on his property. He had been unwilling to sell slaves lest families be broken up, even though the increase in their numbers placed a burden on him for their upkeep and gave him a larger force of workers than he required, especially after he gave up the cultivation of tobacco. In his will, he bequeathed the slaves in his possession to his wife and ordered that upon her death they be set free, declaring also that the young, the aged, and the infirm among them "shall be comfortably cloathed & fed by my heirs." Still, this accounted for only about half the slaves on his property. The other half, owned by his wife, were entailed to the Custis estate, so that on her death they were destined to pass to her heirs. However, she freed all the slaves in 1800 after his death.

For diversion Washington was fond of riding, fox hunting, and dancing, of such theatrical performances as he could reach, and of duck hunting and sturgeon fishing. He liked billiards and cards and not only subscribed to racing associations but also ran his own horses in races. In all outdoor pursuits, from wrestling to colt breaking, he excelled. A friend of the 1750s describes him as "straight as an Indian, measuring six feet two inches in his stockings"; as very muscular and broad-shouldered but, though large-boned, weighing only 175 pounds; and as having long arms and legs. His penetrating blue-gray eyes were overhung by heavy brows, his nose was large and straight, and his mouth was large and firmly closed. "His movements and gestures are graceful, his walk majestic, and he is a splendid horseman." He soon became prominent in community affairs, was an active member and later vestryman of the Episcopal church, and as early as 1755 expressed a desire to stand for the Virginia House of Burgesses.

Traditions of John Washington's feats as an Indian fighter and Lawrence Washington's talk of service days helped imbue George with military ambition. Just after Lawrence's death, Lieutenant Governor Robert Dinwiddie appointed George adjutant for the southern district of Virginia at £100 a year (November 1752). In 1753 he became adjutant of the Northern Neck and Eastern Shore. Later that year, Dinwiddie found it necessary to warn the French to desist from their encroachments on Ohio Valley lands claimed by the crown. After sending one messenger who failed to reach the goal, he determined to dispatch Washington. On the day he received his orders, October 31, 1753, Washington set out for the French posts. His party consisted of a Dutchman to serve as interpreter, the expert scout Christopher Gist as guide, and four others, two of them experienced traders with the Indians. Theoretically, Great Britain and France were at peace. Actually, war impended, and Dinwiddie's message was an ultimatum: the French must get out or be put out.

The journey proved rough, perilous, and futile. Washington's party left what is now Cumberland, Maryland, in the middle of November and, despite wintry weather and impediments of the wilderness, reached Fort LeBoeuf, at what is now Waterford, Pennsylvania, 20 miles (32 km) south of Lake Erie, without delay. The French commander was courteous but adamant. As Washington reported, his officers "told me, That it was their absolute Design to take possession of the Ohio, and by God they would do it." Eager to carry this alarming news back, Washington pushed off hurriedly with Gist. He was lucky to have gotten back alive. An Indian fired at them at 15 paces but missed. When they crossed the Allegheny River on a raft, Washington was jerked into the ice-filled stream but saved himself by catching one of the timbers. That night he almost froze in his wet clothing. He reached Williamsburg, Virginia, on January 16, 1754, where he hastily penned a record of the journey. Dinwiddie, who was laboring to convince the crown of the seriousness of the French threat, had it printed, and when he sent it to London, it was reprinted in three different forms.

The enterprising governor forthwith planned an expedition to hold the Ohio country. He made Joshua Fry colonel of a provincial regiment, appointed Washington lieutenant colonel, and set them to recruiting troops. Two agents of the Ohio Company, which Lawrence Washington and others had formed to develop lands on the upper Potomac and Ohio rivers, had begun building a fort at what later became Pittsburgh, Pennsylvania. Dinwiddie, ready to launch into his own war, sent Washington with two companies to reinforce this post. In April 1754 the lieutenant colonel set out from Alexandria with about 160 men at his back. He marched to Cumberland only to learn that the French had anticipated the British blow; they had taken possession of the fort of the Ohio Company and had renamed it Fort Duquesne. Happily, the Indians of the area offered support. Washington therefore struggled cautiously forward to within about 40 miles (60 km) of the French position and erected his own post at Great Meadows, near what is now Confluence, Pennsylvania. From this base, he made a surprise attack (May 28, 1754) upon an advance detachment of 30 French, killing the commander, Coulon de Jumonville, and nine others and taking the rest prisoners. The French and Indian War had begun.

Washington at once received promotion to a full colonelcy and was reinforced, commanding a considerable body of Virginia and North Carolina troops, with Indian auxiliaries. But his attack soon brought the whole French force down upon him. They drove his 350 men into the Great Meadows fort (Fort Necessity) on July 3, besieged it with 700 men, and, after an all-day fight, compelled him to surrender. The construction of the fort had been a blunder, for it lay in a waterlogged creek bottom, was commanded on three sides by forested elevations approaching it closely, and was too far from Washington's supports. The French agreed to let the disarmed colonials march back to Virginia with the honors of war, but they compelled Washington to promise that Virginia would not build another fort on the Ohio for a year and to sign a paper acknowledging responsibility for "*l'assassinat*" of de Jumonville, a word that Washington later explained he did not rightly understand. He returned to Virginia, chagrined but proud, to receive the thanks of the House of Burgesses and to find that his name had been mentioned in the London gazettes. His remark in a letter to his brother that "I have heard the bullets whistle; and believe me, there is something charming in the sound" was commented on humorously by the author Horace Walpole and sarcastically by King George II.

The arrival of General Edward Braddock and his army in Virginia in February 1755, as part of the triple plan of campaign that called for his advance on Fort Duquesne and on New York Governor William Shirley's capture of Fort Niagara and Sir William Johnson's capture of Crown Point, brought Washington new opportunities and responsibilities. He had resigned his commission in October 1754 in resentment of the slighting treatment and underpayment of colonial officers and particularly because of an untactful order of the British war office that provincial officers of whatever rank would be subordinate to any officer holding the king's commission. But he ardently desired a part in the war; "my inclinations," he wrote a friend, "are strongly bent to arms." When Braddock showed appreciation of his merits and invited him to join the expedition as personal aide-de-camp, with the courtesy title of colonel, he therefore accepted. His self-reliance, decision, and masterfulness soon became apparent.

At table he had frequent disputes with Braddock, who, when contractors failed to deliver their supplies, attacked the colonials as supine and dishonest while Washington defended them warmly. His freedom of utterance is proof of Braddock's esteem. Braddock accepted Washington's unwise advice that he divide his army, leaving half of it to come up with the slow wagons and cattle train and taking the other half forward against Fort Duquesne at a rapid pace. Washington was ill with fever during June but joined the advance guard in a covered wagon on July 8, begged to lead the march on Fort Duquesne with his Virginians and Indian allies, and was by Braddock's side when on July 9 the army was ambushed and bloodily defeated.

In this defeat Washington displayed the combination of coolness and determination, the alliance of unconquerable energy with complete poise, that was the secret of so many of his successes. So ill that he had to use a pillow instead of a saddle and that Braddock ordered his body servant to keep special watch over him, Washington was, nevertheless, everywhere at once. At first he followed Braddock as the general bravely tried to rally his men to push either forward or backward, the wisest course the circumstances permitted. Then he rode back to bring up the Virginians from the rear and rallied them with effect on the flank. To him was largely due the escape of the force. His exposure of his person was as reckless as Braddock's, who was fatally wounded on his fifth horse; Washington had two horses shot out from under him and his clothes cut by four bullets without being hurt. He was at Braddock's deathbed, helped bring the troops back, and was repaid by being appointed, in August 1755, while still only 23 years old, commander of all Virginia troops.

But no part of his later service was conspicuous. Finding that a Maryland captain who held a royal commission would not obey him, he rode north in February 1756 to Boston to have the question settled by the commander in chief in America, Governor Shirley, and, bearing a letter from Dinwiddie, had no difficulty in carrying his point. On his return he plunged into a multitude of vexations. He had to protect a weak, thinly settled frontier nearly 400 miles (650 km) in length with only some 700 ill-disciplined colonial troops, to cope with a legislature unwilling to support him, to meet attacks on the drunkenness and inefficiency of the soldiers, and to endure constant wilderness hardships. It is not strange that in 1757 his health failed and in the closing weeks of that year he was so ill of a "bloody flux" (dysentery) that his physician ordered him home to Mount Vernon.

In the spring of 1758 he had recovered sufficiently to return to duty as colonel in command of all Virginia troops. As part of the grand sweep of several armies organized by British statesman William Pitt the Elder, General John Forbes led a new advance upon Fort Duquesne. Forbes resolved not to use Braddock's road but to cut a new one west from Raystown, Pennsylvania. Washington disapproved of the route but played an important part in the movement. Late in the autumn the French evacuated and burned Fort Duquesne, and Forbes reared Fort Pitt on the site. Washington, who had just been elected to the House of Burgesses, was able to resign with the honorary rank of brigadier general.

Although his officers expressed regret at the "loss of such an excellent Commander, such a sincere Friend, and so affable a Companion," he quit the service with a sense of frustration. He had thought the war excessively slow. The Virginia legislature had been niggardly in voting money; the Virginia recruits had come forward reluctantly and had proved of poor quality—Washington had hanged a few deserters and flogged others heavily. Virginia gave him less pay than other colonies offered their troops. Desiring a regular commission such as his half-brother Lawrence had held, he applied in vain to the British commander in North America, Lord Loudoun, to make good a promise that Braddock had given him. Ambitious for both rank and honor, he showed a somewhat strident vigor in asserting his desires and in complaining when they were denied. He returned to Mount Vernon somewhat disillusioned.

Immediately on resigning his commission, Washington was married (January 6, 1759) to Martha Dandridge, the widow of Daniel Parke Custis. She was a few months older than he, was the mother of two children living and two dead, and possessed one of the considerable fortunes of Virginia. Washington had met her the previous March and had asked for her hand before his campaign with Forbes. Though it does not seem to have been a romantic love match, the marriage united two harmonious temperaments and proved happy. Martha was a good housewife, an amiable companion, and a dignified hostess. Like many well-born women of the era, she had little formal schooling, and Washington often helped her compose important letters.

Some estimates of the property brought to him by this marriage have been exaggerated, but it did include a number of slaves and about 15,000 acres, much of it valuable for its proximity to Williamsburg. More important to Washington were the two stepchildren, John Parke ("Jacky") and Martha Parke ("Patsy") Custis, who at the time of the marriage were six and four, respectively. He lavished great affection and care upon them, worried greatly over Jacky's waywardness, and was overcome with grief when Patsy died just before the Revolution. Jacky died during the war, leaving four children. Washington adopted two of them, a boy and a girl, and even signed his letters to the boy as "your papa." Himself childless, he thus had a real family.

From the time of his marriage Washington added to the care of Mount Vernon the supervision of the Custis estate at the White House on the York River. As his holdings expanded, they were divided into farms, each under its own overseer; but he minutely inspected operations every day and according to one visitor often pulled off his coat and performed ordinary labor. As he once wrote, "middling land under a man's own eyes, is more profitable than rich land at a distance." Until the eve of the Revolution he devoted himself to the duties and pleasures of a great landholder, varied by several weeks' attendance every year in the House of Burgesses in Williamsburg. During 1760–74 he was also a justice of the peace for Fairfax County, sitting in court in Alexandria.

In no light does Washington appear more characteristically than as one of the richest, largest, and most industrious of Virginia planters. For six days a week he rose early and worked hard; on Sundays he irregularly attended Pohick Church (16 times in 1760), entertained company, wrote letters, made purchases and sales, and sometimes went fox hunting. In these years he took snuff and smoked a pipe; throughout life he liked Madeira wine and punch. Although wheat and tobacco were his staples, he practiced crop rotation on a three-year or five-year plan. He had his own water-powered flour mill, blacksmith shop, brick and charcoal kilns, carpenters, and masons. His fishery supplied shad, bass, herring, and other catches, salted as food for his slaves. Coopers, weavers, and his own shoemaker

turned out barrels, cotton, linen, and woolen goods, and bro-
gans for all needs. In short, his estates, in accordance with his
orders to overseers to "buy nothing you can make yourselves,"
were largely self-sufficient communities. But he did send large
orders to England for farm implements, tools, paint, fine tex-
tiles, hardware, and agricultural books and hence was painfully
aware of British commercial restrictions.

Washington was an innovative farmer and a responsible
landowner. He experimented at breeding cattle; acquired at
least one buffalo, with the hope of proving its utility as a meat
animal; and kept stallions at stud. He also took pride in a peach
and apple orchard.

His care of slaves was exemplary. He carefully clothed and
fed them, engaged a doctor for them by the year, generally
refused to sell them—"I am principled against this kind of traf-
fic in the human species"—and administered correction mildly.
They showed so much attachment that few ran away.

He meanwhile played a prominent role in the social life of
the Tidewater region. The members of the council and House of
Burgesses, a roster of influential Virginians, were all friends. He
visited the Byrds of Westover, the Lees of Stratford, the Carters
of Shirley and Sabine Hall, and the Lewises of Warner Hall;
Mount Vernon often was busy with guests in return. He liked
house parties and afternoon tea on the Mount Vernon porch
overlooking the grand Potomac; he was fond of picnics, barbe-
cues, and clambakes; and throughout life he enjoyed dancing,
frequently going to Alexandria for balls. Cards were a steady
diversion, and his accounts record sums lost at them, the largest
reaching nearly £10. His diary sometimes states that in bad
weather he was "at home all day, over cards." Billiards was a
rival amusement. Not only the theater, when available, but also
concerts, cockfights, circuses, puppet shows, and exhibitions of
animals received his patronage.

He insisted on the best clothes—coats, laced waistcoats,
hats, colored silk hose—bought in London. The Virginia of the

Randolphs, Corbins, Harrisons, Tylers, Nicholases, and other prominent families had an aristocratic quality, and Washington liked to do things in a large way. It has been computed that in the seven years prior to 1775, Mount Vernon had 2,000 guests, most of whom stayed to dinner if not overnight.

Washington's contented life was interrupted by the rising storm in imperial affairs. The British ministry, facing a heavy postwar debt, high home taxes, and continued military costs in America, decided in 1764 to obtain revenue from the colonies. Up to that time, Washington, though regarded by associates, in Colonel John L. Peyton's words, as "a young man of an extraordinary and exalted character," had shown no signs of personal greatness and few signs of interest in state affairs. The Proclamation of 1763 interdicting settlement beyond the Alleghenies irked him, for he was interested in the Ohio Company, the Mississippi Company, and other speculative western ventures. He nevertheless played a silent part in the House of Burgesses and was a thoroughly loyal subject.

But he was present when Patrick Henry introduced his resolutions against the Stamp Act in May 1765 and shortly thereafter gave token of his adherence to the cause of the colonial Whigs against the Tory ministries of England. In 1768 he told George Mason at Mount Vernon that he would take his musket on his shoulder whenever his country called him. The next spring, on April 4, 1769, he sent Mason the Philadelphia nonimportation resolutions with a letter declaring that it was necessary to resist the strokes of "our lordly masters" in England; that, courteous remonstrances to Parliament having failed, he wholly endorsed the resort to commercial warfare; and that as a last resort no man should scruple to use arms in defense of liberty. When, the following May, the royal governor dissolved the House of Burgesses, he shared in the gathering at the Raleigh, North Carolina, tavern that drew up nonimportation resolutions, and he went further than most of his neighbors in adhering to them. At that time and later he believed with most Americans that peace need not be broken.

Late in 1770 he paid a land-hunting visit to Fort Pitt, where George Croghan was maturing his plans for the proposed 14th colony of Vandalia. Washington directed his agent to locate and survey 10,000 acres adjoining the Vandalia tract, and at one time he wished to share in certain of Croghan's schemes. But the Boston Tea Party of December 1773 and the bursting of the Vandalia bubble at about the same time turned his eyes back to the east and the threatening state of Anglo-American relations. He was not a member of the Virginia committee of correspondence formed in 1773 to communicate with other colonies, but when the Virginia legislators, meeting irregularly again at the Raleigh tavern in May 1774, called for a Continental Congress, he was present and signed the resolutions. Moreover, he was a leading member of the first provincial convention or revolutionary legislature late that summer, and to that body he made a speech that was much praised for its pithy eloquence, declaring that "I will raise one thousand men, subsist them at my own expense, and march myself at their head for the relief of Boston."

The Virginia provincial convention promptly elected Washington one of the seven delegates to the First Continental Congress. He was by this time known as a radical rather than a moderate, and in several letters of the time he opposed a continuance of petitions to the British crown, declaring that they would inevitably meet with a humiliating rejection. "Shall we after this whine and cry for relief when we have already tried it in vain?" he wrote. When the Congress met in Philadelphia on September 5, 1774, he was in his seat in full uniform, and his participation in its councils marks the beginning of his national career.

His letters of the period show that while still utterly opposed to the idea of independence, he was determined never to submit "to the loss of those valuable rights and privileges, which are essential to the happiness of every free State, and without which life, liberty, and property are rendered totally insecure." If the ministry pushed matters to an extremity, he wrote, "more blood will be spilled on this occasion than ever before in American history." Though he served on none of the committees, he was a useful member, his advice being sought on military matters and weight being attached to his advocacy of a nonexportation as well as nonimportation agreement. He also helped to secure approval of the Suffolk Resolves, which looked toward armed resistance as a last resort and did much to harden the king's heart against America.

Returning to Virginia in November, he took command of the volunteer companies drilling there and served as chairman of the Committee of Safety in Fairfax County. Although the province contained many experienced officers and Colonel William Byrd of Westover had succeeded Washington as commander in chief, the unanimity with which the Virginia troops turned to Washington was a tribute to his reputation and personality; it was understood that Virginia expected him to be its general. He was elected to the Second Continental Congress at the March 1775 session of the legislature and again set out for Philadelphia.

The choice of Washington as commander in chief of the military forces of all the colonies followed immediately upon the first fighting, though it was by no means inevitable and was the product of partly artificial forces. The Virginia delegates differed upon his appointment. Edmund Pendleton was, according to John Adams, "very full and clear against it," and Washington himself recommended General Andrew Lewis for the post. It was chiefly the fruit of a political bargain by which New England offered Virginia the chief command as its price for the adoption and support of the New England army. This army had gathered hastily and in force about Boston immediately after the clash of British troops and American minutemen at Lexington and Concord on April 19, 1775. When the Second

Continental Congress met in Philadelphia on May 10, one of its first tasks was to find a permanent leadership for this force. On June 15, Washington, whose military counsel had already proved invaluable on two committees, was nominated and chosen by unanimous vote. Beyond the considerations noted, he owed being chosen to the facts that Virginia stood with Massachusetts as one of the most powerful colonies; that his appointment would augment the zeal of the southern people; that he had gained an enduring reputation in the Braddock campaign; and that his poise, sense, and resolution had impressed all the delegates. The scene of his election, with Washington darting modestly into an adjoining room and John Hancock flushing with jealous mortification, will always impress the historical imagination; so also will the scene of July 3, 1775, when, wheeling his horse under an elm in front of the troops paraded on Cambridge common, he drew his sword and took command of the army investing Boston. News of Bunker Hill had reached him before he was a day's journey from Philadelphia, and he had expressed confidence of victory when told how the militia had fought. In accepting the command, he refused any payment beyond his expenses and called upon "every gentleman in the room" to bear witness that he disclaimed fitness for it. At once he showed characteristic decision and energy in organizing the raw volunteers, collecting provisions and munitions, and rallying Congress and the colonies to his support.

The first phase of Washington's command covered the period from July 1775 to the British evacuation of Boston in March 1776. In those eight months he imparted discipline to the army, which at maximum strength slightly exceeded 20,000; he dealt with subordinates who, as John Adams said, quarreled "like cats and dogs"; and he kept the siege vigorously alive. Having himself planned an invasion of Canada by Lake Champlain, to be entrusted to General Philip Schuyler, he heartily approved of Benedict Arnold's proposal to march north along the Kennebec River in Maine and take Quebec. Giving Arnold

1,100 men, he instructed him to do everything possible to conciliate the Canadians. He was equally active in encouraging privateers to attack British commerce. As fast as means offered, he strengthened his army with ammunition and siege guns, having heavy artillery brought from Fort Ticonderoga, New York, over the frozen roads early in 1776. His position was at first precarious, for the Charles River pierced the center of his lines investing Boston. If the British general, Sir William Howe, had moved his 20 veteran regiments boldly up the stream, he might have pierced Washington's army and rolled either wing back to destruction. But all the generalship was on Washington's side. Seeing that Dorchester Heights, just south of Boston, commanded the city and harbor and that Howe had unaccountably failed to occupy it, he seized it on the night of March 4, 1776, placing his Ticonderoga guns in position. The British naval commander declared that he could not remain if the Americans were not dislodged, and Howe, after a storm disrupted his plans for an assault, evacuated the city on March 17. He left 200 cannons and invaluable stores of small arms and munitions. After collecting his booty, Washington hurried south to take up the defense of New York.

Washington had won the first round, but there remained five years of the war, during which the American cause was repeatedly near complete disaster. It is unquestionable that Washington's strength of character, his ability to hold the confidence of army and people and to diffuse his own courage among them, his unremitting activity, and his strong common sense constituted the chief factors in achieving American victory. He was not a great tactician: as Jefferson said later, he often "failed in the field"; he was sometimes guilty of grave military blunders, the chief being his assumption of a position on Long Island, New York, in 1776 that exposed his entire army to capture the moment it was defeated. At the outset he was painfully inexperienced, the wilderness fighting of the French war having done nothing to teach him the strategy of maneuvering whole armies. One of his chief faults was his tendency to subordinate his own judgment to that of the generals surrounding him; at every critical juncture, before Boston, before New York, before Philadelphia, and in New Jersey, he called a council of war and in almost every instance accepted its decision. Naturally bold and dashing, as he proved at Trenton, Princeton, and Germantown, he repeatedly adopted evasive and delaying tactics on the advice of his associates; however, he did succeed in keeping a strong army in existence and maintaining the flame of national spirit. When the auspicious moment arrived, he planned the rapid movements that ended the war.

One element of Washington's strength was his sternness as a disciplinarian. The army was continually dwindling and refilling, politics largely governed the selection of officers by Congress and the states, and the ill-fed, ill-clothed, ill-paid forces were often half-prostrated by sickness and ripe for mutiny. Troops from each of the three sections, New England, the middle states, and the south, showed a deplorable jealousy of the others. Washington was rigorous in breaking cowardly, inefficient, and dishonest men and boasted in front of Boston that he had "made a pretty good sort of slam among such kind of officers." Deserters and plunderers were flogged, and Washington once erected a gallows 40 feet (12 metres) high, writing, "I am determined if I can be justified in the proceeding, to hang two or three on it, as an example to others." At the same time, the commander in chief won the devotion of many of his men by his earnestness in demanding better treatment for them from Congress. He complained of their short rations, declaring once that they were forced to "eat every kind of horse food but hay."

The darkest chapter in Washington's military leadership was opened when, reaching New York in April 1776, he placed half his army, about 9,000 men, under Israel Putnam, on the perilous position of Brooklyn Heights, Long Island, where a British fleet in the East River might cut off their retreat. He spent a fortnight in May with the Continental Congress in Philadelphia, then discussing the question of independence; though no record of his utterances exists, there can be no doubt that he advocated complete separation. His return to New York preceded but slightly the arrival of the British army under Howe, which made its main encampment on Staten Island until its whole strength of nearly 30,000 could be mobilized. On August 22, 1776, Howe moved about 20,000 men across to Gravesend Bay on Long Island. Four days later, sending the fleet under command of his brother Admiral Richard Howe to make a feint against New York City, he thrust a crushing force along feebly protected roads against the American flank. The patriots were outmaneuvered, defeated, and suffered a total loss of 5,000 men, of whom 2,000 were captured. Their whole position might have been carried by storm, but, fortunately for Washington, General Howe delayed. While the enemy lingered, Washington succeeded under cover of a dense fog in ferrying the remaining force across the East River to Manhattan, where he took up a fortified position. The British, suddenly landing on the lower part of the island, drove back the Americans in a clash marked by disgraceful cowardice on the part of troops from Connecticut and others. In a series of actions, Washington was forced northward, more than once in danger of capture, until the loss of his two Hudson River forts, one of them with 2,600 men, compelled him to retreat from White Plains across the river into New Jersey. He retired toward the Delaware River while his army melted away, until it seemed that armed resistance to the British was about to expire.

It was at this darkest hour of the Revolution that Washington struck his brilliant blows at Trenton and Princeton, New Jersey, reviving the hopes and energies of the nation. Howe, believing that the American army soon would dissolve totally, retired to New York, leaving strong forces in Trenton and Burlington. Washington, at his camp west of the Delaware River, planned a simultaneous attack on both posts, using his whole command of 6,000 men. But his subordinates in charge of both wings failed him, and he was left on the night of December 25, 1776, to march on Trenton with about 2,400 men. With the help of Colonel John Glover's regiment, which was comprised of fishermen and sailors from Marblehead, Massachusetts, Washington and his troops were ferried across the Delaware River. In the dead of night and amid a blinding snowstorm, they then marched 10 miles (16 km) downstream and in the early hours of the morning caught the enemy at Trenton unaware. In less than two hours and without the loss of a single man in battle, Washington's troops defeated the Hessians, killed their commander (Johann Rall), and captured nearly 1,000 prisoners and arms and ammunition. This historic Christmas crossing proved to be a turning point in the war, and it was immortalized for posterity by Emanuel Gottlieb Leutze in his famous 1851 painting of the event. (The painting is historically inaccurate: the depicted flag is anachronistic, the boats are the wrong size and shape, and it is questionable whether Washington could have crossed the icy Delaware while standing in the manner depicted.)

The immediate result of this American victory was that General Charles Cornwallis hastened with about 8,000 men to Trenton, where he found Washington strongly posted behind the Assunpink Creek, skirmished with him, and decided to wait overnight "to bag the old fox." During the night, the wind shifted, the roads froze hard, and Washington was able to steal away from camp (leaving his fires deceptively burning), march around Cornwallis's rear, and fall at daybreak upon the three British regiments at Princeton. These were put to flight with a loss of 500 men, and Washington escaped with more captured munitions to a strong position at Morristown, New Jersey. The effect of these victories heartened all Americans, brought recruits flocking to camp in the spring, and encouraged foreign sympathizers with the American cause.

Thus far the important successes had been won by Washington; then battlefield success fell to others, while he was left to face popular apathy, military cabals, and the disaffection of Congress. The year 1777 was marked by the British capture of Philadelphia and the surrender of British General John Burgoyne's invading army to General Horatio Gates at Saratoga, New York, followed by intrigues to displace Washington from his command. Howe's main British army of 18,000 left New York by sea on July 23, 1777, and landed on August 25 in Maryland, not far below Philadelphia. Washington, despite his inferiority of force—he had only 11,000 men, mostly militia and, in the marquis de Lafayette's words, "badly armed and worse clothed"—risked a pitched battle on September 11 at the fords of Brandywine Creek, about 13 miles (21 km) north of Wilmington, Delaware. While part of the British force held the Americans engaged, General Cornwallis, with the rest, made a secret 17-mile (27-km) detour and fell with crushing effect on the American right and rear, the result being a complete defeat from which Washington was fortunate to extricate his army in fairly good order. For a time he hoped to hold the Schuylkill Fords, but the British passed them and on September 26 triumphantly marched into Philadelphia. Congress fled to the interior of Pennsylvania, and Washington, after an unsuccessful effort to repeat his stroke at Trenton against the British troops posted at Germantown, had to take up winter quarters at Valley Forge. His army, twice beaten, ill housed, and ill fed, with thousands of men "barefoot and otherwise naked," was at the point of exhaustion; it could not keep the field, for inside of a month it would have disappeared. Under these circumstances, there is nothing that better proves the true fiber of Washington's character and the courage of his soul than the unyielding persistence with which he held his strong position at Valley Forge through a winter of semistarvation, of justified grumbling by his men, of harsh public criticism, and of captious meddling by a Congress that was too weak to help him. In February Martha Washington arrived and helped to organize entertainment for the soldiers.

Washington's enemies seized the moment of his greatest weakness to give vent to an antagonism that had been nourished by sectional jealousies of north against south, by the ambition of small rivals, and by baseless accusations that he showed favoritism to such foreigners as Lafayette. The intrigues of Thomas Conway, an Irish adventurer who had served in the French army and had become an American general, enlisted Thomas Mifflin, Charles Lee, Benjamin Rush, and others in an attempt to displace Washington. General Gates appears to have been a tool of rather than a party to the plot, expecting that the chief command would devolve upon himself. A faction of Congress sympathized with the movement and attempted to paralyze Washington by reorganizing the board of war, a body vested with the general superintendence of operations, of which Gates became the president; his chief of staff, James Wilkinson, the secretary; and Mifflin and Timothy Pickering, members. Washington was well aware of the hostility in Congress, of the slanders spread by Rush and James Lovell of Massachusetts, and of the effect of forgeries published in the American press by adroit British agents. He realized the intense jealousy of many New Englanders, which made even John Adams write his wife that he was thankful Burgoyne had not been captured by Washington, who would then "have been deified. It is bad enough as it is." But Washington decisively crushed the cabal: after the loose tongue of Wilkinson disclosed Conway's treachery, Washington sent the general on November 9, 1777, proof of his knowledge of the whole affair.

With the conclusion of the French alliance in the spring of 1778, the aspect of the war was radically altered. The British army in Philadelphia, fearing that a French fleet would blockade the Delaware while the militia of New Jersey and Pennsylvania invested the city, hastily retreated upon New York City. Washington hoped to cut off part of the enemy and by a hurried march with six brigades interposed himself at the end of June between Sir Henry Clinton (who had succeeded Howe) and the

New Jersey coast. The result was the Battle of Monmouth on June 28, where a shrewd strategic plan and vigorous assault were brought to naught by the treachery of Charles Lee. When Lee ruined the attack by a sudden order to retreat, Washington hurried forward, fiercely denounced him, and restored the line, but the golden opportunity had been lost. The British made good their march to Sandy Hook, and Washington took up his quarters at New Brunswick. Lee was arrested, court-martialed, and convicted on all three of the charges made against him; but instead of being shot, as he deserved, he was sentenced to a suspension from command for one year. The arrival of the French fleet under Admiral Charles-Hector Estaing on July 1778 completed the isolation of the British, and Clinton was thenceforth held to New York City and the surrounding area. Washington made his headquarters in the highlands of the Hudson and distributed his troops in cantonments around the city and in New Jersey.

The final decisive stroke of the war, the capture of Cornwallis at Yorktown, is to be credited chiefly to Washington's vision. With the domestic situation intensely gloomy early in 1781, he was hampered by the feebleness of Congress, the popular discouragement, and the lack of prompt and strong support by the French fleet. A French army under the comte de Rochambeau had arrived to reinforce him in 1780, and Washington had pressed Admiral de Grasse to assist in an attack upon either Cornwallis in the south or Clinton in New York. In August the French admiral sent definite word that he preferred the Chesapeake, with its large area and deep water, as the scene of his operations; and within a week, on August 19, 1781, Washington marched south with his army, leaving General William Heath with 4,000 men to hold West Point. He hurried his troops through New Jersey, embarked them on transports in Delaware Bay, and landed them at Williamsburg, Virginia, where he had arrived on September 14. Cornwallis had retreated to Yorktown and entrenched his army of 7,000 British regulars. Their works were completely invested before the end of the month; the siege was pressed with vigor by the allied armies under Washington, consisting of 5,500 Continentals, 3,500 Virginia militia, and 5,000 French regulars; and on October 19 Cornwallis surrendered. By this campaign, probably the finest single display of Washington's generalship, the war was brought to a virtual close.

Washington remained during the winter of 1781–82 with the Continental Congress in Philadelphia, exhorting it to maintain its exertions for liberty and to settle the army's claims for pay. He continued these exhortations after he joined his command at Newburgh on the Hudson in April 1782. He was astounded and angered when some loose camp suggestions found expression in a letter from Colonel Lewis Nicola offering a plan by which he should use the army to make himself king. He blasted the proposal with fierce condemnation. When the discontent of his unpaid men came to a head in the circulation of the "Newburgh Address" (an anonymously written grievance) early in 1783, he issued a general order censuring the paper and at a meeting of officers on March 15 read a speech admonishing the army to obey Congress and promising his best efforts for a redress of grievances. He was present at the entrance of the American army into New York on the day of the British evacuation, November 25, 1783, and on December 4 took leave of his closest officers in an affecting scene at Fraunces Tavern. Traveling south, on December 23, in a solemn ceremonial immortalized by the pen of William Makepeace Thackeray, he resigned his commission to the Continental Congress in the state senate chamber of Maryland in Annapolis and received the thanks of the nation. His accounts of personal expenditures during his service, kept with minute exactness in his own handwriting and totalling £24,700, without charge for salary, had been given to the controller of the treasury to be discharged. Washington left Annapolis at sunrise of December 24 and before nightfall was at home in Mount Vernon.

In the next four years Washington found sufficient occupation in his estates, wishing to close his days as a gentleman farmer and to give to agriculture as much energy and thought as he had to the army. He enlarged the Mount Vernon house; he laid out the grounds anew, with sunken walls, or ha-has; and he embarked on experiments with mahogany, palmetto, pepper, and other foreign trees, and English grasses and grains. His farm manager during the Revolution, a distant relative named Lund Washington, retired in 1785 and was succeeded by a nephew, Major George Augustine Washington, who resided at Mount Vernon until his death in 1792. Washington's losses during the war had been heavy, caused by neglect of his lands, stoppage of exportation, and depreciation of paper money, which cost him hardly less than $30,000. He then attempted successfully to repair his fortunes, his annual receipts from all his estates being from $10,000 to $15,000 a year. In 1784 he made a tour of nearly 700 miles (1,125 km) to view the wild lands he owned to the westward, Congress having made him a generous grant. As a national figure, he was constrained to offer hospitality to old army friends, visitors from other states and nations, diplomats, and Indian delegations, and he and his household seldom sat down to dinner alone.

Viewing the chaotic political condition of the United States after 1783 with frank pessimism and declaring (May 18, 1786) that "something must be done, or the fabric must fall, for it is certainly tottering," Washington repeatedly wrote his friends urging steps toward "an indissoluble union." At first he believed that the Articles of Confederation might be amended. Later, especially after the shock of Shays's Rebellion, he took the view that a more radical reform was necessary but doubted as late as the end of 1786 that the time was ripe. His progress toward adoption of the idea of a federal convention was, in fact, puzzlingly slow. Although John Jay assured him in March 1786 that breakup of the nation seemed near and opinion for a constitutional convention was crystallizing, Washington remained noncommittal. But, despite long hesitations, he earnestly supported the proposal for a federal impost, warning the states that their policy must decide "whether the Revolution must ultimately be considered a blessing or a curse." And his numerous letters to the leading men of the country assisted greatly to form a sentiment favorable to a more perfect union. Some understanding being necessary between Virginia and Maryland regarding the navigation of the Potomac, commissioners from the two states had met at Mount Vernon in the spring of 1785; from this seed sprang the federal convention. Washington approved in advance the call for a gathering of all the states to meet in Philadelphia in May 1787 to "render the Constitution of the Federal Government adequate to the exigencies of the Union." But he was again hesitant about attending, partly because he felt tired and infirm, partly because of doubts about the outcome. Although he hoped to the last to be excused, he was chosen one of Virginia's five delegates.

Washington arrived in Philadelphia on May 13, the day before the opening of the Constitutional Convention, and as soon as a quorum was obtained he was unanimously chosen its president. For four months he presided over the convention, breaking his silence only once upon a minor question of congressional apportionment. Although he said little in debate, no one did more outside the hall to insist on stern measures. "My wish is," he wrote, "that the convention may adopt no temporizing expedients, but probe the defects of the Constitution to the bottom, and provide a radical cure." His weight of character did more than any other single force to bring the convention to an agreement and obtain ratification of the instrument afterward. He did not believe it perfect, though his precise criticisms of it are unknown. But his support gave it victory in Virginia, where he sent copies to Patrick Henry and other leaders with a hint that the alternative to adoption was anarchy, declaring that "it or dis-union is before us to chuse from." He received and personally circulated copies of *The Federalist*. When ratification was obtained, he wrote to leaders in the various states urging that men staunchly favorable to it be elected to Congress. For a time he sincerely believed that, the new framework completed, he would be allowed to retire again to privacy. But all eyes immediately turned to him for the first president. He alone commanded the respect of both the parties engendered by the struggle over ratification, and he alone would be able to give prestige to the republic throughout Europe. In no state was any other name considered. The electors chosen in the first days of 1789 cast a unanimous vote for him, and reluctantly—for his love of peace, his distrust of his own abilities, and his fear that his motives in advocating the new government might be misconstrued all made him unwilling—he accepted.

On April 16, after receiving congressional notification of the honor, he set out from Mount Vernon, reaching New York City in time to be inaugurated on April 30. His journey northward was a celebratory procession as people in every town and village through which he passed turned out to greet him, often with banners and speeches, and in some places with triumphal arches. He came across the Hudson River in a specially built barge decorated in red, white, and blue. The inaugural ceremony was performed on Wall Street, near the spot now marked by John Quincy Adams Ward's statue of Washington. A great crowd broke into cheers as, standing on the balcony of Federal Hall, he took the oath administered by Chancellor Robert Livingston and retired indoors to read Congress his inaugural address. Washington was clad in a brown suit of American manufacture, but he wore white stockings and a sword after the fashion of European courts.

Martha was as reluctant as her husband to resume public life. But a month later she came from Mount Vernon to join him. She, too, was greeted wildly on her way. And when Washington crossed the Hudson to bring her to Manhattan, guns boomed in salute. The Washingtons, to considerable public criticism, traveled about in a coach-and-four like monarchs. Moreover, during his presidency, Washington did not shake hands, and he met his guests on state occasions while standing on a raised platform and displaying a sword on his hip. Slowly, feeling his way, Washington was defining the style of the first president of a country in the history of the world. The people, too, were adjusting to a government without a king. Even the question of how to address a president had to be discussed. It was decided that in a republic the simple salutation "Mr. President" would do.

Washington's administration of the government in the next eight years was marked by the caution, the methodical precision, and the sober judgment that had always characterized him. He regarded himself as standing aloof from party divisions and emphasized his position as president of the whole country by touring first through the northern states and later through the southern. A painstaking inquiry into all the problems confronting the new nation laid the basis for a series of judicious recommendations to Congress in his first message. In selecting the four members of his first cabinet—Thomas Jefferson as secretary of state, Alexander Hamilton as secretary of treasury, Henry Knox as secretary of war, and Edmund Randolph as attorney general—Washington balanced the two parties evenly. But he leaned with especial weight upon Hamilton, who supported his scheme for the federal assumption of state debts, took his view that the bill establishing the Bank of the United States was constitutional, and in general favored strengthening the authority of the federal government. Distressed when the inevitable clash between Jefferson and Hamilton arose, he tried to keep harmony, writing frankly to each and refusing to accept their resignations.

But when war was declared between France and England in 1793, he took Hamilton's view that the United States should completely disregard the treaty of alliance with France and pursue a course of strict neutrality, while he acted decisively to stop the improper operations of the French minister, Edmond-Charles Genet. He had a firm belief that the United States must insist on its national identity, strength, and dignity. His object, he wrote, was to keep the country "free from political connections with every other country, to see them independent of all, and under the influence of none. In a word, I want an American character that the powers of Europe may be convinced that we act for ourselves, and not for others." The sequel was the resignation of Jefferson at the close of 1793, the two men parting on good terms and Washington praising Jefferson's "integrity and talents." The suppression of the Whiskey Rebellion in 1794 by federal troops whom Hamilton led in person and the dispatch of John Jay to conclude a treaty of commerce with Great Britain tended further to align Washington with the federalists. Although the general voice of the people compelled him to acquiesce reluctantly to a second term in 1792 and his election that year was again unanimous, during his last four years in office he suffered from a fierce personal and partisan animosity. This culminated when the publication of the terms of the Jay Treaty, which Washington signed in August 1795, provoked a bitter discussion, and the House of Representatives called upon the president for the instructions and correspondence relating to the treaty. These Washington, who had already clashed with the Senate on foreign affairs, refused to deliver, and in the face of an acrimonious debate, he firmly maintained his position.

Early in his first term, Washington, who by education and natural inclination was minutely careful of the proprieties of life, established the rules of a virtual republican court. In both New York and Philadelphia he rented the best houses procurable, refusing to accept the hospitality of George Clinton, for he believed the head of the nation should be no man's guest. He returned no calls and shook hands with no one, acknowledging salutations by a formal bow. He drove in a coach drawn by four or six smart horses, with outriders and lackeys in rich livery. He attended receptions dressed in a black velvet suit with gold buckles, with yellow gloves, powdered hair, a cocked hat with an ostrich plume in one hand, and a sword in a white leather scabbard. After being overwhelmed by callers, he announced that except for a weekly levee open to all, persons desiring to see him had to make appointments in advance. On Friday afternoons the first lady held informal receptions, at which the president appeared. Although the presidents of the Continental Congress had made their tables partly public, Washington, who entertained largely, inviting members of Congress in rotation, insisted that his hospitality be private. He served good wines and the menus were elaborate, but such visitors as Pennsylvania Senator William Maclay complained that the atmosphere was too "solemn." Indeed, his simple ceremony offended many of the more radical anti-federalists, who did not share his sense of its fitness and accused the president of conducting himself like a king. But his cold and reserved manner was caused by native diffidence rather than any excessive sense of dignity.

Earnestly desiring leisure, feeling a decline of his physical powers, and wincing under abuses of the opposition, Washington refused to yield to the general pressure for a third term. This refusal was blended with a testament of sagacious advice to his country in the Farewell Address of September 19, 1796, written largely by Hamilton but remolded by Washington and expressing his ideas. Retiring in March 1797 to Mount Vernon, he devoted himself for the last two and a half years of his life to his family, farm operations, and care of his slaves. In 1798 his seclusion was briefly interrupted when the prospect of war with France caused his appointment as commander in chief of the provisional army, and he was much worried by the political quarrels over high commissions, but the war cloud passed away.

On December 12, 1799, after riding on horseback for several hours in cold and snow, he returned home exhausted and was attacked late the next day with quinsy or acute laryngitis. He was bled heavily four times and given gargles of "molasses, vinegar and butter," and a blister of cantharides (a preparation of dried beetles) was placed on his throat, his strength meanwhile rapidly sinking. He faced the end with characteristic serenity, saying, "I die hard, but I am not afraid to go," and later: "I feel myself going. I thank you for your attentions; but I pray you to take no more trouble about me. Let me go off quietly. I cannot last long." After giving instructions to his secretary, Tobias Lear, about his burial, he died at 10:00 P.M. on December 14. The news of his death placed the entire country in mourning, and the sentiment of the country endorsed the famous words of Henry ("Light-Horse Harry") Lee, embodied in resolutions that John Marshall introduced in the House of Representatives, that he was "first in war, first in peace, and first in the hearts of his countrymen." When the news reached Europe, the British channel fleet and the armies of Napoleon paid tribute to his memory, and many of the leaders of the time joined in according him a preeminent place among the heroes of history. His fellow citizens memorialized him forever by naming the newly created capital city of the young nation for him while he was still alive. Later, one of the states of union would bear his name—the only state named for an individual American. Moreover, counties in 32 states were given his name, and in time it also could be found in 121 postal addresses. The people of the United States have continued to glory in knowing him as "the father of his country," an accolade he was pleased to accept, even though it pained him that he fathered no children of his own. For almost a century beginning in the 1770s, Washington was the uncontested giant in the American pantheon of greats, but only until Abraham Lincoln was enshrined there after another critical epoch in the life of the country.

A CLOSER LOOK

The Presidency of the United States of America

by Forrest McDonald

In contrast to many countries with parliamentary forms of government, where the office of president, or head of state, is mainly ceremonial, in the United States the president is vested with great authority and is arguably the most powerful elected official in the world. The nation's founders originally intended the presidency to be a narrowly restricted institution. They distrusted executive authority because their experience with colonial governors had taught them that executive power was inimical to liberty, because they felt betrayed by the actions of George III, the king of Great Britain and Ireland, and because they considered a strong executive incompatible with the republicanism embraced in the Declaration of Independence (1776). Accordingly, their revolutionary state constitutions provided for only nominal executive branches, and the Articles of Confederation (1781–89), the first "national" constitution, established no executive branch.

The Constitution succinctly defines presidential functions, powers, and responsibilities. The president's chief duty is to make sure that the laws are faithfully executed, and this duty is performed through an elaborate system of executive agencies that includes cabinet-level departments. Presidents appoint all cabinet heads and most other high-ranking officials of the executive branch of the federal government. They also nominate all judges of the federal judiciary, including the members of the Supreme Court. Their appointments to executive and judicial posts must be approved by a majority of the Senate (one of the two chambers of Congress, the legislative branch of the federal government, the other being the House of Representatives).

The Senate usually confirms these appointments, though it occasionally rejects a nominee to whom a majority of members have strong objections. The president is also the commander in chief of the country's military and has unlimited authority to direct the movements of land, sea, and air forces. The president has the power to make treaties with foreign governments, though the Senate must approve such treaties by a two-thirds majority. Finally, the president has the power to approve or reject (veto) bills passed by Congress, though Congress can override the president's veto by summoning a two-thirds majority in favor of the measure.

By the time the Constitutional Convention assembled in Philadelphia on May 25, 1787, wartime and postwar difficulties had convinced most of the delegates that an energetic national executive was necessary. They approached the problem warily, however, and a third of them favored a proposal that would have allowed Congress to select multiple single-term executives, each of whom would be subject to recall by state governors. The subject consumed more debate at the convention than any other. The stickiest points were the method of election and the length of the executive's term. At first, delegates supported the idea that the executive should be chosen by Congress; however, congressional selection would make the executive dependent on the legislature unless the president were ineligible for reelection, and ineligibility would necessitate a dangerously long term (six or seven years was the most common suggestion).

The delegates debated the method of election until early September 1787, less than two weeks before the convention ended. Finally, the Committee on Unfinished Parts, chaired by David Brearley of New Jersey, put forward a cumbersome proposal—the electoral college—that overcame all objections. The system allowed state legislatures—or the voting public if the legislatures so decided—to choose electors equal in number to the states' representatives and senators combined; the electors would vote for two candidates, one of whom had to be a resident of another state. Whoever received a majority of the votes would be elected president, the runner-up vice president. If no one won a majority, the choice would be made by the House of Representatives, each state delegation casting one vote. The president would serve a four-year term and be eligible for continual reelection (by the Twenty-second Amendment, adopted in 1951, the president was limited to a maximum of two terms). Until agreement on the electoral college, delegates were unwilling to entrust the executive with significant author-ity, and most executive powers, including the conduct of foreign relations, were held by the Senate. The delegates hastily shifted powers to the executive, and the result was ambiguous. Article II, Section 1, of the U.S. Constitution begins with a simple declarative statement: "The executive Power shall be vested in a President of the United States of America." The phrasing can be read as a blanket grant of power, an interpretation that is buttressed when the language is compared with the qualified language of Article I: "All legislative Powers herein granted shall be vested in a Congress of the United States."

This loose construction, however, is mitigated in two impor-tant ways. First, Article II itemizes, in sections 2 and 3, certain presidential powers, including those of commander in chief of the armed forces, appointment making, treaty making, receiving ambassadors, and calling Congress into special session. Had the first article's section been intended as an open-ended authoriza-tion, such subsequent specifications would have made no sense. Second, a sizeable array of powers traditionally associated with the executive, including the power to declare war, issue letters of marque and reprisal, and coin and borrow money, were given to Congress, not the president, and the power to make appoint-ments and treaties was shared between the president and the Senate.

The delegates could leave the subject ambiguous because of their understanding that George Washington (1789–97) would be selected as the first president. They deliberately left blanks in Article II, trusting that Washington would fill in the details in a satisfactory manner. Indeed, it is safe to assert that had Washington not been available, the office might never have been created.

Scarcely had Washington been inaugurated when an extra-constitutional attribute of the presidency became apparent. Inherently, the presidency is dual in character. The president serves as both head of government (the nation's chief administrator) and head of state (the symbolic embodiment of the nation). Through centuries of constitutional struggle between the crown and Parliament, England had separated the two offices, vesting the prime minister with the function of running the government and leaving the ceremonial responsibilities of leadership to the monarch. The American people idolized Washington, and he played his part artfully, striking a balance between "too free an intercourse and too much familiarity," which would reduce the dignity of the office, and "an ostentatious show" of aloofness, which would be improper in a republic.

But the problems posed by the dual nature of the office remained unsolved. A few presidents, notably Thomas Jefferson (1801–09) and Franklin D. Roosevelt (1933–45), proved able to perform both roles. More common were the examples of John F. Kennedy (1961–63) and Lyndon B. Johnson (1963–69). Although Kennedy was superb as the symbol of a vigorous nation—Americans were entranced by the image of his presidency as Camelot—he was ineffectual in getting legislation enacted. Johnson, by contrast, pushed through Congress a legislative program of major proportions, including the Civil Rights Act of 1964, but he was such a failure as a king surrogate that he chose not to run for a second term.

Washington's administration was most important for the precedents it set. For example, he retired after two terms, establishing a tradition maintained until 1940. During his first term he made the presidency a full-fledged branch of government instead of a mere office. As commander in chief during the

American Revolutionary War, he had been accustomed to surrounding himself with trusted aides and generals and soliciting their opinions. Gathering the department heads together seemed a logical extension of that practice, but the Constitution authorized him only to "require the Opinion, in writing" of the department heads; taking the document literally would have precluded converting them into an advisory council. When the Supreme Court refused Washington's request for an advisory opinion on the matter of a neutrality proclamation in response to the French revolutionary and Napoleonic wars—on the ground that the court could decide only cases and not controversies—he turned at last to assembling his department heads. Cabinet meetings, as they came to be called, remained the principal instrument for conducting executive business until the late 20th century, though some early presidents, such as Andrew Jackson (1829–37), made little use of the cabinet.

The Constitution also authorized the president to make treaties "by and with the Advice and Consent of the Senate," and many thought that this clause would turn the Senate into an executive council. But when Washington appeared on the floor of the Senate to seek advice about pending negotiations with American Indian tribes, the surprised senators proved themselves to be a contentious deliberative assembly, not an advisory board. Washington was furious, and thereafter neither he nor his successors took the "advice" portion of the clause seriously. At about the same time, it was established by an act of Congress that although the president had to seek the approval of the Senate for his major appointments, he could remove his appointees unilaterally. This power remained a subject of controversy and was central to the impeachment of Andrew Johnson (1865–69) in 1868.

Washington set other important precedents, especially in foreign policy. In his Farewell Address (1796) he cautioned his successors to "steer clear of permanent alliances with any portion of the foreign world" and not to "entangle our peace and prosperity in the toils of European ambition, rivalship, interest, humor, or caprice." His warnings laid the foundation for America's isolationist foreign policy, which lasted through most of the country's history before World War II, as well as for the Monroe Doctrine.

Perils accompanying the French revolutionary wars occupied Washington's attention, as well as that of his three immediate successors. Americans were bitterly divided over the wars, some favoring Britain and its allies and others France. Political factions had already arisen over the financial policies of Washington's secretary of the treasury, Alexander Hamilton, and from 1793 onward animosities stemming from the French Revolution hardened these factions into a system of political parties, which the framers of the Constitution had not contemplated.

The emergence of the party system also created unanticipated problems with the method for electing the president. In 1796 John Adams (1797–1801), the candidate of the Federalist Party, won the presidency and Thomas Jefferson (1801–09), the candidate of the Democratic-Republican Party, won the vice presidency; rather than working with Adams, however, Jefferson sought to undermine the administration. In 1800, to forestall the possibility of yet another divided executive, the Federalists and the Democratic-Republicans, the two leading parties of the early republic, each nominated presidential and vice presidential candidates. Because of party-line voting and the fact that electors could not indicate a presidential or vice presidential preference between the two candidates for whom they voted, the Democratic-Republican candidates, Jefferson and Aaron Burr, received an equal number of votes. The election was thrown to the House of Representatives, and a constitutional crisis nearly ensued as the House became deadlocked. Had it remained deadlocked until the end of Adams's term on March 4, 1801, Supreme Court Chief Justice John Marshall would have become president in keeping with the existing presidential succession act. On February 17, 1801, Jefferson was finally chosen president

by the House, and with the ratification of the Twelfth Amendment, beginning in 1804, electors were required to cast separate
ballots for president and vice president.

Jefferson shaped the presidency almost as much as did
Washington. He altered the style of the office, departing from
Washington's austere dignity so far as to receive foreign
ministers in run-down slippers and frayed jackets. He shunned
display, protocol, and pomp; he gave no public balls or celebrations on his birthday. By completing the transition to republicanism, he humanized the presidency and made it a symbol not
of the nation but of the people. He talked persuasively about
the virtue of limiting government—his first inaugural address
was a masterpiece on the subject—and he made gestures in that
direction. He slashed the army and navy, reduced the public
debt, and ended what he regarded as the "monarchical" practice of addressing Congress in person. But he also stretched the
powers of the presidency in a variety of ways. While maintaining
a posture of deference toward Congress, he managed legislation
more effectively than any other president of the 19th century.
He approved the Louisiana Purchase despite his private conviction that it was unconstitutional. He conducted a lengthy and
successful war against the Barbary pirates of North Africa without seeking a formal declaration of war from Congress. He used
the army against the interests of the American people in his
efforts to enforce an embargo that was intended to compel
Britain and France to respect America's rights as a neutral
during the Napoleonic wars and ultimately to bring those two
countries to the peace table. In 1810 Jefferson wrote in a
letter that circumstances "sometimes occur" when "officers of
high trust" must "assume authorities beyond the law" in keeping
with the "*salus populi* . . . , the laws of necessity, of self-preserva-
tion, of saving our country when in danger." On those occasions
"a scrupulous adherence to written law, would be to lose the law
itself . . . thus absurdly sacrificing the end to the means."

From Jefferson's departure until the end of the century, the presidency was perceived as an essentially passive institution. Only three presidents during that long span acted with great energy, and each elicited a vehement congressional reaction. Andrew Jackson exercised the veto flamboyantly; attempted, in the so-called Bank War, to undermine the Bank of the United States by removing federal deposits; and sought to mobilize the army against South Carolina when that state adopted an Ordinance of Nullification declaring the federal tariffs of 1828 and 1832 to be null and void within its boundaries. By the time his term ended, the Senate had censured him and refused to receive his messages. (When Democrats regained control of the Senate from the Whigs, Jackson's censure was expunged.) James K. Polk (1845–49) maneuvered the United States into the Mexican War and only later sought a formal congressional declaration. When he asserted that "a state of war exists" with Mexico, Senator John C. Calhoun of South Carolina launched a tirade against him, insisting that a state of war could not exist unless Congress declared one. The third strong president during the period, Abraham Lincoln (1861–65), defending the *salus populi* in Jeffersonian fashion, ran roughshod over the Constitution during the American Civil War. Radical Republican congressmen were, at the time of his assassination, sharpening their knives in opposition to his plans for reconstructing the rebellious Southern states, and they wielded them to devastating effect against his successor, Andrew Johnson. They reduced the presidency to a cipher, demonstrating that Congress can be more powerful than the president if it acts with complete unity. Johnson was impeached on several grounds, including his violation of the Tenure of Office Act, which forbade the president from removing civil officers without the consent of the Senate. Although Johnson was not convicted, he and the presidency were weakened.

Although the framers of the Constitution established a system for electing the president—the electoral college—they did not devise a method for nominating presidential candidates or even for choosing electors. They assumed that the selection process as a whole would be nonpartisan and devoid of factions (or political parties), which they believed were always a corrupting influence in politics. The original process worked well in the early years of the republic, when Washington, who was not affiliated closely with any faction, was the unanimous choice of electors in both 1789 and 1792. However, the rapid development of political parties soon presented a major challenge, one that led to changes that would make presidential elections more partisan but ultimately more democratic.

As discussed above, the practical and constitutional inadequacies of the original electoral college system became evident in the election of 1800, when the two Democratic-Republican candidates, Jefferson and Burr, received an equal number of electoral votes and thereby left the presidential election to be decided by the House of Representatives. The Twelfth Amendment (1804), which required electors to vote for president and vice president separately, remedied this constitutional defect.

Because each state was free to devise its own system of choosing electors, disparate methods initially emerged. In some states electors were appointed by the legislature, in others they were popularly elected, and in still others a mixed approach was used. In the first presidential election, in 1789, four states (Delaware, Maryland, Pennsylvania, and Virginia) used systems based on popular election. Popular election gradually replaced legislative appointment, the most common method through the 1790s, until by the 1830s all states except South Carolina chose electors by direct popular vote.

Forrest McDonald is Distinguished University Professor (Emeritus) at the University of Alabama. His books include Novus Ordo Seclorum: The Intellectual Origins of the Constitution *(1985),* The American Presidency: An Intellectual History *(1994),* States' Rights and the Union: Imperium in Imperio, 1776–1876 *(2000), and* Recovering the Past: A Historian's Memoir *(2004).*

▊ Whiskey Rebellion

In American history, the Whiskey Rebellion (1794) was an uprising that afforded the new U.S. government its first opportunity to establish federal authority by military means within state boundaries, as officials moved into western Pennsylvania to quell an uprising of farmers rebelling against the liquor tax. Alexander Hamilton, secretary of the Treasury, had proposed the excise (enacted by Congress in 1791) to raise money for the national debt and to assert the power of the national government. Small farmers of the back country, who distilled and consumed whiskey in prodigious quantities, resisted the tax by attacking federal revenue officers who attempted to collect it.

Enforcement legislation touched off what appeared to be an organized rebellion, and in July 1794 about 500 armed men attacked and burned the home of the regional tax inspector. The following month President George Washington issued a congressionally authorized proclamation ordering the rebels to return home and calling for militia from four neighboring states. After fruitless negotiations, Washington ordered some 13,000 troops into the area, but opposition melted away and no battle ensued. Troops occupied the region and some of the rebels were tried, but the two convicted of treason were later pardoned by the president.

Many Americans, particularly members of the opposition Jeffersonian Republican Party, were appalled by the overwhelming use of governmental force, which they feared might be a first step to absolute power. To Federalists, however, the most important result was that the national authority had triumphed over its first rebellious adversary and had won the support of the state governments in enforcing federal law within the states.

Wilson, James

A colonial American lawyer and political theorist, James Wilson (1742–98) was a signer of the Declaration of Independence and member of the Constitutional Convention of 1787.

Immigrating to North America in 1765, Wilson taught Greek and rhetoric in the College of Philadelphia and then studied law under John Dickinson, statesman and delegate to the First Continental Congress. Wilson's fame spread with publication in 1774 of his treatise *Considerations on the Nature and Extent of the Legislative Authority of the British Parliament*. In this work he set out a scheme of empire in which the British colonies would have the equivalent of dominion status. In 1774 he became a member of the Committee of Correspondence in Cumberland County, Pennsylvania, and he served as a delegate to the Second Continental Congress. In 1779 he was appointed advocate general for France and represented that country in cases rising out of its alliance with the American colonies. He became a champion of the Bank of North America and an associate of merchant-banker Robert Morris in his struggle for currency reform after 1781. As a member of the federal Congress (1783; 1785–86), he pressed for an amendment to the Articles of Confederation to permit Congress to levy a general tax.

During the Constitutional Convention in 1787, Wilson helped to draft the U.S. Constitution; he then led the fight for ratification in Pennsylvania. In 1790 he engineered the drafting of Pennsylvania's new constitution and delivered a series of lectures that are landmarks in the evolution of American jurisprudence. He was appointed an associate justice of the U.S. Supreme Court (1789–98), where his most notable decision was that on *Chisholm* v. *Georgia*. In the winter of 1796–97 financial ruin brought on by unwise land speculation shattered his health and ended his career.

Witherspoon, John

A Scottish-American Presbyterian minister and president of the College of New Jersey (now Princeton University), John Witherspoon (1723–94) was the only clergyman to sign the Declaration of Independence.

After completing his theological studies at the University of Edinburgh (1743), he was called to the parish of Beith in 1745 and in 1757 became pastor at Paisley. A conservative churchman, he frequently involved himself in ecclesiastical controversies, in which he proved himself a keen dialectician and an effective speaker. In 1768 he left Paisley to assume the presidency of the College of New Jersey. He was warmly received by the American Presbyterian Church and contributed significantly to its revitalization and growth. He was a vigorous college president, expanding the curriculum, providing scientific equipment, and working to increase the endowment and enrollment.

From his arrival, Witherspoon was an enthusiast about America, and in the dispute with the mother country he ranged himself uncompromisingly on the side of the colonists. He presided over the Somerset County Committee of Correspondence (1775–76), was a member of two provincial congresses, and was a delegate to the Continental Congress (1776–79, 1780–82), where in 1776 he was a persuasive advocate of adopting a resolution of independence.

Witherspoon wrote extensively on religious and political topics. His works include *Ecclesiastical Characteristics* (1753), *Considerations on the Nature and Extent of the Legislative Authority of the British Parliament* (1774), as well as numerous essays, sermons, and pamphlets.

Wolcott, Oliver

Oliver Wolcott (1726–97) was an American public official who signed the Declaration of Independence (1776) and helped negotiate a settlement with the Iroquois (1784).

Descended from an old Connecticut family long active in public affairs, he was the son of Roger Wolcott, who was the colonial governor in 1750–54. Settling in Litchfield County, where he practiced law and was made sheriff (1751), he became a member of the Connecticut council (1771–86) and a delegate to the Continental Congress in Philadelphia. At the beginning of the Revolution, Wolcott signed the Declaration of Independence, then returned home to raise a state militia, which he commanded in defense of New York City (August 1776). The following year he organized more Connecticut volunteers and took part in the successful campaign against General John Burgoyne. In 1779 he commanded Continental troops during the British invasion of his home state.

Wolcott had been appointed a commissioner for northern Indian affairs in 1775. After the war he helped negotiate the Second Treaty of Fort Stanwix, which redrew the western boundaries of the Six (Iroquois) Nations. He went on to serve as Connecticut's lieutenant governor (1787–96) and governor (1796–97), as well as a member of the Connecticut convention that ratified the new federal Constitution.

His son, Oliver Wolcott (1760–1833), continued the family tradition of public service as U.S. secretary of the treasury (1795–1800) and governor of Connecticut (1817–27).

Wythe, George

George Wythe (1726–1806) was a jurist and one of the first U.S. judges to state the principle that a court can invalidate a law considered to be unconstitutional. He also was probably the first great American law teacher, whose pupils included such well-known figures as Thomas Jefferson, John Marshall, and Henry Clay.

Admitted to the bar in 1746, Wythe was a member (1754–55, 1758–68) and clerk (1769–75) of the Virginia House of Burgesses. In 1764 he drew up a forceful remonstrance from Virginia to the British House of Commons against the Stamp Act. In 1776 Wythe, as a delegate to the Continental Congress, signed the Declaration of Independence. Also in that year he was appointed, with Jefferson, Edmund Pendleton, and George Mason, to revise the laws of Virginia. He was a member of the Constitutional Convention (1787) and of the Virginia convention (1788) that ratified the federal Constitution.

A chancery judge from 1778, Wythe became sole chancellor of Virginia in 1788. As an *ex officio* member of the state supreme court, Wythe, in the case of *Commonwealth* v. *Caton* (1782), asserted the power of courts to refuse to enforce unconstitutional laws.

The future President Jefferson studied law in Wythe's office, at Williamsburg, Virginia, in the 1760s. Appointed through Jefferson's influence, Wythe held (1779–89), at the College of William and Mary, the first U.S. professorship of law. One of his students there in 1780 was John Marshall, later chief justice of the United States. Wythe's appointment as chancellor of Virginia required him to resign from the college and move to Richmond, where he opened a private school of law. Among his pupils in Richmond, and clerk of his court, was the future U.S. senator Henry Clay.

Wythe died of poisoning. A grandnephew and heir, George Wythe Sweeney, was acquitted of the murder in a trial in which the only witness was, as a Negro, disqualified from testifying.

Bibliography

Bibliography

Numerous authors contributed to the material compiled in this book. Many of these writers are listed here, along with a sampling of their books: Samuel Flagg Bemis (*John Quincy Adams and the Foundations of American Foreign Policy, A Diplomatic History of the United States*); Irving Brant (*James Madison*); Betty Boyd Caroli (*First Ladies: From Martha Washington to Laura Bush*); Alexander DeConde (*The Quasi-War: The Politics and Diplomacy of the Undeclared War with France, 1797–1801*); Joseph J. Ellis (*American Sphinx: The Character of Thomas Jefferson, Passionate Sage: The Character and Legacy of John Adams, Founding Brothers: The Revolutionary Generation*); Henry F. Graff (*America: The Glorious Republic, The Presidents: A Reference History*); David L. Holmes (*The Faiths of the Founding Fathers*); Theodore Hornberger (*Benjamin Franklin*); Forrest McDonald (*The American Presidency: An Intellectual History, Novus Ordo Seclorum: The Intellectual Origins of the Constitution, Alexander Hamilton: A Biography*); Allan Nevins (*The American States During and After the Revolution, 1775–1789; A Short History of the United States,* with Henry Steele Commager; *Ordeal of the Union*); William M. Wallace (*Appeal to Arms: A Military History of the American Revolution*); and Gordon S. Wood (*Revolutionary Characters: What Made the Founders Different, The Americanization of Benjamin Franklin, The Radicalism of the American Revolution*).

Founding Fathers

OVERVIEWS

Although the recent scholarship on late-18th century America has tended to focus elsewhere, there are several seminal studies of the Founders as a collective. These include Douglass Adair in Trevor Colbourn (ed.), *Fame and the Founding Fathers: Essays by Douglass Adair*

(1971); Bernard Bailyn, *To Begin the World Anew: The Genius and Ambiguities of the American Founders* (2000); Wesley Frank Craven, *The Legend of the Founding Fathers* (1956); Joseph J. Ellis, *Founding Brothers: The Revolutionary Generation* (2000); David L. Holmes, *The Faiths of the Founding Fathers* (2003); and Gordon S. Wood, *Revolutionary Characters: What Made the Founders Different* (2006). On the debunking side of the coin, the classic work is Charles A. Beard, *An Economic Interpretation of the Constitution* (1913, reissued 1935, 1986). Also useful is John Bach McMaster, *The Political Depravity of the Founding Fathers* (1896, reissued 1964).

RECENT WORKS

The recent surge of interest in the Founding Fathers has produced an impressive collection of volumes that, taken together, have begun to alter the old bimodal paradigm. Here are the major titles: H.W. Brands, *The First American: The Life and Times of Benjamin Franklin* (2000); Richard Brookhiser, *Founding Father: Rediscovering George Washington* (1996); Ron Chernow, *Alexander Hamilton* (2004); Saul Cornell, *The Other Founders: Anti-Federalism and the Dissenting Tradition in America, 1788–1828* (1999); Joseph J. Ellis, *Passionate Sage: The Character and Legacy of John Adams* (1993), *American Sphinx: The Character of Thomas Jefferson* (1997), *Founding Brothers: The Revolutionary Generation* (2000), and *His Excellency: George Washington* (2004); Stanley M. Elkins and Eric L. McKitrick, *The Age of Federalism: The Early American Republic, 1788–1800* (1993); John E. Ferling, *Setting the World Ablaze: Washington, Adams, Jefferson, and the American Revolution* (2000); David Hackett Fischer, *Washington's Crossing* (2004); Peter R. Henriques, *Realistic Visionary: A Portrait of George Washington* (2006); Walter Isaacson, *Benjamin Franklin: An American Life* (2003); Pauline Maier, *American Scripture: Making the Declaration of Independence* (1997); Drew R. McCoy, *The Last of the Founders: James Madison and the Republican Legacy* (1989); David McCullough, *John Adams* (2001) and *1776* (2005); Edmund S. Morgan, *Benjamin Franklin* (2002); Jack N. Rakove, *Original Meanings: Politics and Ideas in the Making of the Constitution* (1996); Jean Edward Smith, *John Marshall: Definer of a Nation* (1996); Anthony F.C. Wallace, *Jefferson and the Indians: The Tragic Fate of the First Americans* (1999); and Henry Wiencek, *An Imperfect God: George Washington, His Slaves, and the Creation of America* (2003).

American Revolution

Bernard Bailyn, *The Ideological Origins of the American Revolution*, enlarged ed. (1992), examines the transmission of English republican ideology and its American reception. John Richard Alden, *The American Revolution, 1775–1783* (1954, reissued 1987), is distinguished for its political and military analyses. Jack P. Greene (ed.), *The American Revolution: Its Character and Limits* (1987), contains a valuable collection of essays. Robert Middlekauff, *The Glorious Cause: The American Revolution, 1763–1789* (1982, reprinted 1985), examines the revolution from a somewhat older point of view than is now fashionable. Piers Mackesy, *The War for America, 1775–1783* (1964, reissued 1993), explains the British side of the war. J.G.A. Pocock (ed.), *Three British Revolutions: 1641, 1688, 1776* (1980), sets the American Revolution in the historical context of British experience. Military histories include John Shy, *Toward Lexington: The Role of the British Army in the Coming of the American Revolution* (1965), on the British army in America; Don Higginbotham, *The War of American Independence: Military Attitudes, Policies, and Practice, 1763–1789* (1971, reprinted 1983), which shows the interrelationship of military and political developments; Charles Royster, *A Revolutionary People at War: The Continental Army and American Character, 1775–1783* (1979, reissued 1986); and William M. Fowler, Jr., *Rebels Under Sail* (1976), on the American navy.

Presidency of the United States

General studies, organized historically, include Forrest McDonald, *The American Presidency: An Intellectual History* (1994); Sidney M. Milkis and Michael Nelson, *The American Presidency: Origins and Developments, 1776–2002*, 4th ed. (2003); and a classic earlier work, Edward S. Corwin, *The President: Office and Powers, 1787–1957*, 4th rev. ed. (1957).

Analyses of the office by its functions are Thomas E. Cronin, *The State of the Presidency*, 2nd ed. (1980); Louis W. Koenig, *The Chief Executive*, 6th ed. (1996); and Richard M. Pious, *The American Presidency* (1979).

A wide-ranging study by a variety of specialists is Thomas E. Cronin (ed.), *Inventing the American Presidency* (1989). An important work whose approach is indicated by its title is Arthur M. Schlesinger,

Jr., *The Imperial Presidency* (1973, reissued 1998). Crucial to understanding the inner dynamics of the office is Richard E. Neustadt, *Presidential Power and the Modern Presidents*, rev. ed. (1990).

Constitution of the United States

Catherine Drinker Bowen, *Miracle at Philadelphia* (1966, reissued 1986), examines the debates in and the events surrounding the Constitutional Convention. Books focusing on the origins and intent of the framers of the Constitution include Jack N. Rakove, *Original Meanings: Politics and Ideas in the Making of the Constitution* (1996); and Forrest McDonald, *Novus Ordo Seclorum: The Intellectual Origins of the Constitution* (1985). Michael Kammen, *A Machine That Would Go of Itself: The Constitution in American Culture* (1986, reissued 1994), discusses the significance of the Constitution in American political culture. Charles A. Beard, *An Economic Interpretation of the Constitution of the United States* (1913, reissued 1998), is a critical analysis of the motives of the Constitution's framers.

George Washington

Washington's writings are collected in John C. Fitzpatrick (ed.), *The Writings of George Washington from the Original Manuscript Sources, 1745–1799*, 39 vol. (1931–44, reprinted 1972), a full compilation, excluding only the diaries; these were published separately as *Diaries of George Washington, 1748–1799*, 4 vol. (1925, reissued 1971); and Donald Jackson and Dorothy Twohig (eds.), *The Diaries of George Washington*, 6 vol. (1976–79). Dorothy Twohig (ed.), *The Journal of the Proceedings of the President, 1793–1797* (1981), is an annotated executive daybook covering years for most of which the diaries have not been found. A more recent edition of Washington's correspondence and documents is *The Papers of George Washington*, in four separate series: W.W. Abbot et al. (eds.), *Colonial Series* (1983–); Philander D. Chase (ed.), *Revolutionary War Series* (1985–); W.W. Abbot et al. (eds.), *Confederation Series* (1992–); and Dorothy Twohig (ed.), *Presidential Series* (1987–).

Much the fullest and best biography and a corrective to earlier works is that by Douglas Southall Freeman, *George Washington, A Biography*, 7 vol. (1948–57)—vol. 7 was written by J.A. Carroll and M.W. Ashworth. M.L. Weems, *A History of the Life and Death, Virtues and Exploits, of General George Washington* (1800), was the first edition of the utterly unreliable but most widely distributed early biography, which has been reissued in numerous later editions, often titled *The Life of Washington*; the 5th ed., retitled *The Life of George Washington the Great* (1806), introduced the fictitious anecdote about the hatchet and the cherry tree. Among the best modern works are Shelby Little, *George Washington* (1929, reissued 1962); John C. Fitzpatrick, *George Washington Himself* (1933, reprinted 1975); James Thomas Flexner, *George Washington: The Forge of Experience, 1732–1775* (1965), *George Washington in the American Revolution, 1775–1783* (1968, reissued 1972), *George Washington and the New Nation, 1783–1793* (1970), *George Washington: Anguish and Farewell (1793–1799)* (1972), and *Washington: The Indispensable Man* (1974, reissued 1984); Marcus Cunliffe, *George Washington, Man and Monument*, rev. ed. (1982); and Richard Brookhiser, *Founding Father: Rediscovering George Washington* (1996). Other works dealing with Washington's life and career are Charles Cecil Wall, *George Washington, Citizen-Soldier* (1980), emphasizing his personal life; John R. Alden, *George Washington: A Biography* (1984), focusing on his role in the military and as president; Robert F. Jones, *George Washington*, rev. ed. (1986); John E. Ferling, *The First of Men: A Life of George Washington* (1988), seeking the correlation between the man and his career, and *Setting the World Ablaze: Washington, Adams, Jefferson, and the American Revolution* (2000); Joseph J. Ellis, *His Excellency: George Washington* (2004); David Hackett Fischer, *Washington's Crossing* (2004); and Peter R. Henriques, *Realistic Visionary: A Portrait of George Washington* (2006). Rosemarie Zagarri (ed.), *David Humphreys' Life of General Washington: With George Washington's "Remarks"* (1991), compiles biographical details written in 1787–89 by a Washington aide-de-camp, complete with Washington's comments and corrections.

Washington's presidency is examined in Thomas G. Frothingham, *Washington, Commander in Chief* (1930); Forrest McDonald, *The Presidency of George Washington* (1974, reissued 1988), a study of the political and economic aspects of his administration; Frank T. Reuter, *Trials and Triumphs: George Washington's Foreign Policy* (1983), a useful introductory study; and Richard Norton Smith, *Patriarch: George Washington and the New American Nation* (1993), a detailed treatment of Washington's presidential days. Washington's role in determining the focus and development of the U.S. Constitution is discussed in John Corbin, *The Unknown Washington* (1930, reprinted 1972); and

Glenn A. Phelps, *George Washington and American Constitutionalism* (1993).

Analyses of his military career can be found in Charles H. Ambler, *George Washington and the West* (1936, reprinted 1971); Hugh Cleland, *George Washington in the Ohio Valley* (1955); George Athan Billias (ed.), *George Washington's Generals* (1964, reprinted 1994), with an essay on Washington's generalship; Burke Davis, *George Washington and the American Revolution* (1975), an account of his role as military commander; Edmund S. Morgan, *The Genius of George Washington* (1980), a brief study; Don Higginbotham, *George Washington and the American Military Tradition* (1985), an examination of his public life and life in the military prior to his becoming president; and Thomas A. Lewis, *For King and Country: The Maturing of George Washington, 1748–1760* (1993), with emphasis on the French and Indian War.

Valuable studies on special aspects of Washington's life include Paul Leland Haworth, *George Washington, Farmer* (1915, reissued as *George Washington, Country Gentleman*, 1925); Eugene E. Prussing, *The Estate of George Washington, Deceased* (1927); Halsted L. Ritter, *Washington as a Business Man* (1931); Charles Wyllys Stetson, *Washington and His Neighbors* (1956); Fritz Hirschfeld, *George Washington and Slavery: A Documentary Portrayal* (1997); and Henry Wiencek, *An Imperfect God: George Washington, His Slaves, and the Creation of America* (2003).

Paul Leicester Ford, *The True George Washington* (1896, reprinted 1971; also published as *George Washington*, 1970), is a classic examination of all sides of Washington's career and personality. Charles Moore, *The Family Life of George Washington* (1926), is a look at the president's private life. Paul K. Longmore, *The Invention of George Washington* (1988), is a study that suggests that Washington created his own public image. That public image and its meaning are further analyzed in Garry Wills, *Cincinnatus: George Washington and the Enlightenment* (1984); and Barry Schwartz, *George Washington: The Making of an American Symbol* (1987).

Anne Hollingsworth Wharton, *Martha Washington* (1897, reprinted 1968), is an excellent biography of Washington's wife; it is supplemented by Paul Wilstach, *Mount Vernon: Washington's Home and the Nation's Shrine* (1916, reissued 1930). Correspondence to and from Martha Washington, 1757–1802, is found in Joseph E. Fields (compiler), *Worthy Partner: The Papers of Martha Washington* (1994).

John Adams

The definitive edition of the Adams papers has been published in separate installments. L.H. Butterfield et al. (eds.), *Diary and Autobiography of John Adams*, 4 vol. (1961, reissued 1964); *Adams Family Correspondence*, 6 vol. (1963–93); and *The Book of Abigail and John: Selected Letters of the Adams Family, 1762–1784* (1975, reissued 1997), launched the project, which continued with Robert J. Taylor et al. (eds.), *Papers of John Adams* (1977–). Adams's legal career is handled separately in L. Kinvin Wroth and Hiller B. Zobel (eds.), *Legal Papers of John Adams*, 3 vol. (1965, reprinted 1968). Because the definitive edition remains a work in progress, the only comprehensive edition in print is Charles Francis Adams (ed.), *The Works of John Adams*, 10 vol. (1850–56, reprinted 1971).

Other pieces of the massive Adams correspondence include: Charles Francis Adams (ed.), *Letters of John Adams, Addressed to His Wife*, 2 vol. (1841, reissued 1965); Alexander Biddle et al., *Old Family Letters*, 2 vol. (1892); Worthington Chauncey Ford (ed.), *Statesman and Friend: Correspondence of John Adams with Benjamin Waterhouse, 1784–1822* (1927); Lester J. Cappon (ed.), *The Adams-Jefferson Letters*, 2 vol. (1959, reprinted in 1 vol., 1988); John A. Schutz and Douglass Adair (eds.), *The Spur of Fame: Dialogues of John Adams and Benjamin Rush, 1805–1813* (1966, reissued 1980).

Among the full-length biographies, four stand out: Page Smith, *John Adams*, 2 vol. (1962–63, reprinted in 1 vol., 1988); Peter Shaw, *The Character of John Adams* (1976); John Ferling, *John Adams: A Life* (1992, reissued 1996); and David McCullough, *John Adams* (2001). Although a fictional biography, Catherine Drinker Bowen, *John Adams and the American Revolution* (1950), is unsurpassed in bringing Adams to life during the early stages of his career. For the latter phase of his life, see Joseph J. Ellis, *Passionate Sage: The Character and Legacy of John Adams* (1993). The Adams presidency is the focus of two books: Stephen G. Kurtz, *The Presidency of John Adams: The Collapse of Federalism, 1795–1800* (1957, reissued 1961); and Ralph Adams Brown, *The Presidency of John Adams* (1975). An old but still valuable rendering of the presidential years is Manning J. Dauer, *The Adams Federalists* (1953, reprinted 1984).

Topical accounts of specific moments in Adams's life include Hiller B. Zobel, *The Boston Massacre* (1970, reissued 1996); James H. Hutson, *John Adams and the Diplomacy of the American Revolution* (1980); Alexander DeConde, *The Quasi-War: The Politics and*

Diplomacy of the Undeclared War with France, 1797–1801 (1966); James Morton Smith, *Freedom's Fetters: The Alien and Sedition Laws and American Civil Liberties,* emended ed. (1966); and Merrill D. Peterson, *Adams and Jefferson: A Revolutionary Dialogue* (1976, reissued 1978).

Adams's political thought is the subject of several books. Zoltán Haraszti, *John Adams & the Prophets of Progress* (1952, reissued 1964), is old but still unsurpassed in its revelations based on the marginalia in Adams's books. John R. Howe Jr., *The Changing Political Thought of John Adams* (1966), argues that Adams went through a conservative phase in the 1780s. C. Bradley Thompson, *John Adams and the Spirit of Liberty* (1998), argues for Adams's abiding consistency and has now become the authoritative account. Edward Handler, *America and Europe in the Political Thought of John Adams* (1964), provides an excellent overview of Adams's reactions to major European thinkers.

Four biographies of Abigail Adams provide important insights into the domestic and personal life of the remarkable Adams family: Charles W. Akers, *Abigail Adams: An American Woman,* 2nd ed. (2000); Lynn Withey, *Dearest Friend: A Life of Abigail Adams* (1981); Phyllis Lee Levin, *Abigail Adams: A Biography* (1987); and Edith B. Gelles, *Portia: The World of Abigail Adams* (1992, reissued 1995). The most negative view of Abigail Adams can be found in Paul C. Nagel, *Descent from Glory: Four Generations of the John Adams Family* (1983, reissued 1999), and *The Adams Women: Abigail and Louisa Adams, Their Sisters, and Daughters* (1987, reissued 1999). The multiple paintings of the Adams family are available in Andrew Oliver, *Portraits of John and Abigail Adams* (1967).

Finally, seminal essays on Adams's personality and ideology can be found in several books that focus on larger themes during the Revolutionary era. These include Bernard Bailyn, *Faces of Revolution: Personalities and Themes in the Struggle for American Independence* (1990, reissued 1992); Edmund S. Morgan, *The Meaning of Independence: John Adams, George Washington, Thomas Jefferson* (1976, reissued 1978); and Gordon S. Wood, *The Creation of the American Republic, 1776–1787* (1969, reissued 1998).

Thomas Jefferson

More has been written about Thomas Jefferson than any other figure in American history save Abraham Lincoln. The authoritative bibliography is Frank Shuffelton, *Thomas Jefferson: A Comprehensive, Annotated Bibliography of Writings About Him (1826–1980)* (1983), and *Thomas Jefferson, 1981–1990: An Annotated Bibliography* (1992).

The definitive edition of Jefferson's papers is Julian P. Boyd et al. (eds.), *Papers of Thomas Jefferson* (1950–), which includes extensive editorial notes, all of Jefferson's known letters and writings, plus all correspondence to him that has survived. This multivolume work is an ongoing project, but this edition stops in the mid-1790s, so material relating to his public career as vice president and president, as well as his long retirement, must be obtained from two older editions: Andrew Adgate Lipscomb (ed.), *The Writings of Thomas Jefferson*, 20 vol. (1903–04), is more comprehensive but less reliable; Paul Leicester Ford (ed.), *The Works of Thomas Jefferson*, 12 vol. (1893–99), is more reliable but less comprehensive. Convenient collections of essential primary sources are Merrill D. Peterson (ed.), *The Portable Thomas Jefferson* (1975, reissued 1997), and *Writings* (1984). Several collections of correspondence provide access to specific phases of his career or particular relationships: James Morton Smith (ed.), *The Republic of Letters*, 3 vol. (1995), reproduces the correspondence with James Madison from 1776 to 1826; Douglas L. Wilson and Lucia Stanton (eds.), *Jefferson Abroad* (1999), covers the years in France, 1784 to 1789; Lester J. Cappon (ed.), *The Adams–Jefferson Letters*, 2 vol. (1959, reprinted 1 vol., 1988), provides the extraordinary correspondence with John and Abigail Adams from 1777 to 1826; Edwin Morris Betts and James Adam Bear, Jr. (eds.), *The Family Letters of Thomas Jefferson* (1966, reprinted 1986), contains a good sample of letters to and from his daughters and grandchildren. Information about Jefferson's library, which became the basis for the Library of Congress collection when Jefferson sold it to the federal government in 1815, is available in E. Millicent Sowerby (compiler), *Catalogue of the Library of Thomas Jefferson*, 5 vol. (1952–59, reprinted 1983).

Among the full-life biographies, the standard against which all are measured is Dumas Malone, *Jefferson and His Time*, 6 vol. (1948–81), which is a monumental scholarly achievement that takes Jefferson's view of all the controversial issues. Less comprehensive but somewhat more critical, especially on the latter years, is Merrill D. Peterson, *Thomas Jefferson and the New Nation* (1970, reprinted 1987). Invaluable because it draws upon conversations with those family and friends who knew Jefferson personally is the early biography by Henry Stephens Randall, *The Life of Thomas Jefferson*, 3 vol. (1857, reprinted

1972). Reliable and reverential accounts include Gilbert Chinard, *Thomas Jefferson: The Apostle of Americanism*, 2nd ed. rev. (1939, reissued 1963); Noble E. Cunningham Jr., *In Pursuit of Reason: The Life of Thomas Jefferson* (1987, reissued 1992); and Alf J. Mapp Jr., *Thomas Jefferson*, 2 vol. (1987–91). Fawn M. Brodie, *Thomas Jefferson: An Intimate History* (1974, reissued 1998), makes the sexual relationship with Sally Hemings the center of the story and also makes extensive use of psychiatric theories. Andrew Burstein, *The Inner Jefferson: Portrait of a Grieving Optimist* (1995), focuses on the sentimentalism of Jefferson's core identity. Joseph J. Ellis, *American Sphinx: The Character of Thomas Jefferson* (1997), provides a more critical portrait, focusing on Jefferson's systemic contradictions.

Jefferson's multiple interests and his long career in public service during a crucial chapter of American history combine to generate a huge array of monographs on particular aspects of his life and legacy. The most convenient collection of essays on the current scholarly perspectives across this vast range of topics is Peter S. Onuf (ed.), *Jeffersonian Legacies* (1993). An older version of the panoramic perspective is Lally Weymouth (ed.), *Thomas Jefferson: The Man, His World, His Influence* (1973).

On Jefferson's political thought, see Garrett Ward Sheldon, *The Political Philosophy of Thomas Jefferson* (1991, reprinted 1993); David N. Mayer, *The Constitutional Thought of Thomas Jefferson* (1994); and Richard K. Matthews, *The Radical Politics of Thomas Jefferson: A Revisionist View* (1984, reissued 1987). For the broader intellectual context, see Daniel J. Boorstin, *The Lost World of Thomas Jefferson* (1948, reissued 1993). Three books offer different interpretations of the Declaration of Independence: Carl Becker, *The Declaration of Independence: A Study in the History of Political Ideas* (1922, reprinted 1972); Garry Wills, *Inventing America: Jefferson's Declaration of Independence* (1978, reissued 1980); and Pauline Maier, *American Scripture: Making the Declaration of Independence* (1997). Jefferson's protean political legacy is the subject of Merrill D. Peterson, *The Jefferson Image in the American Mind* (1960, reissued 1998), a magisterial account. A major new window into Jefferson's thought is provided by Herbert E. Sloan, *Principle and Interest: Thomas Jefferson and the Problem of Debt* (1995).

On slavery and race, John Chester Miller, *The Wolf by the Ears: Thomas Jefferson and Slavery* (1977, reissued 1991), is the standard work. Winthrop D. Jordan, *White Over Black: American Attitudes*

Toward the Negro, 1550–1812 (1968, reissued 1977), is seminal, as is David Brion Davis, *The Problem of Slavery in the Age of Revolution, 1770–1823* (1975, reissued 1999). For the context of slavery at Monticello, see James A. Bear Jr. (ed.), *Jefferson at Monticello* (1967). The great paradox of Jefferson's position as a slaveholder is probed rather brilliantly in Edmund S. Morgan, *American Slavery, American Freedom: The Ordeal of Colonial Virginia* (1975, reissued 1995).

The domestic context at Monticello is the subject of several important books. Sarah N. Randolph, *The Domestic Life of Thomas Jefferson* (1871, reprinted 1978), provides an affectionate portrait by his descendants. Jack McLaughlin, *Jefferson and Monticello: The Biography of a Builder* (1988, reissued 1990), goes beyond architectural issues to explore the daily lives of all the residents on the mountain. Elizabeth Langhorne, *Monticello: A Family Story* (1987, reissued 1989), focuses on the white residents. Edwin Morris Betts (ed.), *Thomas Jefferson's Farm Book* (1953, reprinted 1987), reproduces Jefferson's plantation records. Susan R. Stein, *The Worlds of Thomas Jefferson at Monticello* (1993), recovers the material objects Jefferson gathered inside the mansion. Merrill D. Peterson (ed.), *Visitors to Monticello* (1989), reproduces the accounts of firsthand observers.

Jefferson's five-year stay in France is explored in William Howard Adams, *The Paris Years of Thomas Jefferson* (1997); George Green Shackelford, *Thomas Jefferson's Travels in Europe, 1784–1789* (1995); and Marie Goebel Kimball, *Jefferson: The Scene of Europe, 1784 to 1789* (1950). On the matter of Jefferson's love affair with the French Revolution, Conor Cruise O'Brien, *The Long Affair: Thomas Jefferson and the French Revolution, 1785–1800* (1996, reissued 1998), is a highly critical account.

On his political career in the 1790s, the standard overview is Lance Banning, *The Jeffersonian Persuasion: Evolution of a Party Ideology* (1978, reissued 1980). See also Joseph Charles, *The Origins of the American Party System* (1956, reissued 1961); and Noble E. Cunningham, *The Jeffersonian Republicans: The Formation of Party Organization, 1789–1801* (1957, reissued 1963). The crucial role of the political partnership with James Madison is addressed in Adrienne Koch, *Jefferson and Madison: The Great Collaboration* (1950, reprinted 1986).

In addition to the coverage provided in the full-scale biographies, Jefferson's presidency receives book-length treatment in Forrest McDonald, *The Presidency of Thomas Jefferson* (1976); Robert M. Johnstone Jr., *Jefferson and the Presidency: Leadership in the Young*

Republic (1978); and Noble E. Cunningham Jr., *The Process of Government Under Jefferson* (1978). Foreign policy is best discussed in Robert W. Tucker and David C. Hendrickson, *Empire of Liberty: The Statecraft of Thomas Jefferson* (1990, reissued 1992); Lawrence S. Kaplan, *Entangling Alliances with None: American Foreign Policy in the Age of Jefferson* (1987); and George Dargo, *Jefferson's Louisiana: Politics and the Clash of Legal Traditions* (1975). For the domestic implications of the embargo crisis, a splendid assessment is Leonard Williams Levy, *Jefferson & Civil Liberties: The Darker Side* (1963, reprinted 1989). On his battles with the judiciary, see Richard E. Ellis, *The Jeffersonian Crisis: Courts and Politics in the Young Republic* (1971, reprinted 1974). On his relations with Indians, see Anthony F.C. Wallace, *Jefferson and the Indians: The Tragic Fate of the First Americans* (1999).

Each of Jefferson's multiple dimensions has attracted scholarly interest. For his scientific achievements, see Silvio A. Bedini, *Thomas Jefferson: Statesman of Science* (1990); and I. Bernard Cohen, *Science and the Founding Fathers* (1995, reissued 1997). For his religious views, Edwin S. Gaustad, *Sworn on the Altar of God: A Religious Biography of Thomas Jefferson* (1996). For his aesthetic and architectural contribution, William Howard Adams (ed.), *Jefferson and the Arts: An Extended View* (1976). For his educational vision, Roy J. Honeywell, *The Educational Work of Thomas Jefferson* (1931, reissued 1964); and Harold Hellenbrand, *The Unfinished Revolution: Education and Politics in the Thought of Thomas Jefferson* (1990).

On the question of Jefferson's relationship with Sally Hemings, the pre-DNA argument against the liaison was best summarized in Virginius Dabney, *The Jefferson Scandals: A Rebuttal* (1981, reissued 1991). The argument for the liaison was nicely synthesized by Annette Gordon-Reed, *Thomas Jefferson and Sally Hemings: An American Controversy* (1997). The DNA study appeared in Eugene A. Foster et al., "Jefferson Fathered Slave's Last Child," *Nature*, 396(6706):27–28 (November 5, 1998).

James Madison

William T. Hutchinson et al. (eds.), *The Papers of James Madison*, 17 vol. (1962–91), is the most extensive collection of Madison's writings, annotated and with background notes. Gaillard Hunt (ed.), *The Writings of James Madison*, 9 vol. (1900–10), comprises Madison's public papers and private correspondence, and Hunt also edited *The Journal of the Debates in the Convention Which Framed the Constitution of the United States, May–September 1787, As Recorded by James Madison,* 2 vol. (1908), which is the only continuous and an almost exhaustive record of that convention. James Morton Smith (ed.), *The Republic of Letters: The Correspondence Between Thomas Jefferson and James Madison, 1776–1826,* 3 vol. (1995), includes more than 1,200 letters detailing their friendship. A valuable briefer presentation of this subject is Adrienne Koch, *Jefferson and Madison: The Great Collaboration* (1950, reprinted 1987).

Madison's life is most competently and exhaustively treated by Irving Brant, *James Madison,* 6 vol. (1941–61), which sets out to counter the hitherto prevailing misrepresentation of the Madison and Jefferson administrations and particularly the derogation of Madison relative to Jefferson; Brant's *The Fourth President* (1970) selectively condenses the multivolume work into a single volume. Ralph Ketcham, *James Madison* (1971, reprinted 1990), is also good. Drew R. McCoy, *The Last of the Fathers: James Madison and the Republican Legacy* (1989), tells about the man after his presidential career.

The following works discuss and evaluate Madison's political career and administrations: the first section of John Quincy Adams, *The Lives of James Madison and James Monroe, Fourth and Fifth Presidents of the United States* (1850); William C. Rives, *History of the Life and Times of James Madison,* 3 vol. (1859–68, reprinted 1970), concentrating on the period from the American Revolution until 1797; Sydney Howard Gay, *James Madison* (1884, reissued 1983), covering up to 1797; William Lee Miller, *The Business of May Next: James Madison and the Founding* (1992), detailing the period from 1784 to 1791; and Robert Allen Rutland, *The Presidency of James Madison* (1990), focusing on the War of 1812.

Madison's political philosophy is analyzed in Stuart G. Brown, *The First Republicans: Political Philosophy and Public Policy in the Party of Jefferson and Madison* (1954, reprinted 1976), a work concerned with Madison, Monroe, and Jefferson and the development of the essential partisan ideas that bound together the republican faction; Irving Brant, *James Madison and American Nationalism* (1968), an account of Madison's role in the formation and development of U.S. institutions against the background of the popular attitude, with corroboratory documentary readings; Lance Banning, *The Sacred Fire of Liberty: James Madison and the Founding of the Federal Republic*

(1995), explaining Madison's views on national government; and Richard K. Matthews, *If Men Were Angels: James Madison and the Heartless Empire of Reason* (1995), contending that Madison followed liberal political beliefs.

Benjamin Franklin

Leonard W. Labaree et al. (eds.), *The Papers of Benjamin Franklin* (1959–), is the definitive collection of Franklin's writings; it now has 38 volumes and takes Franklin up through Jan. 30, 1783. Albert Henry Smyth (ed.), *The Writings of Benjamin Franklin*, 10 vol. (1905–07, reprinted 1970), has heretofore been the chief collection. A convenient single-volume collection of Franklin's major writings is J.A. Leo Lemay (ed.), *Benjamin Franklin: Writings* (1987), part of the *Library of America* series. The most reliable editions of the *Autobiography* are Leonard W. Labaree et al. (eds.), *The Autobiography of Benjamin Franklin* (1964); and J.A. Leo Lemay and P.M. Zall (eds.), *Benjamin Franklin's Autobiography: An Authoritive Text, Backgrounds, Criticism* (1986).

Full biographies are Carl Van Doren, *Benjamin Franklin* (1938, reprinted 1991); and H.W. Brands, *The First American* (2000). Other biographical studies include Verner W. Crane, *Benjamin Franklin and a Rising People* (1954, reissued 1990); Thomas Fleming, *The Man Who Dared the Lightning: A New Look at Benjamin Franklin* (1971); Claude-Anne Lopez and Eugenia W. Herbert, *The Private Franklin: The Man and His Family* (1975, reissued 1985); Arthur Bernon Tourtellot, *Benjamin Franklin: The Shaping of Genius: The Boston Years* (1977), a study of his heritage and youth; and Ronald W. Clark, *Benjamin Franklin* (1983), a popular biography. Stacy Shiff, *The Great Improvisation: Franklin, France, and the Birth of America* (2005), is a superb account of Franklin in Paris.

Bruce Ingham Granger, *Benjamin Franklin, an American Man of Letters*, new ed. (1976), is an interpretive study. Brian M. Barbour (ed.), *Benjamin Franklin: A Collection of Critical Essays* (1979), emphasizes Franklin's roles as writer and shaper of the American national character. J.A. Leo Lemay, *The Canon of Benjamin Franklin, 1722–1776: New Attributions and Reconsiderations* (1986), is a scholarly reexamination of Franklin's writings. Lemay has also published two volumes of *The Life of Benjamin Franklin* (2006–), which will be a major multivolume biography. Ormond Seavey, *Becoming Benjamin Franklin: The Autobiography and the Life* (1988), analyzes Franklin's writings and life. Nian-Sheng Huang, *Benjamin Franklin in American Thought and Culture, 1790–1990* (1994), deals with the changing images of Franklin after his death. His inventions and scientific thought are examined in I. Bernard Cohen, *Benjamin Franklin's Science* (1990). Melvin H. Buxbaum, *Benjamin Franklin: A Reference Guide*, 2 vol. (1983–88), is an annotated bibliography of writings on Franklin published between 1721 and 1983. Edmund S. Morgan, *Benjamin Franklin* (2002), provides a portrait of Franklin's life as a politician and diplomat and is the best of the short biographies. Walter Isaacson, *Benjamin Franklin: An American Life* (2003), is a lengthy biography that includes insight into Franklin's family life and relationships. Gordon S. Wood, *The Americanization of Benjamin Franklin* (2004), deals with the complicated ways in which Americans related to Franklin during and after his lifetime.

Samuel Adams

For a general introduction to the period of the Revolution, its causes, developments, and the people, see Stewart Beach, *Samuel Adams: The Fateful Years, 1764–1776* (1965); and Cass Canfield, *Samuel Adams's Revolution, 1765–1776* (1976). Biographies include Ralph Volney Harlow, *Samuel Adams, Promoter of the American Revolution: A Study in Psychology and Politics* (1923, reprinted 1975); John C. Miller, *Sam Adams: Pioneer in Propaganda* (1936, reissued 1960); Paul Lewis (Noel Bertram Gerson), *The Grand Incendiary* (1973); John K. Alexander, *Samuel Adams: America's Revolutionary Politician* (2002); and Mark Puls, *Samuel Adams: Father of the American Revolution* (2006).

Alexander Hamilton

Hamilton's public and private life is examined by Nathan Schachner, *Alexander Hamilton* (1946, reissued 1961), well balanced and readable; Broadus Mitchell, *Alexander Hamilton*, 2 vol. (1957–62), a scholarly study; and John Chester Miller, *Alexander Hamilton: Portrait in Paradox* (1959, reprinted 1979), strong on his public career. Harvey Flaumenhaft, *The Effective Republic: Administration and Constitution in the Thought of Alexander Hamilton* (1992); and Forrest McDonald, *Alexander Hamilton* (1979, reissued 1982), reexamine his political philosophy. Other biographies include Jacob Ernest Cooke, *Alexander Hamilton* (1982); Marie B. Hecht, *Odd Destiny: The Life of Alexander Hamilton* (1982); Richard Brookhiser, *Alexander Hamilton, American* (1999); and Ron Chernow, *Alexander Hamilton* (2004). Douglas

Ambrose and Robert W.T. Martin, editors, *The Many Faces of Alexander Hamilton: The Life and Legacy of America's Most Elusive Founding Father* (2006), is a collection of essays by leading Hamilton scholars.

Patrick Henry

Biographies include Robert D. Meade, *Patrick Henry,* 2 vol. (1957–69), a full, authoritative treatment; William Wirt Henry, *Patrick Henry: Life, Correspondence and Speeches,* 3 vol. (1891, reprinted 1969), still valuable; Moses Coit Tyler, *Patrick Henry* (1915, reprinted 1966); David J. Vaughan, *Give Me Liberty: The Uncompromising Statesmanship of Patrick Henry* (1996, reprinted 2003); and Henry Mayer, *A Son of Thunder: Patrick Henry and the American Republic* (2001). David A. McCants, *Patrick Henry, the Orator* (1990), deals with Henry's speeches and rhetorical techniques.

John Marshall

Albert J. Beveridge, *The Life of John Marshall,* 4 vol. (1916–19), is the standard biography of Marshall and the most detailed and comprehensive account of his life and career; it is, however, pervasively laudatory and almost completely uncritical. James Bradley Thayer, *John Marshall* (1901, reprinted 1967), is a biographical essay, keenly perceptive in its appraisal of Marshall's career and work as chief justice. Charles Warren, *The Supreme Court in United States History,* rev. ed., 2 vol. (1937), which is a study of the Supreme Court as an institution of government, appropriately gives great emphasis to the court and the chief justiceship of John Marshall. Other works include Jean Edward Smith, *John Marshall: Definer of a Nation* (1996); Charles F. Hobson, *The Great Chief Justice: John Marshall and the Rule of Law* (1996); Charles F. Hobson et al., editors, *The Papers of John Marshall* (1974–); and R. Kent Newmyer, *John Marshall and the Heroic Age of the Supreme Court* (2001).

Photo Credits